Robert Lyman is one of Britain's most respected military historians and his previous books include *The Longest Siege: Tobruk – The Battle that Saved North Africa, Slim, Master of War* and *Operation Suicide*. He lives in Berkshire, England.

Also by Robert Lyman

Slim, Master of War: Burma and the Birth of Modern Warfare
First Victory: Britain's Forgotten Struggle in the Middle East, 1941
The Generals: From Defeat to Victory, Leadership in Asia 1941–45
The Longest Siege: Tobruk – The Battle that Saved North Africa
Japan's Last Bid for Victory: The Invasion of India, 1944
Operation Suicide: The Remarkable Story of the Cockleshell Raid

Into the Jaws of Death

The True Story of the Legendary Raid
on Saint-Nazaire

Robert Lyman

Quercus

First published in hardback in 2013 by Quercus Editions Ltd

This paperback edition published in 2014 by
Quercus Editions Ltd
55 Baker Street
Seventh Floor, South Block
London
W1U 8EW

A CIP catalogue record for this book is available
from the British Library

PB ISBN 978 1 78206 447 3
Ebook ISBN 978 1 78206 446 6

10 9 8 7 6 5 4 3 2 1

Text and plates designed and typeset by Ellipsis Digital Ltd

Printed and bound in Great Britain by Clays Ltd. St Ives plc

The image on the title page is of wounded commandos being placed on a flatbed truck at about 9 a.m. on the morning of 28 March 1942 (German casualties were taken away by French ambulance). HMS *Campbeltown* has not yet exploded. The kilted Private Thomas McCormack of the 1st (Liverpool Scottish) Battalion, Queen's Own Cameron Highlanders and of No. 2 Commando, mortally wounded in the head by a German hand grenade, is being laid on the vehicle. He was to die of his wounds two weeks later on 11 April 1942 in Rennes, after being transferred to hospital there from the makeshift hospital in the Hôtel l'Hermitage at La Baule, ten miles west of Saint-Nazaire. His body lies in Rennes Eastern Communal Cemetery.

They that had fought so well
Came thro' the jaws of Death,
Back from the mouth of Hell,
All that was left of them,
Left of six hundred.

Alfred, Lord Tennyson,
'The Charge of the Light Brigade', 1854

This book is dedicated to my parents,
Graham and Beth Lyman,
and in memory of the indomitable
Charioteers,
especially those who made the ultimate sacrifice

Contents

We prayed that this time, no one had blundered.
Lance Corporal Jack Webb RAMC, No. 2 Commando, ML 341

It was one of those enterprises which could be attempted only because in the eyes of the enemy it was absolutely impossible.
Vice Admiral Lord Louis Mountbatten,
Chief of Combined Operations

. . . a deed of glory intimately involved in high strategy.
Sir Winston Churchill

. . . it was a handful of men going into the jaws of death.
Gordon Holman, *Evening Standard*, 28 March 1943

This brilliant attack was carried out by night under a vicious enemy fire, by a handful of men, who achieved with certainty and precision what the heaviest bombing raid or naval bombardment might well have failed to do.
Vice Admiral Lord Louis Mountbatten,
Chief of Combined Operations

. . . brilliant and heroic exploit . . .
Sir Winston Churchill

You were the first to give us hope.
Monsieur Paul Ramadier, Prime Minister of France,
to veterans, Saint-Nazaire, 1947

Surely by far the highest number of VCs ever awarded for a single operation; and this is the measure of the heroism of all who took part in that magnificent enterprise.

Vice Admiral Lord Louis Mountbatten,
Chief of Combined Operations, 1942

The English attack on Saint-Nazaire on the night of 28 March 1942 is a first-class example of a well planned undertaking thought out to the last detail and executed with great courage.

German report on the raid

We would not wish to deny the gallantry of the British. Every German is moved by a feeling of respect for the men who carried out this action. The crew of the Campbeltown *under fierce fire forced their ship through the northern lock gates, and carried out a crazy enterprise as well as it could be done. They fought until death or capture.*

German naval spokesman, radio broadcast, 31 March 1942

Preface

The telephone rang shrilly. The officer of the watch shook off his sleep, picked it up almost instinctively, awoke in an instant and listened intently to the voice at the other end of the line. But the message was confusing, and hard to comprehend. Attacks? Saint-Nazaire? Kapitänleutnant Herbert Sohler, commanding officer of the *Kriegsmarine's* 7th U-boat Flotilla (7 *Unterseebootsflottille*), was on the telephone from the Celtic Hotel in La Baule, talking some nonsense about a British raid on the submarine port. He wanted urgently to talk to the submarine chief.

The duty officer noted the time: 1.45 a.m. Vice Admiral Karl Dönitz had only arrived back at his château overlooking the River Scorff at Kernével, near Lorient, a few hours before, following a major tour of inspection of the massive U-boat base at Saint-Nazaire. Now, only a handful of hours later, a British attack seemed to be unfolding in the very place where Germany's submarine chief (*Befehlshaber der Unterseeboote*, *BdU*, the 'Commander of the Submarines') had inspected his nine Type-VII U-boats and their feted and dramatically successful crews. Certainly, the Führer had warned only that week of the heightened risk of Commando attacks on Germany's European littoral, but this seemed different, even sinister. The coincidence of the British attacking the same place where Dönitz had been only hours before seemed too remarkable to be true. Was it not probable that this was an attempt on Dönitz's life, as British commandos had attempted to do recently to General Rommel in North Africa? After all, it seemed reasonable to assume that the German U-boat commander was a figure of hate in the Anglo-Saxon world, given that it was his hand on the helm in the Battle of the Atlantic.

He rang the Admiral's aide-de-camp, elsewhere in the building, to brief him fully on this momentous news. It would be up to the ADC to awaken Dönitz. Meanwhile the duty officer would warn the guard commander to call out the reserve guard, increasing security around the château. With what was almost certain to have been an attempt on the life of Dönitz himself, Germany's most senior naval commander, no precaution seemed excessive. He picked up the telephone and rang the guard commander. Minutes later Sohler was on the telephone to Dönitz.

'Admiral, I have received a message from the port commander of Saint-Nazaire that the British are landing in the dockyards at this very moment, and have occupied half the port.'

'Sohler, what is happening with my submarines? Are they safe?' a shocked Dönitz barked out in reply.

'Right now I don't know, sir,' came Sohler's response. 'I'm going straight to Saint-Nazaire and will call you back as soon as I've found out what's going on. In the meantime I am evacuating the crews to La Roche-Bernard.'

With that he leapt into his staff car (no one had thought to awaken his driver) and raced the eight miles to Saint-Nazaire, driving along the D213, which meant that he could stay away from the by now dangerous coast road. When he reached the northern outskirts a roadblock barred his way. The sky over the port was lit up by searchlights and rent by the thunder of gunfire and explosions. It would have been foolhardy to proceed, although he was full of fear for his nine completed U-boat pens and their precious steel occupants.

As Sohler was wondering what to do, three truckloads of soldiers from Kapitän zur See Karl-Conrad Mecke's 22 *Marineartillerieregiment* pulled up behind him. Sohler took charge at once, and ordered the men to clear a path through the streets. They reached the massive concrete pens with no trouble shortly after 3 a.m. To Sohler's immense relief it was intact: no enemy troops had broken through its perimeter. In accordance with standing orders, however, he ordered that explosive scuttling charges be placed in each vessel, and that every submarine submerge itself onto the floor of the pen, to prevent the enemy placing magnetic mines on the hulls. Sohler then called Dönitz to tell him that the U-boats were intact.

An hour later a second call to Dönitz confirmed that the danger was past: the British did not seem to be targeting the U-boat base, but for some reason the other parts of the dock infrastructure. After the first hours of anxious panic, Sohler at last began to relax. He couldn't understand what else might attract the British to Saint-Nazaire other than his precious submarines. Clearly, the British raid was a pathetic failure.

Dramatis Personae

The War Office, Whitehall, London

Anthony Eden MC	Secretary of State for War (11 May 1940–22 December 1940); Secretary of State for Foreign Affairs (22 December 1940–26 July 1945)
General Sir John Dill DSO	Chief of the Imperial General Staff (until December 1941)
General Sir Alan Brooke DSO	Chief of the Imperial General Staff (from December 1941)
Major General Dick Dewing	Director of Operations and Plans, War Office (until October 1941)
Major General John Kennedy	Director of Operations and Plans, War Office (from October 1941)
Colonel Dudley Clarke RA	Chief, MO9 (until October 1941)
Major David Niven, The Rifle Brigade	Planning Staff, MO9

Combined Operations HQ, 1a Richmond Terrace, London

Admiral Sir Roger Keyes RN	Director Combined Operations (July 1940–November 1941)
Vice Admiral Lord Louis Mountbatten RN	Adviser, Combined Operations (from October 1941) and Chief, Combined Operations (from March 1942)

Wing Commander The Marquis de Casa Maury RAF	Head of Intelligence, Combined Operations
Major David Wyatt RE	SOE Liaison Officer with COHQ
Captain John Hughes-Hallett RN	Naval Adviser
Group Captain Alfred ('Fred') Henry Willetts DSO RAF	RAF Adviser
Commander David Luce RN	Naval Planner

Special Service Brigade

Brigadier Charles Haydon DSO OBE	Commander, Special Service Brigade (the 'Commandos') and Military Adviser to COHQ
Lieutenant Colonel Hughie Stockwell	First Commandant, STC Lochailort
Lieutenant Colonel Ronnie Tod	Commanding Officer, No. 11 Independent Company
Lieutenant Colonel John Durnford-Slater	Commanding Officer, No. 3 Commando

Royal Navy, Operation *Chariot*

Commander Robert ('Bob') Ryder RN	Naval Force Commander
Lieutenant Commander Sam Beattie RN	Commanding Officer, HMS *Campbeltown*
Lieutenant Nigel Tibbits RN	Explosive Ordnance Officer, HMS *Vernon*
Lieutenant A.R. ('Bill') Green RN	Navigating Officer, HMS *Campbeltown*
Lieutenant Commander Robin Jenks RN	Commanding Officer, HMS *Atherstone*
Lieutenant Commander Hugo Tweedie RN	Commanding Officer, HMS *Tynedale*

Commander Guy Sayer RN	Commanding Officer, HMS *Cleveland*
Lieutenant Commander Michael Tufnell DSC RN	Commanding Officer, HMS *Brocklesby*
Lieutenant Commander Mervyn Wingfield RN	Commanding Officer, HM Submarine *Sturgeon*
Lieutenant Reginald Verity RNVR	Beach Master
Sub-Lieutenant John O'Rourke RCNVR	Communications Officer, HMS *Campbeltown*
Lieutenant Dunstan Curtis RNVR	MGB 314. Scuttled when crew had been transferred to HMS *Atherstone*.
Lieutenant Commander William ('Billie') Stephens RNVR	Commanding Officer 20th Motor Launch Flotilla; Senior Officer of ML force. ML 192 (Flotilla No. 1)[1]; Leader, Starboard Column. Destroyed during the raid.
Lieutenant Edward Burt RNVR	ML 262 (No. 2), 20th Flotilla. Destroyed during the raid.
Lieutenant Eric Beart RNVR	ML 267 (No. 3), 20th Flotilla. Destroyed during the raid.
Lieutenant A.B. ('Bill') Tillie RNVR	ML 268 (No. 4), 20th Flotilla. Destroyed during the raid.
Lieutenant Leslie Fenton RNVR	ML 156 (No. 5), 7th Flotilla. Abandoned when crew transferred to HMS *Atherstone* after the raid.
Sub-Lieutenant Mark Rodier RNVR	ML 177 (No. 6), 7th Flotilla. Destroyed during the raid.
Lieutenant Charles Stuart Irwin RNVR	ML 270 (No. 7), 7th Flotilla. Scuttled when crew transferred to HMS *Brocklesby*.
Lieutenant Thomas Boyd RNVR	ML 160 (No. 8), 7th Flotilla. Successfully returned to England.

1. Denotes the position of each vessel in the Order of Battle. This is shown diagrammatically at Appendix 1

Lieutenant Thomas Platt RNVR	ML 447 (No. 9), 28th Flotilla; Leader, Port Column. Destroyed during the raid.
Lieutenant Douglas Briault RNVR	ML 341 (No. 10), 28th Flotilla. Returned to England with engine trouble before the raid.
Lieutenant Thomas Collier RNVR	ML 457 (No. 11), 28th Flotilla. Destroyed during the raid.
Lieutenant Norman Wallis RANVR	ML 307 (No. 12), 28th Flotilla. Successfully returned to England.
Lieutenant Kenneth Horlock RNVR	ML 443 (No. 13), 28th Flotilla. Successfully returned to England.
Lieutenant Ian Henderson RNVR	ML 306 (No. 14), 28th Flotilla. Lost during the raid but salvaged by the Germans.
Lieutenant Henry Falconer RNVR	ML 446 (No. 15), 28th Flotilla. Scuttled when crew transferred to HMS *Atherstone*.
Sub-Lieutenant Bob Nock RNVR	ML 298 (No. 16), 28th Flotilla. Destroyed during the raid.
Sub-Lieutenant R.C.M (Micky) Wynn RNVR	MTB 74 (No. 17). Destroyed during the raid.

Commandos, Operation *Chariot*

Lieutenant Colonel Charles Newman	Military Force Commander. Commanding Officer, No. 2 Commando, Old Entrance
WO1 Alan Moss	Group 2B, Regimental Sergeant Major, No. 2 Commando, Old Entrance
Major William (Bill) Copland	Second-in-Command, No. 2 Commando, HMS *Campbeltown*. In command of Group 3 targets
Captain Stanley Day	Adjutant, No. 2 Commando

Lieutenant Ronald ('Ronnie') Swayne	Group 1A, Demolition Party, Old Mole
Lieutenant John Vanderwerve	Group lA, Protection Party, Old Mole
Captain Bill Bradley	Group lB, Demolition Party, Old Mole
Lieutenant Philip Walton	Group lC, Demolition Party, Old Mole
Second Lieutenant William ('Tiger') Watson	Group lC, Protection Party, Old Mole
Lieutenant A.D. Wilson	Group 1D, Demolition Party, Old Mole
Second Lieutenant Paul Bassett-Wilson	Group 1D, Demolition Party, Old Mole
Lieutenant John Bonvin	Group 1D, Demolition Party, Old Mole
Lieutenant Joe Houghton	Group 1D, Protection Party, Old Mole
Captain Eric ('Bertie') Hodgson	Group 1E, Assault Party, Old Mole. In command of Group 1 targets.
Captain David Birney	Group 1F, Assault Party, Old Mole
Captain William ('Bill') Pritchard MC RE	Group lG, Demolition Control, Old Mole
Lieutenant Mark Woodcock	Group 2A, Demolition Party, Old Entrance
Lieutenant Dick Morgan	Group 2A, Protection Party, Old Entrance
Captain Harold Pennington	Group 2C, Demolition Party, Old Entrance
Second Lieutenant Morgan Jenkins	Group 2C, Protection Party, Old Entrance
Captain Michael ('Micky') Burn	Group 2D, Assault Party, Old Entrance. In command of Group 2 targets
Captain Richard Hooper	Group 2E, Special Task Party, Old Entrance

Captain Robert ('Bob') Montgomery RE	Group 3, Demolition Control, Southern Caisson
Lieutenant Robert ('Bertie') Burtinshaw	Group 3A, Demolition Party, Southern Caisson
Lieutenant Christopher Smalley	Group 3A, Demolition Party, Southern Caisson
Lieutenant Stuart Chant	Group 3A, Demolition Party, Southern Caisson
Lieutenant H.G.L 'Hoppy' Hopwood	Group 3A, Protection Party, Southern Caisson
Lieutenant Bill Etches	Group 3B (in overall command of Group 3B)
Lieutenant Gerard Brett	Group 3B, Demolition Party, Southern Caisson
Lieutenant Corran Purdon	Group 3B, Demolition Party, Southern Caisson
Lieutenant M.C. 'Bung' Denison	Group 3B, Protection Party, Southern Caisson
Lieutenant John Roderick	Group 3C, Assault Party, Southern Caisson
Captain Donald Roy	Group 3D, Assault Party, Southern Caisson

German Armed Forces

Admiral Wilhelm Marschall	C-in-C, Navy Group West (*Oberbefehlshaber des Marinegruppenkommando West*), Paris
Admiral Wilhelm Meisel	Chief of Staff, Navy Group West, Paris
Generalfeldmarschall Hugo Sperrle	Commander, *Luftflotte* 3
Vice Admiral Karl Dönitz	Commander of Submarines, *Kriegsmarine* (*Befehlshaber der Unterseeboote*, BdU)

General Karl Ritter von Prager	25th Army Corps, Army Group D
Lieutenant General Rudolf Pilz	GOC 333 Infantry Division
Oberst Hans-Hugo von Schuckmann	Commanding Officer, 679th Infantry Regiment (part of 333 Infantry Division)
Kapitän zur See Adalbert Zuckschwerdt	*See Kommandant* Loire, February 1941 to November 1942
Vice Admiral Wolf von Trotha	Director (*Oberwerftdirektor*) of the German naval shipyard (*Kriegsmarinewerft*), Saint-Nazaire
Kapitän zur See Edo Dieckmann	Commanding Officer, *Marineartilleriebataillon* 280
Kapitän zur See Karl-Conrad Mecke	Commanding Officer, 22 *Marineflakregiment*
Korvettenkapitän Thiessen	Commanding Officer, *Marineflakbataillon* 703, Villès-Martin
Korvettenkapitän Koch	Commanding Officer, *Marineflakbataillon* 705
Korvettenkapitän Burhenne	Commanding Officer, *Marineartilleriebataillon* 809
Korvettenkapitän Kellermann	Commanding Officer, Harbour Defences, Saint-Nazaire
Kapitänleutnant Herbert Sohler	Commanding Officer, 7th U-boat Flotilla (7 *Unterseebootsflottille*), Saint-Nazaire
Kapitänleutnant[2] Gerd Keibling	Commanding Officer, *U-593*, attacked by HMS *Tynedale*
Korvettenkapitän Friedrich Paul	Commanding Officer, *Jaguar*
Korvettenkapitän Moritz Schmidt	Commander, Torpedo Boat Flotilla (*Seeadler, Jaguar, Iltis, Falke* and *Kondor*) and commanding officer, *Seeadler*

2. Lieutenant Commander, German Navy.

Author's Note

I have standardised all times into a.m. and p.m. rather than using the 24-hour clock. All time, including that in France (including timings given in the German records), has been converted to British Double Summer Time (BDST), the time zone used by Combined Operations during the raid. Since 1916 British Summer Time (BST) had been an hour ahead of GMT. In 1940, however, the clocks in Britain were not put back by an hour at the end of Summer Time, and continued to be advanced by one hour each spring and put back by an hour each autumn, until July 1945. During these summers, therefore, operating on BDST, Britain was two hours ahead of GMT. French time, usually an hour ahead of UK time, was therefore an hour behind BDST. So, when the *Campbeltown* exploded at a local time of 10.35 a.m. on Saturday 28 March 1942, the BDST time was 11.35 a.m. Confusingly most contemporary accounts mistakenly refer to the British time zone in use as BST rather than the correct BDST.

All sources are listed at the end of the book, but are not directly referenced. This has saved many precious pages that can otherwise be used for text. To the academic purists who dislike this practice, I apologise.

I have standardised all references to the great dry dock and lock at Saint-Nazaire as the Normandie Dock, in deference to the great French liner for which it was first constructed in 1934. Its other names are the 'Louis Joubert' dock and the 'Forme Ecluse'. For further clarity, I have attempted to standardise references to the three entrances to the Bassin. The South Lock is referred to as the Southern Entrance, the Middle Lock is the Old Entrance and the Northern Lock is the great Normandie Dock itself.

I have used individuals' common names where they are known, rather than their more formal initials, or indeed their Christian names. For instance, Lieutenant R.O.C. Swayne of the Herefordshire Regiment and No. 1 Commando (later Sir Ronald Swayne MC) was universally known as Ronnie (although the nickname used by his soldiers was 'Rocky'), and it is as such that he is recorded in this account.

Ranks given are those that pertained at the time.

ONE

Britain, early 1942

At least the weather over most of Britain on the evening of Friday 27 March 1942 was pleasant. The sun had shone during the day over a mostly cloudless sky, the prevailing winds were gentle, the seas calm. In peacetime this would have been a perfect spring day, ushering in the hopeful joys of a long, warm summer after one of the most miserable Februaries on record. Sir Alexander Cadogan, the British Permanent Under-Secretary for Foreign Affairs, noted in his diary for Sunday 29 March with something of relief that the wind 'dropped last night and it was a God-given day today – sun the whole time. Like summer, and swarms of bees busy on the crocuses – which are *lovely!*'

But there was little else for Britons to enjoy at the end of another week of seemingly endless conflict. Now in its thirty-first month, the war, for most Britons, dragged interminably on, with no prospect of any resolution, let alone success, in sight. The widely held view across all strata of society was that the military situation was continuing to decline. For some that decline was considered irreversible. Worrying about the mental health of the Prime Minister a few weeks before on 4 March, Cadogan had noted in his diary: 'Poor old PM in a sour mood and a bad way.' Sir Henry ('Chips') Channon, Member of Parliament for Southend, recalled in his diary on 30 March: 'We are living in a Gibbonian age – Decline and Fall . . .' In January the Cabinet received a report from the Ministry of Information in which they were told that the prevailing mood across the country was fatalistic; a lack of British military success was leading to a sense of 'frustration and loss of interest in the war and war news'.

It has long been demonstrated that rates of suicide among the general population decline in wartime. Émile Durkheim in 1897 suggested that this was because of the greater social cohesion evidenced during times of conflict, although subsequent commentators have suggested more prosaic reasons, such as a reduction in unemployment, a recognised risk factor for suicide. In Britain during the Second World War, however, there was a significant increase in the male rate of self-destruction, reaching a peak in 1942. A 2006 study demonstrated in Scotland, for instance, that suicide rates among men aged 15–24 years rose during the Second World War, peaking at 148 per million during 1942 before declining to 39 per million by 1945, while the rate among men aged 25–34 years reached 199 per million during 1943 before falling to 66 per million by 1946. The year 1942 seems to represent the nadir of hopelessness in the face of the relentless march of fascist militarism across the globe. As the historian Robert Mackay has convincingly demonstrated, many in Britain by 1942, despite official propaganda and the Prime Minister's rhetoric that 'We Can Take It', simply could not take it at all. Even the most optimistic seemed to fall into a death-embracing depression, exemplified most poignantly by the suicide of Staff Sergeant Felix Lloyd Powell of the Peacehaven Home Guard. In 1915 he had written, with his brother George, the popular and optimistic First World War marching song 'Pack Up Your Troubles in Your Old Kit Bag and Smile, Smile, Smile'. On 10 February 1942 he shot himself through the heart with his service rifle.

It is reasonable to surmise that the apparent hopelessness of seemingly endless war, reinforced by the randomness of death from the sky, reached a low point in 1942. The news was sometimes good, but more often horrifyingly bad. On the balance sheet of war the sinking the previous May of the predatory German leviathan *Bismarck* (56,000 tons) would be far outweighed by a sequence of unprecedented humiliations. 1942 was to be a year of defeat and pessimism. Life was bleak, and dangerous, for soldier and civilian alike, and the news from the front was rarely anything but gloomy. It was a sense of hopelessness exacerbated, or so the Prime Minister believed, by the depredations of woe-mongering sections of the British media – most particularly the *Daily Mirror*, *Daily Mail* and *Daily Herald* – that were salivating like vultures over the soon-to-be-dead carcass of British freedom.

As the new year of 1942 dawned this gloom was compounded by the astounding reports of rapid Japanese gains down the Malayan Peninsula, including the startling news that the battleship *Prince of Wales* and the battle cruiser *Repulse* had been lost to Japanese air attack. To a British population imbued with the myth of *their* vessels ruling the waves to enforce Pax Britannica, the loss of these capital ships – to Japanese pilots widely derided as having such poor eyesight as to be virtually blind – was almost incomprehensible.

Although he never displayed his fears in public, even the Prime Minister was depressed. Assailed on every side by bad news, Averell Harriman, Roosevelt's special envoy to London, noted to the President that Churchill's confidence had been shattered, 'to such an extent that he has not been able to stand up to this adversity [the relentless news of defeat] with his old vigour'. Churchill's doctor, Charles Wilson (later Lord Moran), recalled that the news of Singapore 'stupefied the Prime Minister'. A month later, Wilson observed, 'something of the old crusading fire had already left him'. Cadogan agonised to his diary on 10 February: 'News all round frightful. Singapore is going to be a bloody disaster and sinkings – especially of tankers – are climbing up to a murderous figure.' Two days later, his diary reached a new level of despair:

The blackest day, yet, of the war. Singapore evidently only a drawn out agony. Burma threatened . . . Meanwhile, [the German battle cruisers] 'Scharnhorst', 'Gneisenau' and 'Prinz Eugen' cockily steamed out of Brest this morning [where they had been block-aded for a year] and up the *Channel* in broad daylight, and so far I have been unable to hear that we have been able to knock any paint off them. We are nothing but failure and inefficiency everywhere and the Japs are murdering our men and raping our women in Hong Kong . . .

In the same breath, perhaps demonstrating the true priority of his concerns, Cadogan noted that he was 'running out of whisky and can get no more drink of any kind. But if things go on as they're going, that won't matter.' The limited military successes of 1941, several of which had consequences of strategic significance for the Allies, such as the defence of the Middle East (Iraq, Syria and Iran) against Axis expansion in the region, together with the 242-day defence of the siege of Tobruk, which prevented Rommel from steamrolling his Afrika Korps all the way to the Nile, were now long forgotten in the anxiety of the present moment.

For all the while, the Battle of the Atlantic was raging unabated, threatening Britain's very survival as a country, let alone her ability to fight back against her enemies. The German North Sea surface raiders such as the massive battleships *Bismarck* and *Tirpitz* threat-ened to join the massive U-boat campaign in the Atlantic against shipping en route to the British Isles, a shockingly effective offen-sive that Churchill later described as the only thing that ever really frightened him. Churchill felt – but did not publicly express – this despair, as Wilson was to observe at first hand:

One day when things at sea were at their worst, I happened to go to the Map-room. There I found the P.M. He was standing with his back to me, staring at the huge chart with the little black beetles representing German submarines. 'Terrible,' he muttered. I was about to retreat when he whipped round and brushed past me with his head down. I am not sure he saw me. He knows that we may lose the war at sea in a few months and that he can do nothing about it. I wish to God I could put out the fires that seem to be consuming him.

On that particular Friday the daily distillation of air, naval and 'military' activity (the latter denoting events on land), prepared for the Chiefs of Staff Committee and the Prime Minister, noted that there had been thirteen sweeps of the French coast that day, during which the RAF had claimed thirteen German aircraft destroyed, with six damaged and a further six 'probables'. British losses amounted to six aircraft and five pilots, one of whom was the much-decorated 39-year-old fighter pilot Group Captain Victor Beamish DSO and Bar, DFC, AFC, who was not seen by his colleagues to exit his burning Spitfire, and was therefore presumed dead. The previous night Bomber Command had sent 234 Wellingtons and Stirlings to bomb the venerable Hanseatic city of Lübeck, and twenty-three other sorties of various kinds, including leaflet-dropping, were recorded. The ancient wooden city was devastated, to the delight of the British popular press, the *Daily Express* exulting in the fact that at long last the Germans had been made to experience a British version of the 'blitz'.

The attack on Lübeck was the harbinger of dreadful things to come, as it constituted the first in a series of violent British assaults on German cities designed to undermine the German war effort by direct attacks on civilian morale. It was hoped, by the architect of this onslaught in London ('Bomber' Harris) and the Defence Council which gave it sanction, that revulsion at the destruction wrought from the skies would quickly turn the German people away from their political masters and therefore against the war. The German leadership was horrified at the ramifications for its regime of the attack. Joseph Goebbels, the propaganda minister, recorded in his diary:

The damage is really enormous; I have been shown a newsreel of the destruction. It is horrible. One can well imagine how such a bombardment affects the population . . . We can't get away from the fact that the English air-raids have increased in scope and importance; if they can be continued on these lines, they might conceivably have a demoralising effect on the population.

But, as in the impact of the 'blitz' on the inhabitants of British cities during the two great aerial assaults in 1940 and 1944, the German people proved more resilient to horror than might have been expected. The eventual judgement was that this furious nocturnal onslaught did not have the desired effect, but these were early days, and it was one of the few means by which puny Britain could, at this desperate stage of the war, fight back against the overwhelming strength of the German juggernaut.

Further afield the impact of the war was being felt in new corners. Mrs Eleanor Roosevelt returned to New York that night by plane from the west coast. She recorded in her diary that the flight was unusually comfortable. But during her journey she was informed that two US destroyers had been lost at sea. 'I cannot bear to think of the many women whose hearts ache for the boys and men who are lost with each of these ships,' she wrote that night:

> as well as any one of the airplanes that fail to come back from a raid, or that crash somewhere in this country or in foreign parts. These days are terrible ones for the men themselves and for the women who wait at home for news. So many of the boys are very young and, under ordinary circumstances, would have their whole lives still before them. I wonder if women in every country are making up their minds that out of this war there shall come some kind of permanent peace.

As she was writing, Lieutenant Commander Harry Hicks and the 140-man crew of the USS *Atik*, a 3,200-ton American 'Q' Ship, were fighting and losing their own lonely, brutal war three hundred miles into the Western Atlantic, off the coast of Virginia. The *Atik*'s men were victims of Vice Admiral Dönitz's U-boat campaign against Allied shipping. *U-123* successfully sank the *Atik*, and her crew, whose survivors took to the life rafts. All perished in an ensuing storm. *U-123*'s home base was Lorient, on the newly captured French Atlantic coast.

On the same day in France, the first transport of Jews destined for Auschwitz, all of whom had been arrested in Paris the previous December, made their way by train from their transit and detention camp at Royallieu in the Compiègne Forest, 50 miles north of the capital. They were the first of 45,000 French civilians to be transported east, Frenchmen delivered into the hands of the Nazis by Frenchmen. It was this chilling conclusion that had first struck the young resistance leader Marie-Madeleine Fourcade a few months before: 'The implacable reality that I had been refusing to face for so many months now became crystal clear to me. So far . . . all our friends had been hunted and struck down by Frenchmen.'

It was another day, and night, therefore, of total war. In Britain, the home fires burned but dimly. In 1941 food had become severely rationed as a consequence of German success in sinking vast quantities of precious shipping, a situation that was to worsen dramatically in 1942 as the Battle of the Atlantic reached its destructive peak. The loss of Malaya and Singapore stopped supplies of rubber, tin and rice at a stroke. The wartime coalition government, forced against its natural inclination to practise the politics of austerity, oversaw a draconian rise in taxes, the basic rate reaching an unprecedented 50 per cent.

The fact had now sunk in as never before that this was a no-holds-barred war to the death, in which the entire resources of the nation had to be applied, without exception. Accordingly the National Service Act was extended to introduce conscription for unmarried women between the ages of twenty and thirty, to add to that for men which had been brought in at the outbreak of war. The gloom reflected in diaries of the period remained pervasive. On Saturday 21 March Sir Alexander Cadogan wrote in his diary: 'Not much doing. We are in a period of awful – and perhaps disastrous – stagnation. I hope we are planning aggressive action . . . I am personally convinced, in spite of all the obvious risks, and chances of disaster, that we must do something active in the next four months.' Ten days later General Alan Brooke, the Chief of the Imperial Staff, observed:

> The last day of the first quarter of 1942, fateful year in which we have already lost a large proportion of the British Empire, and we are on the high road to lose a great deal more of it! During the last fortnight I have had for the first time since the war started a growing conviction that we are going to lose this war unless we control it very differently and fight it with more determination . . .
>
> It is all desperately depressing . . .
>
> I wonder if we shall muddle through this time as we have done in the past? There are times when I wish to God I had not been placed at the helm of a ship that seems to be heading inevitably for the rocks.

And yet, the truth was that amidst this gloom the portents of victory were there for those who could see them. Two in particular were significant. The first was Operation *Barbarossa*, Hitler's invasion of the Soviet Union in June 1941. The second, eagerly anticipated by Winston Churchill, was the arrival in the war of the United States, propelled by Japan's offensive in the Pacific and the Far East. Within days of the attack on Pearl Harbor on 7 December 1941 Churchill was on RMS *Queen Mary*, in great secret, en route to embrace his new co-belligerent. It was a moment for which he had long hoped, recognising that without the might of the United States on her side it was only a matter of time before Britain, too, succumbed and slid beneath the waves of the totalitarian tidal wave that had already drowned the old countries of Europe in blood and terror.

TWO

Enter the Commandos

Even as the defeated British Expeditionary Force was struggling off the beaches near Dunkirk in early June 1940 the British Prime Minister was urging the consideration of means whereby offensive operations, even if on a small scale, could be mounted against the German armies now sweeping over northern France. The impulse to strike back was, for Winston Churchill, urgent and strong. On Tuesday 4 June 1940 – the final day of the Dunkirk evacuation – Churchill sent a memo to his Chief of Staff, General Hastings ('Pug') Ismay, urging that:

> . . . we should immediately set to work to organise raiding forces on these coasts where the populations are friendly. Such forces might be composed of self-contained, thoroughly-equipped units of say 1,000 up to not more than 10,000 when combined. Surprise would be ensured by the fact that their destination would be concealed until the last moment. What we have seen at Dunkirk shows how quickly troops can be moved off (and I suppose on) to selected points if need be. How wonderful it would be if the Germans could be made to wonder where they were going to be struck next, instead of forcing us to try to wall in the Island and roof it over! An effort must be made to shake off the mental and moral prostration to the will and initiative of the enemy from which we suffer.

Independently, but at precisely the same time, the restive mind of Lieutenant Colonel Dudley Clarke, a South African-born officer in the Royal Artillery who was at the time military assistant to the newly appointed Chief of the Imperial General Staff, General Sir John Dill, was trying to solve the same problem. Clarke, whose ideas were later to help develop some of the war's most imaginative deceptions, was described by the Countess of Ranfurly in 1943 as 'quite small, brilliantly clever and imaginative and always on the edge of laughter' and by Field Marshal Wavell as someone in whom he 'recognised an original, unorthodox outlook on soldiering'. Some of that imagination and unorthodoxy were put to good use in 1940. That same warm, early summer evening, wandering the mile home from the War Office on Whitehall – a journey that took him twenty minutes, along Pall Mall, up St James's Street, crossing Piccadilly at The Ritz and then to his flat in the garret of an old seventeenth-century house in Stratton Street in Mayfair – Clarke asked himself how Britain, given the disaster on the Continent, might fight back against the triumph of the Wehrmacht.

Pondering the subject that night, he sketched out a paper that he gave to Dill the next morning. Clarke's suggestion was to form bands of uniformed guerrillas that could carry out attacks on the overstretched German supply lines reaching deep into Europe. His ideas were framed by his knowledge of the Boer commandos who had wreaked havoc on the ponderous British in the South African war, making up for their weakness in conventional terms by mounting pinprick raids against their more conservatively organised opponents. He also had personal experience of the impact made by 'ill-armed fanatics on native ground of their own choosing' in Palestine during the Arab Revolt in 1936, far outweighing their tiny numbers. 'Guerrilla warfare was always in fact the answer of the ill-equipped patriot in the face of a vaster though ponderous military machine,' Clarke considered, 'and that seemed to me to be precisely the position in which the British Army found itself in June 1940. And, since the commando seemed the best exponent of guerrilla warfare which history could produce, it was presumably the best model we could adopt.' Dill was an instant convert: he showed the paper to the Prime Minister the day after he had received it from Clarke.

Churchill responded as enthusiastically as Dill when he received Clarke's paper on 6 June. The day before he had fired off a missive to his Chiefs of Staff demanding that enterprises be prepared to conduct a ceaseless 'offensive against the whole German occupied coastline' using 'specially trained troops of the hunter class, who can develop a reign of terror first of all on the "butcher and bolt" policy'. Now, when he heard Clarke's ideas, he told Dill to waste no time in organising their implementation. To Clarke's surprise he found himself, later that day, catapulted into the Directorate of Operations to command a new branch (MO9) responsible for converting his bright idea into some form of military reality. 'Your Commando scheme is approved,' Dill had told him, 'and I want you to get it going at once. Try to get a raid across the Channel mounted at the earliest possible moment.' The name Clarke had instinctively given to these new troops – 'commandos' – was picked straight out of the title of Deneys Reitz's exciting account of the activities of mobile columns of Boer fighters: men who, despite their inferiority in numbers and supplies, had struck back vigorously and successfully against the British in South Africa forty years before. The name resonated deeply with fighting soldiers, though less so with the more instinctively conservative military caste that populated Whitehall at the time. Despite some resistance, the name stuck, although for some time the formal designation of the Commando organisation was the Special Service Brigade, a name regarded with deep hostility by commandos because of the Nazi connotations of the 'SS' (*Schutzstaffel*) abbreviation.

The Commando concept was, like its Boer precursor, conceived in the midst of failure. Without the humiliation that faced the British Army in 1940 it seems unlikely that the idea would have gained any traction in military thinking. Hilary St George Saunders, the wartime 'recorder' on the staff of HQ Combined Operations, and the then anonymous author of *Combined Operations: The Official Story of the Commandos* published in New York in 1943 to publicise British feats of arms to an American audience, admitted that the sole reason for the establishment of the new organisation was because, at the time, 'there was no existing unit of the British Army which could be made available for raiding operations. That is the bald truth.' With the loss of the British Expeditionary Force in France, Britain's armoury was suddenly, and most grievously, impoverished, and those troops that remained were required to defend their own shores. At the time, explains Dudley Clarke, there were only forty Thompson sub-machinegun carbines ('Tommy guns') in the whole of Britain. The Commandos suffered, as Clarke admitted, from a debilitating and 'stringent economy':

> So urgent was the need of every sort of arm and equipment to refit the B.E.F. that raiding had to be carried out on a Woolworth basis. For this reason the Commandos were armed, equipped, organised and administered for one task and one task only – tip-and-run raids of not more than 48 hours from bases in England against the Continent of Europe . . . So short, in fact, had been the supplies of arms that the Commandos at first had only a small training scale of weapons and each in turn drew up its full complement of Tommy-guns etc., from a communal store on the eve of a raid!

Within a week Clarke, who had rushed to Scotland the day following his appointment to interview and recruit men from the Independent Companies that had been formed from the Territorial Army for operations in Norway, and who were now kicking their heels guarding Glasgow against the threat of German parachutists, had drafted a memorandum which was dispatched under the signature of the Director of Military Operations and Plans, Major General Dick Dewing, on 13 June. 'The object of forming a commando,' the memorandum explained, 'is to collect together a number of individuals trained to fight independently as an irregular and not as a formed military unit. For this reason a commando will have no unit equipment and need not necessarily have a fixed establishment. Any establishment that may be produced will be for the purposes of allotting appropriate ranks in the right proportions to each other.'

The procedure proposed for raising and maintaining commandos is as follows. One or two officers in each Command will be selected as Commando Leaders. They will each be instructed to select from their own Commands a number of Troop Leaders to serve under them. The Troop Leaders will in turn select the officers and men to form their own Troop.

While no strengths have yet been decided upon I have in mind commandos of a strength of something like 10 troops of roughly 50 men each. Each troop will have a commander and one or possibly two other officers . . .

Once the men have been selected the commando leader will be given an area (usually a seaside town) where his commando will live and train while not engaged on operations. The officers and men will receive no Government quarters or rations but will be given a consolidated money allowance to cover their cost of living. They will live in lodgings, etc., of their own selection in the area allotted to them and parade for training as ordered by their Leaders. They will usually be allowed to make use of a barracks, camp, or other suitable place as a training ground. They will also have an opportunity of practising with boats on beaches nearby . . .

The commando organisation is really intended to provide no more than a pool of specialised soldiers from which irregular units of any size and type can be very quickly created to undertake any particular task.

The main characteristics of a commando in action are:

a. Capable only of operating independently for 24 hours;

b. Capable of very wide dispersion and individual action;

c. Not capable of resisting an attack or overcoming a defence of formed bodies of troops, i.e., specialising in tip and run tactics dependent for their success upon speed, ingenuity and dispersion.

Recruitment began straight away, but as this had never been done before, it proved to be a rather hit-or-miss affair. On 20 June a notice went out across the Army for volunteers for hazardous service. When Captain John Durnford-Slater RA, adjutant of the 23rd Medium and Heavy Training Regiment at Plymouth, saw the letter his heart jumped. Like many of his fellows, stuck in jobs a long way from the fighting, and desperate to contribute in some positive way to the fighting, he was bored rigid in his important but nevertheless humdrum job, and pestered his commanding officer relentlessly to allow him to apply. Grudging permission was granted. An application and interview followed. On 28 June 1940, a few days after returning from London, he was surprised to receive a signal:

CAPT. J.F. DURNFORD SLATER IS APPOINTED TO RAISE AND COMMAND NUMBER 3 COMMANDO IN THE RANK OF LIEUTENANT COLONEL. GIVE EVERY ASSISTANCE AND RELEASE FROM PRESENT APPOINTMENT FORTHWITH AS OPERATIONAL ROLE IMMINENT.

The operational role to which the signal referred was that of countering what was considered by many to be the imminent invasion of Britain. So urgent was the requirement that Durnford-Slater was ordered to raise his new unit within two weeks, forming it in Plymouth. The most daunting part was selecting men on the basis of a ten-minute interview, but very quickly Durnford-Slater worked out his formula. It was not perfect, but it seemed to work:

> On the whole the type I looked for was the quiet, modest type of Englishman, who knew how to laugh and how to work. Other Commandos were formed especially for the Scots and the Irish, although we had quite a few of these mixed up with our core of Englishmen. I always avoided anyone who talked too much, and soon learned a lesson in this when a fine athletic-looking fellow who had taken part in many sports proved useless and boastful and had to be discharged. We never enlisted anybody who looked like the tough-guy criminal type, as I considered that this sort of man would be a coward in the battle.

Lieutenant Stuart Chant, a pre-war Territorial Army soldier who had been with the British Expeditionary Force that escaped from Dunkirk, arrived by small coaster at Ramsgate on 31 May 1940:

> Shortly after our return to England an order was circulated seeking volunteers for 'special service'. Certain qualifications were listed: an ability to march long distances – I reckoned I must have marched hundreds of miles in my three-and-a-half years' service in the Artists' Rifles; the ability to swim, which I could, well; and a knowledge of small boats – I used to spend weekends sailing and fishing at sea. I applied and, in October 1940, was accepted and ordered to join No 5 Commando, then stationed in Felixstowe.

Another recruit was the Hollywood actor David Niven, who had returned from Tinsel Town to 'do his bit' for the Old Country, and at the time of the evacuation of the remnants of the BEF from Dunkirk was kicking his heels on regimental duty (as a company commander) with the 2nd Battalion, The Rifle Brigade in Tidworth. Seeing him restless at the thought of spending the remainder of the war in a military backwater without firing a shot, during what many of his contemporaries were calling the 'Bore War', the adjutant, Captain Mark Kerr, in a moment of kindness (or so Niven thought), showed him the note calling for volunteers. 'There followed qualifications about age and questions about liability to air- and sea-sickness,' Niven recalled.

'I think it must be parachuting,' said Mark. 'I heard rumours that they are forming something like that.'

'Jesus!' I said. 'I don't want any part of that.' But the Tidworth boredom prevailed and 'anything to make a change', I put my name down.

He was interviewed and accepted for the job by Dudley Clarke, who described him as having – happily – 'the least trace of the rigidity of the professional soldier. His was just the character, it seemed, to gain the confidence of the enterprising young leaders whom we hoped to attract into the Commandos . . .'

It was the responsibility of the newly appointed officers then to trawl the local military units for volunteers to join the new organisation. There were no instructions for doing this, however, and the officers had to make it up as they went along. Inevitably, they made mistakes. Major Milton of No. 7 Commando selected those who looked and talked tough, and regretted it immediately:

We tended to go for men who stood out because they had done something unusual in civilian life, like the one who had gone around the Horn in a Finnish sailing ship or another who had been with the International Brigades in Spain or one who had been the leading light in a Glasgow razor gang.

These wilder spirits, however, tended not to respond well to the hard discipline required of Commando troops, and soon found themselves back in their original units, tails between their legs. Because members of the Commandos were on secondment from their parent units, the threat of being Returned to Unit – RTU'd for short – remained the most effective penalty for misbehaviour, or poor performance. On the whole, however, only the best soldiers tended to volunteer, with the result, as Tom Sherman of No. 2 Commando was to attest, that 'the standards were so high we'd cream off the best in the regiments'.

Second Lieutenant Peter Young of the 2nd Battalion, The Bedfordshire and Hertfordshire Regiment and of No. 3 Commando, also recently returned from Dunkirk, took a more pragmatic line from the outset, as he told the historian Robin Neillands: 'Well, you talk to them, don't you. See if they have something to offer, weed out the bullshitters, select the men with potential, the kind who will always get their shot in first.' He was to add in his book *Storm from the Sea*:

We did not take our full complement of N.C.O.s, preferring to promote our own men when they had proved themselves, a stroke of genius for which we were to be deeply thankful later on. The great majority of our men were reservists, who had served seven years with the colours, mostly in India. Their average age was about twenty-six, and they were well-trained, keen, professional soldiers in the prime of life. They knew their weapons, had seen some fighting and wanted more.

For Dudley Clarke the ideal mixture entailed 'the dash of the Elizabethan pirate, the Chicago gangster and the Frontier tribesman, allied to a professional efficiency and standard of discipline of the best Regular soldier'. For his part Lieutenant Colonel Charles Newman, commanding officer of No. 2 Commando, told the writer David Mason that he chose 'to recruit people for their brains and common sense, people such as schoolmasters and business executives, bank clerks and solicitors, men on whom he could rely to carry out their tasks with the right combination of daring and caution'. Lieutenant Ronnie Swayne of No. 1 Commando regarded Newman's No. 2 Commando as having a 'very high rate of intelligence and quality, both officers and men . . . They were very good. In a Commando like No 2 it was much more like a well-run public school. I mean they were put more on their honour. Tough discipline wasn't necessary. In my Commando there was a lot of tough discipline.'

Large numbers of commando soldiers, such as Charles Newman himself (The Essex Regiment) and Lieutenant Stuart Chant (The Artists' Rifles), had been members of the pre-war Territorial Army, the TA or 'Terriers' who were mobilised 'for the duration' at the outset of war. The TA had seen a dramatic growth in applications in the late 1930s, as many thinking young men, recognising the clouds of war for what they were, determined to do their bit to stop Hitler when the balloon went up, as they were certain it would. Major James Dunning, who joined No. 4 Commando in 1940, believed that there were three main characteristics in those who volunteered. The first – common to all – was a desire above all else 'to have a go at Jerry'. When he was called up in 1939 Newman recalled: 'I'd been Territorial for sixteen years, having started for a year as a Private Soldier, and loved every minute of it.' The 'embodiment' of the Territorial Army on 1 September 1939,* he admitted

although one at heart hated the idea of war, was the fulfilment of nearly all Territorial minds, to serve with one's own County Regiment and have a smack at the Hun who'd been asking for it for so long. The one desire was to soldier with one's friends, to have under one's command all those lads from Barking, East Ham, and outer London whom we had trained from raw recruits.

---

* Embodiment entailed the calling out of the Territorial Army, or parts of it, for full-time military service in defence of the country.

We knew all their families and loved them all and now was the
chance to fight with them.

The second group were the professional soldiers, regular, reserve
and TA, who felt deeply let down by the fall of France and Dunkirk,
and were inspired by revenge. Charles Newman wrote in 1970:
'We had all been through a period of everything going wrong for
Britain . . . and as we all loved Britain we had an earnest desire
to do something about it, to strike back.'

The third group were those from the traditionally non-combatant
arms and services of the Army (i.e. those not in the 'Teeth Arms'
– infantry, armour or artillery) 'who welcomed and cherished the
prospects offered by Special Service'. Whatever their motives, all
were volunteers, and all were on secondment from their parent
corps and regiments, with the result that from the outset commandos were a rich mixture of virtually every cap badge in the Army.
The vast majority were highly motivated (those who weren't did
not last long), and demonstrated throughout five long years of
war that they were the crème de la crème of British soldiery.

The Commandos recruited from the broadest possible spectrum
of military service, age and experience, with the result that they
became cultural melting pots in the Army, breaking down tradition, social background and military custom to create a genuinely
meritocratic force probably unique in the modern history of the
British Army. In 6 Troop of No. 2 Commando, for instance, the
three officers, as the historian Peter Stanley demonstrates, were of
a social mix that would have been inconceivable in a British fighting regiment before the war. Lieutenant Micky Burn was a
deep-thinking man of action from a prosperous upper-middle-class
home, public school-educated, who had joined the Territorial Army
in 1937 because he saw the war clouds looming, and felt that the
country was in a very feeble state and needed defending. In civilian
life he had started a career as a journalist for *The Times* and early
developed a passionate hatred of social inequality that led to an

infatuation with Hitler's Germany, which he soon dropped in favour of socialism when he saw through Nazi propaganda. Gris Davies-Scourfield of the King's Royal Rifles Corps, who was to spend time incarcerated with Burn in Colditz, described him affectionately as 'one of these ex-public school intellectual communists whom one often encountered during the Thirties. Micky, whom I came to like enormously, actually told me one day that I was a typical barrier to all social progress and would undoubtedly end up one day, nice fellow though I might be, hanging from a lamp post!'

Second Lieutenant Tommy Peyton was another ex-public school-boy, who had joined the regular Army in the late 1930s, the son of an upper-middle-class family which had produced Army offic-ers for generations. He was twenty years old. By contrast, Lieutenant Morgan Jenkins was the son of a miner from Tynewydd in Glamor-gan who had made his way through Brecon County School. His route to the Commandos had also led, like Micky Burn's, through the Territorial Army, and by November 1940 he had been commissioned.

The men of each Commando became one large, extended family, common to the British regimental tradition where esprit de corps during the times of peace creates bonds that are hard to break in time of war. For Lieutenant Corran Purdon of the Royal Ulster Rifles and No. 12 Commando the friendships developed amongst his fellow officers were profound. Not for nothing was No. 12 Commando nicknamed 'The Happy Commando':

Gerard Brett, who was in my own No 12 Commando and also in my Regiment, had been a curator at the Victoria and Albert Museum and had written a book on the Byzantine Age. We had joined the Commando together. Bill Etches of No 3 Commando was another good friend. We had been at the Royal Military College, Sandhurst, together before the War. Bill was at Vaagso with No 3 Commando while Gerard and I had sailed on the second Lofoten Islands raid.

Ronnie Swayne of No 1 Commando, huge, black-haired, amusing and a music lover, had just missed his Blue for rugger at Oxford, due to injury. Ronnie had raided the French coast already. Stuart Chant was another fine rugger player, dark, good looking and great fun. Tall, thin Paul Bassett-Wilson was in my Commando and went on to win an MC and Bar. Harry Pennington, the Oxford rugger Blue, was another officer whom I liked very much, immensely fit and tough.

Mark Woodcock of 3 Commando, a delightful, ever-cheerful chap, who had broken both legs mountaineering, really should not have been with us but for his terrific guts and enthusiasm. Chris Smalley, a quiet, reliable man with a heavy moustache and ruddy face, inspired confidence; he and the huge, slightly stooping, powerful extrovert, Bertie Burtinshaw were both from No 5 Commando. Bill Bradley of 3 Commando and I had been babies together in India where our parents were friends.

Relationships between officers and men tended to be quite different in the Territorial Army and the Commandos from those that prevailed across most of the Army, which tended to absorb the traditions of the pre-war Army and in any case reflected the starker class divisions that existed in society at the time. Charles Newman commanded by virtue of a powerful, friendly personality, compelling loyalty by leading from the front, and demonstrating an intense, personal and very genuine interest in and affection for his men. He was, by every measure, an outstanding commanding officer. Micky Burn remembered him as 'convivial, gregarious, a non-intellectual, ringside, rugger-playing hearty, who also played jazz and music-hall on the piano'. Every photograph of him has a pipe clenched firmly between his teeth. The young Lieutenant Corran Purdon, who saw his commanding officer through the distance imposed by rank, described him like an uncle, with the appearance of a 'battered old elephant'. The newspaperman Gordon Holman described him, at first glance, as 'hardly the type one would have expected to find commanding special service troops. His jolly, easy-going manner, his pipe held loosely in the corner of his mouth, his soft, unhurried speech gave hardly a hint of the tremendous courage, determination and power of leadership he possessed. In a matter of hours I realised that every one of his men believed in him utterly.'

Private Bob Bishop recalled an occasion at a regimental boxing match between No. 2 Commando and a neighbouring artillery unit, whilst at Ayr, which displayed Newman's leadership credentials to the full:

Before the first bout commenced, the artillery CO entered the hall and took his ringside seat amid some mutterings from his own men to the effect of 'officers always getting the best seats'. Then Charlie made his entrance and the difference could be compared to codfish versus caviar. The entire Commando rose up and belted out this verse:

Clap hands! – Here comes Charlie!
Clap hands! – GOOD OLD CHARLIE!
Clap hands! – Here's OUR CHARLIE now!!

The Colonel grinned, and turned with his hands clasped above his head in the prize-fighter manner to acknowledge what he knew was a genuine expression of admiration from his boys. The artillery lads looked on in disbelief. They just could not understand how we respected and admired our Charlie.

This more relaxed relationship between officers and men is exemplified by the attitude of Lieutenant Corran Purdon to his NCOs, one of deeply felt mutual respect that he still retained in his ninetieth year when interviewed for this book:

As an original member of No. 12 Commando I knew every man who had been selected for the operation. Sergeant Deery, a fair-haired, cheery Royal Inniskilling Fusilier and Corporal Johnson of the Gordons, a trifle dour and rock-steady, were both to win Military Medals on the Raid.

Corporal Jumbo Reeves, a former RAF pilot, complete with appropriate handlebar moustache and his guitar, extrovert and amusing; Corporal Joe Molloy, a staunch and dependable southern Irishman; little Corporal Blount of the South Wales Borderers, a tiger in action; Corporal Jones 'the Post', strong, large and, like so many of his fellow countrymen in Wales, possessed of a fine voice; Corporal Chetwynd of the Sherwood Foresters, a tough reliable soldier; Corporal Bob Wright RE, intelligent, brave, cheerful and strong; Corporal Ferguson and Corporal Lemon, two grand Ulster soldiers from the North Irish Horse; and then the remaining three corporals of the four comprising my own splendid team.

Corporal Ron Chung RE was powerful, brave, half-Chinese, with a strong and amusing personality. Corporals 'Cab' Callaway, gallant, reliable and ever-cheerful, and Bob Hoyle, who had a great sense of humour under a slightly serious appearance, very courageous, steady, intelligent and resilient.

Commandos lived in the community amongst which they trained, rather than in barracks. Although initially an administrative convenience – there was no time to try to find military accommodation to house these units when they were raised – it proved to be a stroke of unplanned genius, for in these arrangements lay the first requirement of a commando, namely to be self-motivated and self-reliant. With an allowance of six shillings and eightpence per day, the men had to find their own accommodation and provide for their own subsistence. Most rose to the challenge, as did the thousands of willing landladies across the country's seaside towns, where the various Commandos were based, who found themselves suddenly part and parcel of the Commando community. A myriad of unprepossessing domestic sanctuaries in Salcombe, Falmouth, Dartmouth, St Ives, Paignton, Tenby, Weymouth, Brighton, Bexhill, Seaford, Worthing, Bridlington, Largs, Ayr, Girvan and Troon overnight became mini-armouries, full of the heavy clobber of the soldier's life, with rifles propped up in hallways, packs, ropes and boots in the sitting room, unprimed hand grenades and tommy gun ammunition piled up in the kitchen.

Mrs Cécilie Birney recalled in exasperation rather than annoyance the ubiquitous presence of deadly weapons in the house. When stationed in Langholm on one occasion Cécilie and her new husband, Captain David Birney, watched in amusement as Tom Peyton tried to persuade Micky Burn to dispose of a mortar bomb in his possession, about which Tom was concerned. On another occasion, when stationed in Paignton, Mickey turned up for a party one evening with a bag of gelignite. He explained to Cécilie that he felt uncomfortable keeping it under his bed in the hotel: would she look after it instead? Without a moment's hesitation the young Mrs Birney found a place for the offending item in her kitchen.

The story of the soldier reprimanded on parade for the state of his dirty rifle or unpolished boots blaming it on his landlady is part of Commando lore. 'This was in every way a splendid arrangement,' remarked Lieutenant Colonel John Durnford-Slater, as 'it increased a man's self-reliance and self-respect, developed his initiative and made him available for training; the old barrack-room boredom and bad language were eliminated.' It was common, commented Hilary St George Saunders, for the men to be dismissed at one place one afternoon and 'told that the next parade will be at 6 a.m. on the following morning at a place 60, 70, sometimes 100 miles away. How each Commando soldier gets to that place is his own affair.'

THREE

Training for War

A period of structural consolidation took place later in 1940, with the Commandos merging with the existing Independent Companies that had been quickly formed for operations in Norway, to become 'Special Service' companies, and then battalions. But these arrangements did not last long, and by the spring of 1941 their organisation had settled into the form they were to retain until the end of the war. It 'started the ball rolling for the happiest and most exciting part of the war for me,' confessed Charles Newman, who was given command of No. 2 Commando. '[Major] Bill Copland was to be my Second-in-command and [Captain] Stan Day [the] Adjutant. The Commando was about 460 strong. I moved over to Paignton and got down to work with my new command.'

From October 1940 the commander of the entire Commando structure was a 41-year-old Irish Guardsman who had distinguished himself commanding 2nd Battalion, Irish Guards in the fighting in France earlier in the year, Brigadier Charles Haydon DSO OBE. Newman was later to comment of Haydon that 'a finer soldier I have yet to meet'. With his twelve Commandos spread across the length and breadth of the United Kingdom, Haydon established his headquarters at Theale, a small village south-west of Reading. In a letter to *The Times* on 6 November 1945 Lieutenant Micky Burn, recently released from captivity in Germany as a prisoner of war, explained the paramount role Haydon played between

1940 and 1942 in successfully establishing the Commandos in the British Order of Battle:

> His object was set down lucidly in his training programmes, which were carried out conscientiously during the experimental period before action . . . He wanted all his soldiers to be self-reliant, able to use individual initiative without harm to discipline, physically perfectly fit, instructed in explosives and first aid, as well as in the usual weapons, and trained to assume that no obstacle could not be overcome. He had to keep the experiment alive against the prejudice of those who thought it a waste of time, and against the impatience of his own volunteer force, who were constantly keyed up to undertake raids that were often cancelled at the last moment. At a period in 1941, when the lurid Press were describing the Commandos as thugs and cat-burglars, he insisted that their discipline should be as strict in essential respects as that of the Regular Army and their appearance as smart. He aimed at a regular irregularity. This training had a stimulating effect on character; after a few months of it, officers and men were transformed.

There were eventually twelve Commandos under Haydon's charge, numbered 1 through to 12. Each comprised three hundred men in six troops, each of which was commanded by a troop leader (a captain), supported by a troop sergeant major (TSM) (a staff sergeant or warrant officer). The fifty men in each troop had two sections, each commanded by a lieutenant, both of which again were divided into two fighting teams, commanded by lance corporals or corporals and armed with Bren guns, rifles and the famous Thompson sub-machine carbine, known in military lists simply as the TSMC. The latter, able to spit out a heavy, bull-nosed .45 slug at an average rate of 600 rounds a minute, became an inextricable part of the Commando identity.

Commando training was, from the very inception of the

organisation, tough. To a large extent this was self-imposed by the earliest commando soldiers who felt somehow that to beat the Germans they needed to be stronger, fitter and better trained than they would otherwise be as standard infantrymen. As a result it proved to be imaginative and challenging, extending through all weathers, seasons and terrain. Significant characteristics of this training were the emphasis placed on night work, boatmanship, practice with live ammunition (and an acceptance of the small number of inevitable casualties) and explosive demolitions. Training extended beyond 9 a.m. to 5 p.m., and Monday to Friday. At the beginning there was no template: commanding officers competed with each other to draw up regimes that tested their men to the limits of their physical and mental endurance, and their own. It was in the absence of any comprehensive training plan that Lieutenant Colonel Charles Newman came up with his own set of requirements for the men of No. 2 Commando, through which a strong sense can be gained of the physical and mental demands made on this new type of soldier:

1. The object of Special Service is to have available a fully trained body of first class soldiers, ready for active offensive operations against an enemy in any part of the world.

2. Irregular warfare demands the highest standards of initiative, mental alertness and physical fitness, together with the maximum skill at arms. No Commando can feel confident of success unless all ranks are capable of thinking for themselves; of thinking quickly and of acting independently, and with sound tactical sense, when faced by circumstances which may be entirely different to those which were anticipated.

3. Mentally. The offensive spirit must be the outlook of all ranks of a Commando at all times.

4. Physically. The highest state of physical fitness must at all times be maintained. All ranks are trained to cover at great speed any type of ground for distances of five to seven miles

in fighting order. Examples:

(a) Fighting Order (seven miles in one hour (march and run).

(b) FSMO (Full Service Marching Order) 5 miles in one hour (marching)

9 miles in two hours (marching)

15 miles in 4¼ hours

25 miles in 8 hours

35 miles in 14 hours

After all these distances and times, troops must be ready, in para (a) to fight, and in para (b) to fight after two hours rest.

5. Cliff and mountain climbing and really difficult slopes climbed quickly form a part of Commando training.

6. A high degree of skill in all branches of unarmed combat will be attained.

7. Seamanship and Boatwork. All ranks must be skilled in all forms of boatwork and landing craft whether by day or by night, as a result of which training the sea comes to be regarded as a natural working ground for a Commando.

8. Night sense and night confidence are essential. All ranks will be highly trained in the use of the compass.

9. Map reading and route memorising form an important part of Commando training.

10. All ranks of a Commando will be trained in semaphore, Morse and the use of W[ireless]/T[elegraphy].

11. All ranks will have elementary knowledge of demolitions and sabotage. All ranks will be confident in the handling of all types of high explosive, Bangalore torpedoes, and be able to set up all types of booby traps.

12. A high standard of training will be maintained in all forms of street fighting, occupation of towns, putting towns into a state of defence and the overcoming of all types of obstacles, wire, rivers, high walls etc.

13. All ranks in a Commando should be able to drive motor cycles, cars, lorries, tracked vehicles, trains and motor boats.
14. A high degree of efficiency in all forms of fieldcraft will be attained. Every man in a Commando must be able to forage for himself, cook and live under a bivouac for a considerable period.
15. All ranks are trained in first aid and will be capable of dealing with the dressing of gun-shot wounds and the carrying of the wounded.
16. These are a few among the many standards of training that must be attained during service in a Commando. At all times a high standard of discipline is essential, and the constant desire by all ranks to be fitter and better trained than anyone else.
17. The normal mode of living is that the Special Service Soldier will live in a billet found by himself and fed by the billet for which he will receive 6s 8d per day to pay all his expenses.
18. Any falling short of the standards of training and behaviour on the part of a Special Service Soldier will render him liable to be returned to his unit.

The initial selection requirements demanded men who were perhaps tougher than the norm, and the training that followed became renowned for its rigour. The British Army had always had a tradition of punishing route marches, but the Commandos seemed determined to break all previous records. The standard was to cover 60 miles in twenty-four hours: in one celebrated instance B Troop, No. 12 Commando marched the 63 miles from Crumlin to Londonderry in Northern Ireland in 19 hours. Ten miles in 90 minutes carrying full kit, and 35 miles in 9 hours and 20 minutes (4 hours and 40 minutes less than Newman's original instructions), became the benchmarks for the commando soldier. When Newman decided to take his No. 2 Commando to new quarters in Weymouth he declined the offer of transport and marched them all the way from Paignton, carrying weapons and full fighting order, weighing in excess of 60 pounds. They completed the 120 miles in a leisurely four days.

These long, hard marches proved to be a new approach to physical training in the Army, which had previously focused on gym-based muscle-building and organised games. Of his training for No. 11 Commando in 1940 the 23-year-old Captain Geoffrey Keyes wrote to his mother: 'We march and swim and do other violent things. I go to bed weary and sleep like a dog . . .' Of a later training exercise he told her: 'The first day was a shocker, as we started from scratch with eleven miles cross-country, non-stop in three hours twenty minutes, halt for lunch and then on again. It was no joke.'*

Lieutenant Arthur Kellas of the Border Regiment described being given a group of volunteers from the Grenadier Guards to train at Lochailort in early 1941. He took them on a strenuous three-day march across the hills from Glen Dessary to Loch Nevis and the west coast and back through Fedden in 'foul February sleet':

> The object was a test of endurance on a diet of pemmican, 'that pelican or pemmican stuff', as it was known to the troops, experimental slabs of synthetic nourishment which could be eaten raw like chocolate, or crumbed and cooked like oatmeal, or fried, or chopped up and stewed, according to taste and convenience . . .
>
> As we straggled above Glen Garry on the second day of this campaign, clambering over rocks and floundering in bog, soaked and weary, splashing through rivers in spate and the spray flying, even that sturdy Yorkshireman Duncan, out of the wool business in Bradford, was flagging. In the event it should be confessed that the pemmican ration was supplemented by more illicit

---

* Lieutenant Colonel Keyes was awarded a posthumous VC in late 1941 during a raid on a building in Libya believed (wrongly) to be Rommel's HQ.

venison, a hind brought down by a fusillade on the first evening as we came over the pass in the rain to the sea at Loch Nevis; although indeed most of the men were too tired that night to eat anything, and fell asleep at once in a damp peat-shed at Finiscaig, the Black Place. 'Got pless them', said the old lady there in her soft Highland tone, when she had recovered from her fright to see a column of soldiers come down from the rocks, drenched to the skin, in the dark. 'Sure it iss a far, far way they are after coming, the poor dear souls.'

. . . For a shared discomfort like the Pemmican March makes friends; and the worse the conditions the better the friendship, mysterious product of adversity.

The Commandos pioneered a new approach to physical training in the British Army, which emphasised 'Battle PT', in which exercise was undertaken in the field, wearing boots and equipment. Carrying logs and heavy weapons on runs across the hills helped sections and troops to learn to work together as teams, as well as hardening men for the sort of heavy physical activity they would expect to undergo on live operations. Likewise, exercises were repeatedly carried out in darkness. James Dunning of No. 4 Commando believed that evening or night exercises were undertaken by his troop at least three times a week.

Hilary St George Saunders, in *Combined Operations: The Official Story of the Commandos*, told his American readership that a Commando soldier needed to become proficient in the tools of his trade of war. But this of itself was insufficient, as success in war was as much psychological as it was physical:

He must do more than this; he must master his mind as well as his body and become not only a specially trained soldier but a trained individual soldier. In other words, self-reliance and self-confidence form an integral, a vital part of his mental and moral makeup. To achieve these mutually dependent qualities the men, on entering the depot, are treated as far as possible as individuals. They are required to do everything for themselves. It is not for them to await orders from their officer or their N.C.O. They must do the sensible, obvious thing just because it is the sensible, obvious thing.

He observed that there were four main objects of Commando training, namely:

1. To produce a sense of discipline and esprit de corps, second to none in the armed forces of any country
2. To learn the lesson that darkness is a help and not a hindrance
3. To endow him with a degree of physical fitness approaching that of a trained athlete, and at the same time to give him skill in the handling of all infantry weapons
4. To make him eager always to attack

Recognising early on the virtues of centralised training across his brigade, particularly for its leaders, Charles Haydon took over the Irregular Training Centre. Established at the ruins of Inverailort Castle, Lochailort, in the remote Western Highlands in May 1940 in order to train military saboteurs, it was now, until its disbandment in 1942, handed over to Combined Operations and called the Special Training Centre (STC). Twenty miles west of Fort William, this remote place, brooding over the cold, dark waters of the deep sea loch, retains its lonely beauty still, although a tarmac road now links it to the world. Through its ancient gates walked some of the most remarkable men in the history of British Special Forces, and it was here that David Niven was able to meet other volunteers for 'special duty'. 'Volunteers usually fall into two groups' he observed. 'There are the genuinely courageous who are itching to get at the throat of the enemy, and the restless who will volunteer for anything in order to escape from the boredom of what they are presently doing. There were a few in my category but most of the people I was thrown together with were made of sterner stuff.'

The STC was commanded by Lieutenant Colonel 'Hughie' Stockwell of the Royal Welch Fusiliers, who had distinguished himself in Norway earlier in the year, and who would command a division in Burma in 1945. These included Surgeon-Commander George Murray Levick RN, who had accompanied Captain Scott on his historic expedition to the Antarctic in 1910–13 and whose discovery of the appallingly promiscuous sexual predilections of Adélie penguins so shocked him that he wrote up his results in Greek to hide them from common perusal; Simon 'Shimi' Fraser (Lord Lovat), previously of the Scots Guards and now of the Lovat Scouts, a Territorial Army regiment, and later to become one of the most famous Commando soldiers of the war; his two cousins, David and William ('Bill') Stirling, the former of whom set up the Special Air Service in North Africa; Major James 'Jim' Gavin RE, who had been on the 1936 Everest expedition and had been preparing for another, now aborted, assault in 1940; the Arctic explorer Major Andrew Croft, The Essex Regiment; together with the Spanish Civil war veteran and later Special Operations Executive (SOE) agent Major Peter Kemp.

Other famous names who made significant, even extraordinary personal contributions to the war included 'Mad Mike' Calvert RE of Burma and Chindit fame; Freddie Spencer Chapman, who was to spend three and a half years working for SOE behind Japanese lines in Malaya; Lieutenant (later Colonel) David Sutherland of the SAS and SBS; the senior SOE agent in the Balkans, Fitzroy Maclean; Lieutenant Arthur Kellas (later of SOE and a distinguished diplomat); the adventurer and writer Colonel Peter Fleming (brother of Ian Fleming, inventor of James Bond); the mountaineer Alexander 'Sandy' Wedderburn and the actor Anthony Quayle.

Two of the instructors at the Special Training Centre, Lochailort, were, David Niven recalled, 'two very formidable Shanghai police,

Mr. Sykes and Mr. Fairbairn, who concentrated on teaching us a dozen different ways of killing people without making any noise'. The fighting knife they designed whilst at Lochailort in November 1940 became the famous symbol of the Commandos and their fighting techniques became embedded in the standard training regime for all soldiers, not just of commandos. At Lochailort they trained secret agents for both MI6 and SOE, as well as commandos, and did more than anyone else to introduce successful methods of hand-to-hand fighting (initially called 'self-preservation' and thereafter Unarmed Combat) to the British Army. Corran Purdon described Fairbairn and Sykes as 'looking like two benevolent, square-shaped padres'. They 'took us close combat shooting in their sandbagged, basement range, when moving targets suddenly materialised from the gloom. They gave us all great encourage-ment and confidence.' Marcus Binney tells the story of the unsuspecting Major Henry Hall of the Dorsetshire Regiment in February 1941 when he and a group of other trainees met the two men for the first time:

We gathered at the foot of a large staircase in a big house and two old gentlemen aged approximately fifty-eight and fifty-six dressed in battledress with the rank of captain and both wearing glasses appeared at the top of the stairs and proceeded to fall down the stairs together and landed in battle crouch position with a handgun in one hand and a Fairbairn-Sykes knife in the other.

All commandos were to spend several weeks training in the demanding conditions of the Highland terrain. Micky Burn observed that the innovation in Commando training was to enable men to fight on the assumption that all their officers were dead, a factor that stimulated their own initiative, self-confidence and self-reliance, perhaps for the first time in their lives. Lieutenant Corran Purdon remembered how the 'tremendous amount of fitness training, and the long exercises over the rugged, mountainous countryside which surrounded us were designed to increase our powers of endurance, to accustom us to direction finding, self-reliance and to teach us battle tactics by day and night.' Conspicuous by his presence was the commanding officer of the STC, Lieutenant Colonel 'Hughie' Stockwell, who was, according to Stuart Chant, 'a real fire-eater'. 'Led by Colonel Stockwell,' Purdon recalled, 'we splashed through hip high, freezing sea loch estuaries, forded icy torrents holding boulders to combat the force of the rushing spate, climbed seemingly interminably high mountains and ran down steep scree slopes'. Captain Joe Nicholl MC of No. 2 Commando recalled Commando training in the Highlands (at the successor to the STC, Achnacarry) in 1942. Speaking in the third person, he wrote:

> For P.T. all were stripped to the waist, wearing only denim trousers and boots and gaiters. The exercises were designed to strengthen muscles, rather than simply to get fit. Joe had to learn to handle a length of Scots pine in such a way that, with 8 men underneath, it could be thrown over the head to the other arm. In fact, the team spirit came to be accepted, whether they realised it or not.
>
> Everything had a purpose. Unarmed combat was not just an attempt to learn judo in 3 easy lessons. Nothing was taught that couldn't be learnt and practised by the weakest or dimmest – and put into practice on the toughest. A Toggle rope bridge was an astonishing contraption. With the aid of anything up to 40 of these lengths of rope with an eye at one end and a small smoothed stick at the other, attached together, a three-span bridge could be made and fitted across a swiftly-flowing burn.
>
> The Death Slide consisted of wire stretched across the stream from 20ft up in one tree down to a low tree stump on the other side . . .
>
> The Speed March was an organised attempt to get a Troop a distance of 15 miles in three hours. It was not a race, but it was

deemed a failure if any member of the Troop had to fall out. All were fully equipped and carried rifles or Thompson sub-machine guns. The unfortunates who had been selected to carry the Bren guns were usually helped by others in the Section, or by the Officer, who in any case was expected to be that amount fitter than his men and to set a good example. Eventually this almost became a 'moral obligation'. As a team exercise it was first rate, as well as being planned so that an average rate for each mile was kept up, and any dropping below that meant picking it up again later on. Those Troops which went off too fast to begin with, nearly always found themselves staggering in a long staggering line . . . The route to Spean Bridge and back (7½ miles each way) was impossibly hilly, but it did mean that a swift walk up the inclines left the Section the joy of trotting down the other side . . .

'Me and my Pal' provided a real learn effort. Armed with Thompson sub-machine guns with full magazines and two grenades, two men would start for the first 'mock-up' of the front of a house. As one man moved, the other watched. As soon as one of the cardboard figures appeared, pulled out at the lug of a wire by an instructor, 'Jack' had to fire. Then 'Bill' would rush forward, break the imaginary glass of the window with the butt of his Tommy gun, and throw an imaginary grenade. He waited 2 seconds, and then hurled himself over the window-sill, with Jack following closely. As they came out on the other side, Jack sprinted across to the wall, covered by Bill. Here it was a bit tricky for one to keep an eye on the other while he scrambled over the wall. Then came 'grenade confidence'. Each had to throw a 4-second grenade, and watch it land in the ditch below before taking cover. The first throw and glimpse was always very rapid. The second became almost casual.

David Niven left Lochailort after two months feeling 'unbearably fit'. Stuart Chant remembered Lochailort perhaps not with fondness, but certainly with respect:

The impact on us of this specialist training and of these feats of endurance was extraordinary. Even the humblest and smallest soldier quickly developed into a man 'twice his height', as it were, who thought nothing of hardships which would have seemed impossible to him and his mates a few weeks before arriving in that lonely part of Scotland.

To the officers and men of the newly raised Commandos there was no thought but that one day they would be victorious against an otherwise currently all-powerful enemy. The twenty-year-old Lieutenant Corran Purdon exemplified the view of his peers, in his belief in the certainty of ultimate victory. He and his band of brothers did not despise the regular Army, but knew that in the Commandos they were the vanguard of its resurrection. They knew that, with their adopted principle of 'fast marching and straight shooting' they represented the best that then was in the British Army. They knew, in their heart of hearts, that their time would come, however painful the journey might have to be.

FOUR

The First Raids

Almost immediately after Churchill's injunction in May 1940 to waste no time in striking back against the enemy by launching raids against the German-occupied coastline, attacks across the Channel got under way. It was clear at once, however, especially to those taking part, that there was much to learn about this novel type of warfare. Raids were fine in theory, but proved extremely hard to achieve in practice, and required specialist skills, training, weapons and equipment – especially purpose-designed landing craft – before they could hope to have any kind of measurable success.

The story of the following two years was one of raids of various sizes – some very small and some substantial – and for different purposes, as well as of rapid learning. Many raids had a specific technical purpose, as in the capture of the Würzburg radar system at Bruneval in February 1942, the destruction of the hydroelectric dam at Glomfjord in Norway in September, and the sinking of Axis blockade-runners by Royal Marine canoeists at Bordeaux in December. Some had at their heart the trialling of a new piece of equipment, or design of attack, such as Captain Gerald Montanaro's canoe and limpet-mine raid on a German freighter in Boulogne harbour on the night of 11 April 1941. But raids, as the chief planner at Combined Operations, Captain John Hughes-Hallett, was to assert, could be and often were an end in themselves. Although ideally the resources for a raid could seamlessly be applied to a higher, perhaps even a strategic, purpose, the aim of hurting the Germans wherever they could, by whatever means (within the constraints of the Laws of Armed Conflict), was reason enough for action.

Indeed, the early raids were designed merely to remind the Germans that they had not yet subdued a still recalcitrant and defiant Britain. Planned as well as they could be in the circumstances, many mistakes were made. Some were almost comical, although there was no doubting the enthusiasm of those taking part, and their determination to hit back against the Hun, even though, looking back, their efforts sometimes seem more suited to an episode of *Dad's Army* than a serious act of war.

Within three weeks of Dunkirk, and the day after France's capitulation, the newly promoted Colonel Dudley Clarke accompanied a group of men on the first raid against the coast of France. Operation *Collar*, hastily devised, comprised 115 officers and men of the unit he had been building since the day he had been transferred to MO9, with the cover name of 'No. 11 Independent Company', an early group of commandos recruited from men who had fought in the Norwegian campaign. Commanded by Lieutenant Colonel Ronnie Tod of the Argyll and Sutherland Highlanders, the men, travelling in seven noisy RAF air-sea rescue launches and a steam yacht, headed across the Channel to raid an area north of Boulogne, with the stated aim of gathering intelligence. The real aim, of course, was simply to strike a blow against the all-conquering Hun, to demonstrate that although France had fallen, Britain had not, and – if these men had anything to do with it – would not.

The outcome of the raid, described by Clarke in his book *Seven Assignments*, was an utter shambles. Almost everything that could go wrong, did. Boats were threatened in the Channel by the very same RAF fighters who were supposed to be escorting them, then became separated from each other in the darkness as compasses failed. Others landed in the wrong place. A 'Wehrmacht HQ' attacked with tommy-gun fire and grenades at Le Touquet turned out to be a dance hall, in which the local beauties were having their first introduction to the jackbooted gallants of the newly arrived master race. The steam yacht very nearly collided with a German seaplane taking off outside Boulogne harbour. And Tod, attempting to fire a tommy gun in anger for the first time at a separate landing north of Boulogne (no one knew where, exactly), found to his consternation that when he pulled the trigger to engage a German patrol, the magazine fell off. His training on this weapon had been non-existent.

On the beach preparing to be taken off, Lieutenant Ronnie Swayne encountered two Germans. Attempting to fire his .38 revolver he discovered that he had forgotten to load it, so was forced to knock one of the Germans on the head with the butt of the weapon, while his batman managed to bayonet the other, before turning to finish off Swayne's assailant. 'It wasn't really serious soldiering,' he was later to muse. In the rush to escape, Clarke himself received a bullet that knocked him flat and nearly severed his ear. Like many other operations before and since, it achieved little of military merit, but was loudly propagandised at home, excessively as it turned out. When the Prime Minister was offered the newspapers in bed on the morning of 24 June it was to read the absurdly exaggerated headline in *The Times*:

BRITISH RAIDERS LAND ON ENEMY COAST! SUCCESSFUL RECONNAISSANCE

Churchill was not best pleased at the magnification of what had been a trivial raid, in the midst of the havoc of the fall of France. Clarke accepted the criticism, but was interested to note the *Times* leader comment that morning. 'The point,' it read, 'is that this incident shows the offensive spirit, which is exactly what the public wants . . .'

It was because of his desperation for the success of this novel method of warfare that the Prime Minister denounced, more in frustration than anger, the raid by members of No. 3 Commando and No. 11 Independent Company, led by Lieutenant Colonels John Durnford-Slater and Ronnie Tod respectively, on the Channel Island of Guernsey in July 1940, as a 'silly fiasco'. He was being unfair. Durnford-Slater's account of Operation *Ambassador* in his book *Commando* certainly contained all the elements of a farce, but it was only by experiencing what could go wrong, as he acknowledged, that they could ever hope to get it right.

The plan (explained to Durnford-Slater by Major David Niven, on the staff of MO9) was that Tod's Independent Company was to attack the island's airfield, with a single troop (i.e. about fifty men) of No. 3 Commando acting as a diversion on the south-eastern side of the island. Unfortunately, No. 11 Independent Company, transported in four RAF air-sea rescue launches, never managed to arrive at Guernsey: two launches broke down on the way, one launch became geographically embarrassed and landed instead on the German-free island of Sark (where the troops enjoyed a pint at a local pub), whilst the other hit rocks off Guernsey and was forced to return, without disembarking its troops. All this was unknown to Durnford-Slater and Lieutenant Peter Young of No. 3 Commando, as they reached the foot of cliffs in launches sent from their escorting destroyer, at about 00.50 hours on the morning of 15 July 1940. They had misjudged the tide, however, and when the heavily laden men jumped from the RAF launches (these were not designed to land on beaches, or to disembark fighting troops) they found themselves up to their necks in seawater on a rocky shore in a heavy swell. The story of the two hours they then spent exhaustingly climbing the hundreds of steep steps up the cliffs (hauling rolls of barbed wire for a planned roadblock), prowling around the island, sodden wet, meeting no Germans and seeming to set every dog on the island barking, was somewhat deflating to the men, who had come for action and had found none. Anticipated German positions were empty, and no military target of any value could be found.

Suddenly, Durnford-Slater realised that their time had nearly run out, and they had to get back down the cliffs if they had any hope of rendezvousing with the launches and getting back to their waiting destroyer before dawn. The journey back was bungled just as badly as their coming, however. Durnford-Slater fell during the rapid descent of the cliffs and his cocked Webley revolver went off, alerting a German machinegun post on the opposite cliff, which responded at once by spurting tracer fire into the darkness. The swell had risen even more strongly by then, and the launches were unable to approach the shore, so the men had to strip off and swim, leaving their weapons, equipment, and in some cases uniforms behind. Then, to cap it all, Durnford-Slater discovered that three of his men could not swim. They had to be left behind, on the promise that a submarine might be sent to collect them the following night. It was only luck that the destroyer, a long way from the comforting umbrella that could be provided by friendly fighter escort and uncomfortably close to the threat of prowling Messerschmitts based on the nearby French coast, waited behind for another 30 minutes to pick up the wet and chastened commandos, their martial ardour much dampened by their experience. No submarine could be made available to collect the non-swimmers the following night, however, with the result that they paid for falsifying their application forms to join the Commandos with five years as prisoners of war, a harsh punishment by any standard.

Part of the problem was that in 1940 there was no clear raiding strategy, arguably something that did not emerge with any clarity until Lord Louis Mountbatten took over the reins from Keyes in November 1941. Until then the policy tended to bow to the loudest voice. In particular there was little clarity in policy terms between large raids by formed bodies of troops, and smaller, more pinprick or guerrilla-type 'hit-and-run' or 'butcher-and-bolt' attacks. For his part Churchill demanded size and scale from the outset, despite the reality that Clarke's slowly expanding Commando operation would take time to grow in size and capability. Clarke was fearful of 'being jockeyed into a trot before we had really learned to walk. We would have liked the first few raids to be humble affairs carried out with a degree of obscurity . . .'

The Prime Minister, however, wanted immediate, large-scale action. He envisaged a series of substantial raids by regular, well-trained troops against the entire extent of the Nazi seaboard, which would harass the occupiers and compel them to tie down troops, in which armoured vehicles would debouch on to an enemy shore, 'do a deep raid inland, cutting vital communication, and then back, leaving a trail of German corpses behind them'. In his more expansive moments he envisaged 'large armoured eruptions' that would reach as far, perhaps, as Paris, although given the catastrophic haemorrhage of trained manpower after Dunkirk this aspiration was impossible to achieve, in the short term at least. He made his views clear to his planners and policymakers alike. In a minute sent to Anthony Eden, at that time the Secretary of State for War, on 25 August 1940, he argued:

> If we are to have any campaign in 1941 it must be amphibious in its character and there certainly will be many opportunities [for] minor Operations all of which will depend on surprise landings of lightly equipped mobile forces accustomed *to work like packs of hounds* instead of being moved about in the ponderous manner which is appropriate. These have become so elaborate, so complicated in their equipment, so vast in their transport that it is very difficult to use them in any operation in which time is vital.
>
> For every reason therefore we must develop the storm troop or Commando idea. I have asked for 5,000 parachutists and we must also have *at least 10,000 of these small 'bands of brothers'* who will be capable of lightning action. In this way alone will

those positions be secured which afterwards will give the opportunity for highly trained regular troops to operate on a larger scale. [my italics]

The truth is that he also wanted pinprick raids by soldiers acting as guerrillas to commit murder and mayhem behind enemy lines in occupied Europe, and therefore to achieve the psychological dislocation of the enemy, but in the very early months of thinking about raids the confusions in policy and priority, together with establishing the appropriate boundaries between Combined Operations and the newly formed SOE, took some time to iron out. It took time to identify the best way of responding to the challenge posed by a newly militarised Europe and a paucity of resources with which to hit back in a way that would cause Germany and its rapidly expanding empire the most harm.

In the military memory of the time, Britain's last great raiding victory had been that staged against the German-held port of Zeebrugge in April 1918, a largely ineffectual though successfully propagandised enterprise designed to remove access to the English Channel to German U-boats entering from their hides along the Bruges canal. The raid had been commanded by Vice Admiral Sir Roger Keyes: who better, thought Churchill, to take command of raiding operations in 1940? Keyes had been at Gallipoli and so had some experience of amphibious operations. He took up his appointment thinking in terms of raids of significant size and scale, reversing Dudley Clarke's previous policy of 'little-and-often', but found himself instantly stymied by serious deficiencies in resources and equipment across an Army attempting to reconstitute itself and a Navy desperately stretched by challenges in both home and foreign waters.

Whether large or small, it seems clear that raiding in 1940 and 1941 was a gut reaction to the impotence Britain felt in the face of newly won German military hegemony in Europe. In so far as the policy could be said to have been designed, it was to benefit the morale of Britons whilst undermining that of Germans watching on the other side of the grey Channel moat. Perhaps also it was an instinctive response to a need to create an outlet for British martial testosterone at a time when the opportunities for striking back against the military arrogance of Germany's Goliath were otherwise severely limited.

As it turned out, raids did have a positive military consequence for Britain, as they forced the Germans to disperse their forces across the length and breadth of their occupied coast, from the south of France to the north of Norway, but it is clear that this strategic outcome was a happy side-effect, not a policy objective. Major General John Kennedy (who took over as director of Military Operations and Plans at the War Office from Dick Dewing in October 1940) affirmed that by the end of 1940 planning was under way for the eventual descent on the Normandy coast, even though most recognised that this event lay many years ahead of them. '[The] correct raiding policy at this period of the war,' he commented – perhaps wanting but tactfully declining to suggest that this wasn't actually the policy pursued by Keyes – 'was to harry the enemy with small detachments on a wide front, and thus force him to maintain troops all along the coast-line for the purposes of defence.' But if the raids were too small, they would lack any real effect.

Throughout 1941 responsibility for designing and conducting raids lay in the hands of the Army commands on the southern and south-eastern coasts. The idea was that the Army would ask Combined Operations for the requisite resources and then undertake the operations themselves. The process did not work well, as it lacked coordination and strategic coherence and was compounded by a profound lack of resources. In 1940, for example, there were only nine heavy landing craft in Royal Navy service, and only six of these in British waters. The result was that no serious raids took place on the French coast that year and Combined Operations found that its operations tended to be in Norwegian waters, far from the purview of the regional Army commanders-in-chief.

It was, therefore, a frustrating year for Keyes, who believed that the War Office and Admiralty in particular needed to pay much more attention to the raiding agenda. Much time was spent in planning for substantial raids – against Vichy-held Dakar, for example; to capture the Azores from Portugal and the Canary Islands from Spain; and to seize the Italian island of Pantelleria, lying between Sicily and Tunis and thus a potential aid in the defence of Malta – but it was a year marred by squabbling at the highest levels. The service chiefs had other priorities and derided what some called 'Churchill's Private Army'.

Nevertheless, three well organised and well executed raids were carried out in Europe (in addition to three conducted in the Mediterranean) by Combined Operations in 1941. All were against German interests in occupied Norway. A number of much smaller intelligence-gathering raids on the French coast centred on the Pas-de-Calais port of Boulogne were also undertaken, but it was to Norway that Keyes initially looked to mount the first raids of real substance. In April 1940 Britain and France, yet to suffer the humiliation inflicted on both countries the following month in the Low Countries, had launched what they had fondly anticipated to be a protective mission to defend Norway from German aggression. It had not gone well, and despite inflicting substantial casualties on the German fleet the British expeditionary force found itself withdrawing in some ignominy in June. Thereafter Norway loomed large in the consciousness of both sides. In 1941 it presented itself as an ideal target for Combined Operations raids, where measured British attacks could be made without fear of engaging the full might of the Wehrmacht, whilst at the same time causing the Germans some (perhaps incidental) harm, and keeping the spirit of the offensive alive both in the hearts of the British and those in occupied Europe who were quickly learning the hard facts of Nazi occupation.

A harsh reality was the need to use, or else to lose, the four thousand superbly trained commandos in British service, who the British Army was now looking at with a jealous and acquisitive eye. Indeed a fierce battle for control of the raiding agenda took place in 1941, as General Alan Brooke attempted to bring this stray force under direct Army command. He was to fail.

Equally, many commandos, some of whom had been training intensively for six months, were now losing heart at the lack of action. One of the most dispiriting things about being a commando in 1940–42 was the absence of regular, meaningful operations. There were, of course, a few, but they were not conducted either in numbers or with frequency enough to motivate the men. Operations were regularly prepared for, but were often cancelled at the last minute. This was profoundly dispiriting to the men, and it was difficult to maintain morale in these circumstances for long periods of time. Micky Burn recalled that the constant cancellation of raids for which men were preparing 'created a very high degree of tension. It was beginning to have an impact on morale.' Indeed, at the end of 1941 Burn was looking to leave the Commandos because he saw no prospect of action.

FIVE

Raids in 1941

So it was that a raid – Operation *Claymore* – was prepared by Keyes against the remote Lofoten Islands, just inside the Arctic Circle, in early March 1941. The purpose was to strike a blow against the enemy, its military targets the fish-oil production facilities at the small ports of Stamsund, Henningsvaer, Svolvær and Brettesnes, which produced half of Norway's total pre-war oil output and which the Germans had taken immediate steps to exploit. Fish oil produced glycerine, an important component of explosives, so the raid was easy to justify in London in terms of resources and effort. A subsidiary though important purpose was to gladden the hearts of Norwegian patriots by striking a blow against their oppressors, an express aim of the raid being the arrest of local supporters of Vidkun Quisling's pro-Nazi party, the capture and removal to prison camps in Britain of German personnel, the evacuation of recruits for the Free Norwegian Forces and the destruction or capture of enemy ships and of Norwegian vessels found to be working for the Germans.

In fact, Operation *Claymore* demonstrated all the virtues of joint operations between the services (in this case the Army and Royal Navy), a subject in its infancy during these early days, and which would not begin to bear fruit in terms of combat on a tri-service basis until the raid on Saint-Nazaire itself, and then more fully in November 1942 with the Anglo-American amphibious invasion of North Africa – Operation *Torch*. (Its ultimate expression was to be Operation *Overlord*, the invasion of France, two years later.) Under the direct command of Brigadier Charles Haydon two fast, modern, requisitioned Dutch cross-Channel passenger ferries, carrying five hundred commandos of Durnford-Slater's No. 3 Commando (HMS *Prinses Beatrix*) and David Lister's No. 4 Commando (HMS *Queen Emma*), together with a group of demolition experts from the Royal Engineers and Norwegian patriots led by the actor Captain Martin Linge, all protected by a screen of five destroyers, travelled the 900 stomach-churning miles from Scotland via the Orkney and Faroe Islands, arriving off the four surprisingly well lit and unsuspecting ports just before dawn on 4 March. The prospect of action was a considerable relief to the seasick soldiers following their week-long traverse of an extremely rough Atlantic and Norwegian Sea.

Just over six hours later the raiders were back on their ships heading for the sanctuary of the open ocean, leaving a scene of comprehensive destruction behind them, and having suffered no loss. The Germans had been caught by surprise, and in the process the raiders destroyed eleven factories and some 800,000 gallons of fish oil, sank five ships and took 225 Germans and sixty 'Quislings' prisoner. Local Norwegians initially assumed that it was a German exercise, but before long were plying the commandos with ersatz coffee and cakes and volunteering in large numbers to return with the Norwegian soldiers to Britain. A total of 314 Norwegian volunteers agreed to return with Martin Linge to Britain, most to join the Free Norwegian forces.

A most significant though at the time unremarked success came from a discovery made in the captain's cabin on the *Krebs*, an armed trawler which had the temerity to fire on the British destroyers with her puny gun. Heavily outgunned, and after a short firefight that killed the captain and others on the bridge, the burning *Krebs* was beached. The small boarding party from the destroyer HMS *Somali* was led by Lieutenant Sir Marshall Warmington, who searched the dead captain's cabin for incriminating papers. He knew nothing of the battle raging at the time to discover the secrets of the German Enigma cipher machine, but in a drawer whose lock he removed with a shot from his Webley revolver, Warmington discovered a pile of papers, as well as some rotors that he immediately recognised as belonging to a cipher machine.

The discovery proved to be of immense value to Alan Turing and Peter Twinn, who had been attempting to break the German naval codes at the Code and Cipher establishment Bletchley Park. It was in fact a momentous breakthrough. Luftwaffe codes had been broken as early as the summer of 1940, but the *Kriegsmarine*'s had proven harder to crack. An important means of breaking into Enigma messages was by tracking the lazy errors made by operators who had to change rotor sequences every day, but often failed to change their personal message settings, allowing Bletchley Park to decrypt each day's codes by comparing them with the operator's previous day's settings.

Martin Linge, although jubilant at the warmth of reception given by the local population, was worried nevertheless at the consequences of the raid for them. He was right to be concerned. Berlin's reaction was one of vengeful fury. Hitler's personal injunction was to burn the town of Svolvær to the ground, although in the event only a partial destruction was attempted with the arrival of a unit of the feared SS. Meanwhile in Oslo, as an act of retribution, some 100 Norwegian military prisoners of war whose homes were in Svolvær and Lofoten were moved into the Grin prison camp, where they remained hostages to the citizens' continuing good behaviour. Thereafter Hitler's focus became increasingly fixed on Norway as the back door through which a major Allied invasion might be directed.

Seven further raids were conducted during 1941, although a full five months were to pass before the tiny reconnaissance, Operation *Chess*, was launched against Ambleteuse (between Calais and Boulogne) on the night of 27 July 1941 by seventeen men of No. 12 Commando, commanded by Second Lieutenant Philip

Pinckney RA of the Berkshire Yeomanry.* The plan was to secure intelligence whilst testing a prototype landing craft that had recently arrived from the United States. Private John Huntingdon recalled the raid:

'E' Troop was chosen to carry out a small operation against the French coast. The plan was to use an armoured landing craft, a small vessel newly designed for use in landing troops on beaches . . . The bows consisted of a ramp which could be lowered and raised for us to run off onto the beach side. Inside the ramp were double gates of steel, inside the body or well of the craft were fitted three rows of low benches running along the sides and one down the centre for the troops to sit on . . . Amongst the men on the craft was [Lieutenant-Commander Sir Geoffrey Congreve, DSO, the Special Service Brigade's Senior Landing Officer] . . . we were to attack a small beach which was supposed to be un-defended, or so they said. All was well until we got quite near to the beach, it was beautifully dark and all seemed well when suddenly flares shot up from the shore line. We were exposed and a heavy machine gun opened fire on us, the gun was firing down from the top of a small sand hill. The gun had to be silenced so a small party led by Captain Pinckney got ashore under the fire and threw hand grenades onto the cliff top. The gun was silenced.

The 44-year-old Congreve, who had joined the raid as an observer, and who had led the landing operation at Lofoten, was killed in the exchange of machinegun fire.

The four raids that followed were as frustratingly small and inconsequential as *Chess*. Operation *Acid Drop* (against the towns of Hardelot and Merlimont, west of Boulogne) on 30 August by

* Pinckney, later a member of the Special Air Service, was caught by the Germans after being injured parachuting into Baigno, Italy, on 7 September 1943 and executed in cold blood.

thirty men of No. 5 Commando, designed to gain intelligence and, hopefully, a prisoner, achieved neither. Operation *Chopper* (against Saint-Vaast, on the Cherbourg Peninsula and Saint-Aubin, near Courcelles) on 27 September by 5 Troop, No. 1 Commando saw the two small Commando patrols engaging in firefights with the enemy, but with no outcome either way. Operation *Astrakhan* (near Calais) on 12 November by Captain Gerald Montanaro's 101 Troop, Special Boat Section, was a canoe reconnaissance for Operation *Sunstar* (Houlgate, east of Ouistreham), which took place on 23 November by No. 9 Commando (led by Lieutenant Colonel Ronnie Tod), designed to attack a newly built German gun battery overlooking the coast. In the event nothing tangible was achieved. John Hughes-Hallett, who took over planning for COHQ under Mountbatten in December 1941, considered that tiny raids had been conducted 'on account of their stimulating effect on morale. Nevertheless these raids achieved nothing, and a number of very gallant young officers, such as Commander Congreve, lost their lives to no avail.'

It was only in Norway that two further raids of substance were mounted in 1941, and these then reinforced German paranoia about Britain's intentions towards its fragile Scandinavian flank. The first was against Vaagso (Operation *Archery*) and the second a simultaneous and repeat raid against Lofoten (Operation *Anklet*), on 26 December. The attack on Vaagso and Maaloy, between Bergen and Trondheim, was undertaken by 570 men of Lieutenant Colonel Durnford-Slater's No. 3 Commando, together with elements from three other Commandos. The cruiser HMS *Kenya*, four destroyers and two landing craft arrived off the target on the morning of 27 December, and began a preparatory bombardment. RAF Hampdens, Beaufighters and Blenheims, flying at the edge of their range from bases in Scotland, bombed targets and defended the airspace above for seven hours as the commandos landed and destroyed with explosive charges the power station and coastal defences, the radio transmitter, factories and lighthouse. The raid was marked by fierce infantry combat in which, for the loss of twenty-one British dead and eleven aircraft, the enemy suffered 252 casualties, lost nine merchant ships and four Heinkel bombers.

One of those who died was Captain Martin Linge, killed in a gun battle for possession of one of the town's hotels. His concerns about the consequences of the Lofoten raid at the start of the year for the local civilian population were now borne out in full after Operation *Archery*. Only seventy-one Norwegians returned to Britain with the raiders, but the simultaneous attack on Lofoten the same day by some 300 commandos, designed as a diversion for the raid on Vaagso, was the cause of savage reprisals. In one case a group of forty-three men caught on a ship making its way secretly to Britain were executed without mercy.

Quite rightly the raids caused a storm of protest among the exiled Norwegian government in London, which accused the British of launching attacks on the country with no thought for the consequences for those who lived there and who might inadvertently get caught up in the fighting. In any case, they asked, should not Combined Operations be attacking German targets, rather than economic ones on which the local population depended not merely in these hard times for their livelihood, but for their survival? As a result a mechanism in the form of an Anglo-Norwegian Collaboration Committee, chaired by Brigadier Colin Gubbins of SOE, was established to ensure that the Norwegian government-in-exile had a say in future operations that affected their benighted homeland.

The raids on Norway that year confirmed Hitler's suspicions that Britain saw the country as the launch pad for an eventual attack into Europe, and he redeployed a further thirty thousand troops to Norway to meet this threat. Admiral Raeder likewise was persuaded that Norway was the right place for his new battleship, the *Tirpitz*. The two raids, mounted on Boxing Day 1941, were the first undertaken by Keyes's successor, the newly promoted

Commodore Lord Louis Mountbatten, extracted – much against his will – from the longed-for command of HMS *Illustrious*, then refitting in the United States, to be 'adviser' on Combined Operations, a less decisive and divisive term than the 'Director' that Keyes had been.*

Keyes's passionate defence of his prerogatives as Chief of Combined Operations had alienated the three service chiefs, damaging their confidence in Churchill's grand plan with respect to amphibious raiding. Unwilling to have this imperilled and despite their friendship, the Prime Minister removed him, ensuring that his replacement was a man whose will could be bent to his own. The first imperative, Churchill told Mountbatten, following a year of meagre pickings (not all of them Keyes's fault), was to escalate and embolden the raiding agenda. 'You will continue Commando raids,' the Prime Minister told Mountbatten, 'for they are important for the morale of this country and of our allies. But the primary task will be to prepare for the great invasion, for unless we return to the Continent and beat the Germans on land we shall never win the war.'

Seeking to inject pace into his newly inherited empire, Mountbatten called for two raids a week. In December 1941 Captain John Hughes-Hallett RN, the man who was to play a key role in designing D-Day two and a half years later, joined Mountbatten's team as naval adviser. Group Captain Fred Willetts RAF, who had been awarded the DSO for the air plan supporting the attack on Vaagso (he had piloted the lead Hampden bomber during the raid), was the air adviser and Charles Haydon the military adviser. In practice, the roles of the three men were different. Willetts ended up fulfilling more or less a liaison role with the RAF's functional commanders-in-chief (of Coastal, Fighter and Bomber Commands), Haydon remained the independent commander of

---

* Mountbatten was elevated from 'Adviser' to 'Chief' on 18 March 1942, and promoted from Commodore to Acting Vice Admiral.

raiding troops and Hughes-Hallett became Mountbatten's chief planner.

Under Mountbatten Combined Operations grew rapidly in size, capability and competence, the staff at the HQ on Richmond Terrace increasing from twenty-three to over four hundred. Responsibility for the planning and coordination (but not always control) of raids came under their remit. COHQ thus became a critical focal point for planning raids that would then be carried out by whatever fighting organisation proposed them. Pug Ismay was to note thankfully in March 1942 that Mountbatten's new broom was working well, Combined Operations 'functioning in complete accord with the Service departments and Home Forces'.

Although many were less generous, particularly those with tribal drums to beat, what is undoubtedly true is that Mountbatten's arrival served to energise COHQ. His eagerness to engage staff from outside the traditional ranks of service officers introduced much-needed genetic variety into the Combined Operations corporate body. A remarkably eclectic mix of adventurers, scientists, university dons and writers offered ideas and suggestions far from the beaten track of military orthodoxy; the many technical successes of Operation *Overlord* in June 1944 were due in large measure to Mountbatten's adventurous iconoclasm in 1942. For the Director of Operations in the War Office, Major General John Kennedy, Mountbatten's appointment – and Keyes's departure – could not have come at a more opportune time:

> For over a year we had been trying to persuade the War Cabinet that we needed an active raiding policy to tide us over until we had the capacity for offensive action on a bigger scale. Keyes had been against such raids on the grounds that they would fritter away resources with which he hoped to be allowed to carry out bigger projects – projects on which he had set his heart, but which we regarded as wild, or unprofitable, or even impossible. Mountbatten, who had succeeded Keyes as Chief of Combined

Operations, had been instrumental in winning Churchill to our way of thinking . . .

Churchill and Roosevelt, following the arrival of the United States in the war in December 1941, had agreed that raiding would continue, in order to maintain offensive spirit, encourage morale, take the war to the enemy, demonstrate to Stalin their willingness to open a Second Front as soon as practicable and serve to prepare for the eventual invasion of Europe. Combined Operations was eventually to have both a Search Committee, responsible for identifying targets, or develop those presented to it from outside agencies, and an Examinations Committee, which determined what raids and operations would go to Mountbatten (and thence to the Chiefs of Staff) for approval and final planning. But in the New Year of 1942, responsibility for planning for a new year of raids, under Mountbatten's keen eye, fell to Captain John Hughes-Hallett and his two staff officers, Commander David Luce RN (a successful submarine commander) and Lieutenant Commander Ackroyd de Costabadie RN, who had won a DSC during the Dunkirk evacuation and had been on the Vaagso raid. All three had recently joined Combined Operations, and were tasked with translating the Prime Minister's new instructions to Mountbatten into an executable programme. 'Our most urgent task,' Hughes-Hallett recalled in his memoirs, 'was to select suitable targets for raids on France and Norway. Everyone agreed that in the first instance it must fall to the Navy to suggest objectives since it was no use suggesting places which could not be reached by the appropriate landing craft or other vessels.'

The only project scheduled at the time was a parachute raid on the German radar installation at Bruneval timed for 27 or 28 February (Operation *Biting*). There was nothing else in the pipeline, leaving Hughes-Hallett and his team with a blank canvas. The planning took only a day – 21 January 1942 – when the three men sat down in Richmond Terrace in front of a map of the

European seaboard to make tentative proposals for one raid every
month up to and including August that year. They were not so
much concerned at this stage with determining the objectives of
a particular raid, but rather with the feasibility of reaching the
place undetected. They soon concluded that Norway was not as
attractive as had first been assumed: the distances were so great,
the weather too unpredictable, and Norway had seen three raids
already in 1941. They therefore concentrated their attention on
the Channel area:

> Our first choice (for early March 1942) was a house on the Ostend
> sea front which the Germans were using as a rehabilitation centre
> for Luftwaffe pilots who had recovered from wounds. For the
> end of March we suggested a raid on Saint-Nazaire to be followed
> a few days later with one on Bayonne. For May we proposed an
> attack on Alderney; the island to be held for as long as practicable
> providing the raiding force was able to occupy it completely and
> quickly. By the occupation of Alderney we hoped it would at last
> be possible to cut the German coastal route to the Atlantic ports
> by which they had sustained much of the U-boat campaign since
> the French railway system was reported to be inadequate to keep
> the U-boats supplied. For June we chose Dieppe, as by that time
> we expected to have sufficient landing craft to lift an entire Divi-
> sion. For July we felt that a repeat raid on Dieppe would achieve
> surprise and lead to the slaughter of specialist German engineers
> likely to be at work repairing and strengthening the fortifications.
> Finally, for August we visualized a landing on the south bank of
> the Somme, to seize a beach head through which a large force
> of armoured cars could pass and make a dash towards Paris.

With this programme agreed with Charles Haydon and Fred
Willetts, a detailed intelligence study of each of the targets was
put in motion. Two days later Hughes-Hallett briefed Mountbatten
on the approach. He agreed in principle, and asked for outline

plans to be prepared and discussed with him as soon as possible.

It is clear from Hughes-Hallett's testimony that Saint-Nazaire was chosen as a target because of the desire to surprise the Germans by mounting a couple of major raids on the Atlantic coast, and not because of any strategic virtue the place might otherwise have boasted in relation to the maritime balance of power. Saint-Nazaire happened to be the most distant objective that could be reached by a raiding force with only one daylight period on the voyage. The team thought that with luck and careful timing this force might get there unobserved, and repeat the famous 1918 *coup de main* assault by the Royal Navy and Royal Marines on the German-held port of Zeebrugge. Two daylight periods, they felt, would be tempting providence too far, and therefore although a raid on Bayonne near the Spanish border had many attractions, it was felt wise to time it for a few days after Saint-Nazaire.

Saint-Nazaire was also attractive because, although one of the most heavily defended ports in Europe, a glance at the charts revealed a fatal defect in the siting of its defensive batteries. The main approach channel (the dredged Passe des Charpentiers) ran close inshore for some miles on the northern bank, where most of the enemy's heavy coastal defence batteries were sited. To seaward there was a great area of shoal water that dried out at low water to form huge mudflats. However, the range of the tide in the Loire is very great, and Hughes-Hallett thought it possible that there would be enough water over the flats for vessels drawing not more than twelve feet at the 'extraordinary spring tides', that is to say, twice a year. If this were so, it would be possible for the raiders to pass over the shoal water and enter the deep-water channel very close to Saint-Nazaire itself, and run the gauntlet of only one of the batteries. Consultation with the Admiralty's wonderfully titled 'Superintendent of Tides' and liaison with the Liverpool Observatory and Tidal Institute (LOTI) confirmed that this was so, and he advised that the end of March would be the ideal date for an attack in 1942. After selecting these possible objectives, the next step was to study the detailed intelligence and ask for scale models to be made.

The raids that were planned by COHQ in 1942 did not all fit the same pattern. As in 1940 and 1941 some were tiny (despite Hughes-Hallett's aversion to small raids) – a few brave men carried in flimsy craft launched from a submarine, for example – while some were considerably larger, designed to test the techniques necessary to launch, in due course, the invasion of the Continent. Following the eight raids mounted in 1941 a further fifteen were launched in 1942, conducted, supported or coordinated by Combined Operations. The raids were carried out by a variety of fighting organisations but the purpose was clear: raiding in and of itself was considered a strategic necessity.

Britain's raiding policy together with increasingly strident (and public) demands from Stalin for the opening of a Second Front along Europe's Atlantic seaboard served to worry Hitler. Alarmed by the prospect of an increasing number of raids against his European seaboard following the heavy Combined Operations raids in the last two months of the previous year, on 24 March 1942 he issued a detailed warning (Führer Directive No. 40):

The coastline of Europe will, in the coming months, be exposed to the danger of an enemy landing in force.

The time and place of the landing operations will not be dictated to the enemy by operational considerations alone. Failure in other theatres of war, obligations to allies, and political considerations may persuade him to take decisions which appear unlikely from a purely military point of view . . .

The many important military and industrial establishments on the coast or in its neighbourhood, some of them equipped with particularly valuable plant, may moreover tempt the enemy to undertake surprise attacks of a local nature.

Particular attention must be paid to English preparations for landings on the open coast, for which they have at their disposal many armoured landing craft, built to carry armoured fighting vehicles and heavy weapons. The possibility of parachute and airborne attacks on a large scale must also be envisaged . . .

In the meantime, Britain did what it could. In Churchill it had what the SOE agent Lieutenant Benjamin Cowburn described as 'the greatest living orator in the world', noting that in France in late 1941 and early 1942 the British Prime Minister's prestige was immense. 'When words were almost all we had to hurl at the enemy, he had found the right ones and spoken them with the simplicity and directness which only a complete command of the richest language ever spoken by man could ever bring . . . We shall never surrender!' In France and in other German-occupied territories SOE could begin the process of sponsoring subversion and fanning the flames of resistance. It could plan for raids large and small, and the escalating bomber offensive in the air had to continue. But it was principally through what Churchill described as the 'hand of steel from the sea' that beleaguered Britain could demonstrate to its own people that the war was winnable, to the subject peoples of Europe that their nightmare would one day be over, and to its own planners that a successful large-scale amphibious assault on the shores of France was possible.

Major General John Kennedy ascribed to Mountbatten the credit for revitalising Britain's offensive credentials for, according to the War Office's Director of Operations, it was he who 'displayed immense drive in organizing the descent on Saint-Nazaire, which was . . . a resounding success'. An attack on the French port of Saint-Nazaire, described by its first chronicler, Brigadier Cecil Lucas Phillips, as *The Greatest Raid of All*, was to be the next Commando target.

SIX

Tirpitz

Mountbatten's success in 1942 in building credibility for Combined Operations lay not so much in his fresh new approach, his sympathetic ear, or in his inclusive and non-confrontational approach to the rights and privileges of the powerful service chiefs, as in his ability to combine his own aims with a compelling strategic imperative that sufficed to secure essential Admiralty support.

The port of Saint-Nazaire boasted the only dry dock on the Atlantic seaboard that could provide sanctuary to the single remaining German warship that could still strike fear deep into British hearts: the *Tirpitz*. Laid down in 1936, this fast, enormously strong 45,500-ton steel monster, boasting eight 15-inch guns and foot-deep armour, had been launched by Hitler to much Nazi pomp and fanfare in the boatyards of Wilhelmshaven on 1 April 1939 and was the sister ship to the *Bismarck*, scuttled in mid-Atlantic in May 1941 after being crippled by British torpedo bombers and then attacked by the massed guns of the Royal Navy. It began its work-up trials in the Baltic after being commissioned on 25 February 1941. In a detailed directive on future strategy in the Mediterranean on 15 October 1940 the Prime Minister described the disabling of *Bismarck* and *Tirpitz* as Bomber Command's 'greatest prize'.

After the loss of the *Bismarck*, Germany's three remaining battleships (*Tirpitz*, *Scharnhorst* and *Gneisenau*), together with the heavy cruiser *Prinz Eugen* (which had left the Bismarck after the battle of the Denmark Strait, to head for Brest), constituted Germany's primary maritime striking force. Even after the loss of the *Bismarck* these ships possessed a psychological hold on British decision-makers in 1941 and 1942 far in excess of their puny numbers. Indeed, the key role of *Tirpitz* in Britain's war leaders' strategic decision-making during this period cannot be overstated. The threat of this mighty new capital ship breaking into the Atlantic sea lanes to join the U-boat wolfpacks in hunting down Allied shipping, the vast trans-atlantic supply chain between Britain and the United States, as the *Bismarck* had attempted unsuccessfully to do, was at the time a horrifying prospect. London believed that if Hitler attempted to use his last remaining battleships in the same way that he had intended to use the *Bismarck* it represented a significant threat to Britain's survival.

At the outbreak of war the *Kriegsmarine* had not been in a position to confront the Royal Navy in a stand-up fight of the type seen, for example, at Jutland in 1915, despite Hitler's grand designs in 1938 for an 800-ship battlefleet to challenge the Royal Navy by 1945 ('Plan Z'). The serried ranks of battleships chal-lenging each other to mortal combat on the high seas were now a thing of the past, as obsolete as the redcoat regiments facing their enemy in squares at Waterloo. At the time war was declared in 1939 the Royal Navy remained too strong in numerical terms to make an engagement of this kind worthwhile for Germany. Indeed, and to the chagrin of their commanders, German warships were expressly forbidden even to engage British convoys if the presence of an enemy battleship riding shotgun was detected, for fear of losing one of her few capital vessels. Instead, German naval policy rapidly evolved to launching attacks – aerial, surface and sub-surface – that did not involve a deliberate, direct confronta-tion with the big guns of the enemy's main fleet. In effect the German battleships became raiders, deploying in small battle groups of fast-moving, heavily gunned vessels designed to strike quickly and decisively before heading for home, or safe sanctuary.

The goal was simple. If Britain were to lose maritime control of the waters in which it held strategic interest, such as the Atlantic bridge to North America, the Suez Canal and Eastern Mediterranean and the Cape of Good Hope, there was every chance it would lose the war for, frustratingly plucky though it might be (to German eyes), perfidious Albion would starve without the sea lanes that provided so much of her essential supplies from both her colonies and the New World: oil, wheat, butter and meat. All that was required was for a stranglehold to be placed on the global lifeline that criss-crossed the oceans sustaining Britain and preventing her starvation.

Britain, of course, had global interests to protect, and the resources it had to execute this defence, as a consequence of policies adopted during the 1930s, were spread very thinly indeed. Germany did not have to do too much to cause Britain harm somewhere in the world – a situation that became especially grave when Japan launched its own onslaught in Asia and the Pacific in December 1941. Following the calamitous loss of HMS *Prince of Wales* and HMS *Repulse* to Japanese dive bombers in the Gulf of Siam in December 1941 after they had ventured from Singapore without air cover in an attempt to disrupt the Japanese amphibious landings in northern Malaya, the entire Royal Naval presence in Asian waters amounted to a mere eleven ships: three ancient cruisers armed with 6-inch guns, six destroyers, and two sloops. Britain had the resources to deliver gunboat diplomacy across the globe, deploying notional capabilities to hint at the reserves of power that lay behind, but it did not have the resources to fight two simultaneous high-intensity wars on either side of the world. In addition, Britain had, by this stage of the war, been fighting for two years, and during this time had sustained grievous losses of major ships in keeping her sea lanes open and the enemy at bay. Japan's arrival merely exacerbated an already dangerous state of affairs.

The strategy that the *Kriegsmarine* was forced to adopt, to attack

Britain's sea lanes of communication rather than her main battle-fleets, worked far better than Hitler ever imagined, and nearly brought Britain to her knees. In their weakness the Germans were forced to use subterfuge and guile, rather than brute force, to achieve their aims, concentrating their forces to exploit British weakness. In this, for some significant spans of time, they were spectacularly successful. Heavy cruisers – the so-called 'pocket' battleships, such as the 16,000-ton *Graf Spee* with its 11-inch guns – could travel far and fast and carry out crippling attacks on merchant vessels plying their trade across the four corners of the globe. Likewise, fast, well-armed raiders could cause considerable damage, sustained by regular rendezvous with refuelling vessels on the high ocean. This enabled them to maintain operations for large parts of the year without ever having to victual in a port.

In particular the ubiquitous U-boat could, with only tiny numbers, hunt down prey and deliver death from the deep. Hitler's grand 'Plan Z' was effectively stillborn in September 1939, and resources allocated to achieve it were diverted to the construction of U-boats. Submarine attacks on Britain's vital maritime interests started immediately at the outbreak of war, although they were hampered by the lack of well placed ports from which to operate – a situation that the fall of France and the conquest of Norway did much to rectify. Their successes against a Royal Navy and Merchant Navy that seemed to have forgotten all the convoy lessons of 1917 and 1918 led the Germans to describe this early part of the U-boat war, despite the small size of the boats deployed (750 tons), as *Der erste glückliche Zeit* ('The First Happy Time'). There were to be others.

Although the U-boat remains the dominant image of the Battle of the Atlantic, it took time for their output to increase to a number that could have any meaningful impact on British maritime traffic. In 1939 only five British ships out of over 5,700 that sailed had been sunk by U-boats, and by mid-1940 Admiral Dönitz possessed a mere twenty-nine vessels. The use of battleships like the ill-fated *Graf Spee* as lone raiders was ultimately counterproductive, because they could relatively easily be isolated and hunted down across the wide expanses of the world's oceans, or starved through the capture or destruction of their supply vessels. Until 1941, when the *Kriegsmarine* received the new U-boats ordered at the outset of war, it had to rely on a mixture of methods to place a stranglehold on Britain's maritime jugular, the sea lanes that supplied her through the Atlantic, both from the Americas and up from the Cape of Good Hope.

In 1941 it was not the U-boat or the surface raider, but the threat of attacks by battleships sallying out of the Baltic or North Sea ports, that most troubled London. In January and February 1941 *Scharnhorst* and *Gneisenau* sank over 115,000 tons of shipping in a bloody spree before escaping into Brest. Worse was to come. Two months later the world's largest and most powerful battleship, the *Bismarck*, prepared to deploy into the Atlantic as a surface raider after completing her sea trials, and during her departure through the Denmark Strait on 24 May 1941 with the *Prinz Eugen* engaged and sank the elderly British battle cruiser HMS *Hood*. Eyewitnesses on HMS *Prince of Wales* described her death in what appeared to be a single, all-consuming explosion, and film shot from the *Prinz Eugen* shows her demise in a sudden, catastrophic cloud of smoke reaching far into the sky. There were only three survivors from a complement of over 1,400 men.

The *Bismarck* appeared a fearsome, even invincible threat, even though within a month the folly of a German naval strategy based on the battleship was to be laid bare: the *Bismarck*, after a desperate battle during which she was trying to seek sanctuary at Saint-Nazaire on the French Atlantic coast, was battered to death by the concentrated firepower of a British air and naval task force hastily assembled to destroy it, much as farmers might set dogs to hunt, trap and kill the threat to their livestock posed by a single marauding predator. In all, six British battleships and battle cruisers, two aircraft carriers, thirteen cruisers and twenty-one destroyers were committed to the hunt. But the do-or-die effort required to defeat her meant that Britain remained, in late 1941 and 1942 and all the way into 1944 – unnecessarily perhaps in retrospect – in thrall to the spectre of a powerful German battleship let loose among the unprotected flocks amidst the watery fields of Britain's Atlantic backyard.

A combination of submarine, fleet action and aerial attack by long-range, four-engined Focke-Wulf FW 200 Kondor anti-shipping bombers of *Kampfgeschwader* 40 (KG40) flying in vast, non-stop sweeps from Bordeaux to Norway created a threat of fearsome proportions to Britain in 1941 and 1942. By the end of 1941 a quarter of Britain's merchant fleet had been sunk, to say nothing of the value of the cargoes they had carried. The situation was so bad that the First Sea Lord (Admiral of the Fleet Sir Alfred Dudley Pound) was to declare in March 1942: 'if we lose the war at sea we lose the war.' No one disagreed with him. Navy losses in 1941 had been severe on both sides of the Atlantic, but especially in the Western Atlantic, as small groups of U-boats sought out unprotected merchant vessels for destruction by torpedo or gunfire. In January and February 1942 a total of forty-four vessels had been sunk by U-boats in Canadian waters, a far greater tally than they were able to achieve in more densely protected oceans, such as the eastern Atlantic and the approaches to the British sea terminals in Londonderry, Liverpool and Glasgow. In the early weeks of the 1942 campaign some thirteen ships totalling 100,000 tons were sunk, at a time when the Germans judged that Britain would be forced to surrender if she lost an average of 700,000 tons per month.

This disastrous and bloody trend continued into February and March, and exacerbated fears in London of what might happen if Germany unleashed into the Atlantic its remaining capital ships, cooped up in Brest and the Baltic. U-boat attacks in January 1942 in all theatres of war accounted for sixty-two ships; in February eighty-five; in March ninety-five. The mathematics of attrition appeared horrifyingly one-sided: between January and July a total of 681 ships were lost, an average of 97 per month, amounting to a loss of 3,556,999 gross tons of shipping.

In late 1941 and early 1942 London accordingly adopted a policy of containment. The battleships *Scharnhorst* and *Gneisenau*, together with the heavy cruiser *Prinz Eugen*, had been holed up in the French Atlantic port of Brest since early June 1941 while the *Tirpitz* was in the Baltic. The large French ports of Brest and Saint-Nazaire offered the sanctuary on the Atlantic seaboard necessary for any forays out of German or Norwegian waters. German battleships could leave their lairs on the Baltic or Norwegian coast only if they had ports to which they could repair for victualling when it was required. The pocket battleship *Graf Spee*, for instance, was forced to scuttle itself in the River Plate when it could find no refuge in the South Atlantic and was hemmed in by the Royal Navy. With too little fuel on board to allow it to flee, and no protective harbour available, the captain believed that the only recourse available to him was scuttling for the ship, and suicide for himself.

And it was this vulnerability that meant that by late 1941 Germany's naval strategy was different to that presumed by the Admiralty. In fact, by now (after the loss of *Bismarck*) Berlin was so scared of losing her remaining capital ships that she pursued an alternative policy. With only one battleship left, Hitler was not prepared to lose her in a single scrap with the massed resources of the Royal Navy and, since December 1941, the United States Navy. Instead, he considered, with good cause, that the battleship would do more harm striking against the Arctic convoys taking precious British and American war materiel to succour the Soviet Union.

What skewed Hitler's judgement was his view that when Britain came to make its strategic counter-attack against Hitler's Europe it would do so through Norway. After all, he considered, outside

North Africa virtually all of British offensive land operations, limited though they were, had been aimed at Norway. Accordingly, in December 1941, at the suggestion of Admiral Erich Raeder, he instructed that the German High Seas Fleet should concentrate in Norwegian waters, there to focus on fighting the war in the east, strangling Stalin's lifeline with the Free World. The Atlantic, and the convoys upon which Britain depended for survival, would be left to the depredations of Dönitz's U-Boats. With luck, a strong German fleet dispersed across the Norwegian fjords would force the Royal Navy to deploy a significant proportion of its own fleet not to protect convoys from U-boats, but to prevent a *Kriegsmarine* breakout, without the *Tirpitz* having to deploy into the Atlantic at all.

The strategy worked beautifully, as *Tirpitz* served to tie up strong British naval resources that would otherwise have been deployed elsewhere just in case the German battleship sallied out of its northern lair. Accordingly *Tirpitz* left Wilhelmshaven on 14 January 1942 and made for Trondheim. This was followed in February by Operation *Cerberus*, in which the battleships *Scharnhorst* and *Gneisenau* and the heavy cruiser *Prinz Eugen* escaped through the English Channel. If London had known more of Raeder's intentions it would have quickly stifled the rampant self-criticism that swept the Admiralty following the escape of the German ships up the English Channel. They were also unaware that a severe shortage of fuel oil for *Tirpitz* significantly reduced Raeder's options: the reality at this stage of the war was that Germany could not launch a battlefleet based on this maritime behemoth into the Atlantic for sheer lack of the fuel required to undertake anything other than short sallies into the Arctic Ocean. Thus *Cerberus* was in fact a strategic advantage to Britain, as it represented an end to the danger of an Atlantic breakout. In other words, there was now no strategic imperative behind an attack on Saint-Nazaire, at least in so far as the Battle of the Atlantic or the balance of maritime power was concerned.

But with the British still ignorant of the shift in German maritime strategy (Churchill would write of Hitler after the war that he was 'obsessed with the idea that we intended to invade Northern Norway at an early date. With his powerful one-track mind he sacrificed the glittering chances in the Atlantic and concentrated every available surface ship and many a precious U-boat in Norwegian waters'), huge efforts were made to find and attack the *Tirpitz*. On the morning of 9 March 1942 twelve Fairey Albacore torpedo bombers attacked the ship; two aircraft were lost but no hits were scored. Then, on 30 March, thirty-three Halifax bombers attacked the ship; they scored no hits and five aircraft (and thirty-five crew) were lost. Similar heavy attacks, with comparable losses, took place in April. No strikes on the vessel were made. Five bombers were lost during the first attack, and two in the second. It was not until late 1944 that a massive attack by eighteen Lancaster bombers carrying five-ton 'Tallboy' bombs eventually managed to capsize the ship. In the context of early 1942, therefore, anything that might remove the threat posed by the *Tirpitz* was urgently considered.

Churchill voiced his concerns to the Chiefs of Staff Committee on Sunday 25 January 1942. In a note he prepared for the meeting he wrote:

The presence of *Tirpitz* at Trondheim has now been known for three days. The destruction or even the crippling of this ship is the greatest event at sea at the present time. No other target is comparable to it. She cannot have ack-ack protection comparable to Brest or the German home ports. If she were even only crippled, it would be difficult to take her back to Germany. No doubt it is better to wait for moonlight for a night attack, but moonlight attacks are not comparable with day attacks. The entire naval situation throughout the world would be altered, and the naval command in the Pacific would be regained.

There must be no lack of co-operation between Bomber

Command and the Fleet Air Arm and aircraft-carriers. A plan should be made to attack both with carrier-borne torpedo aircraft and with heavy bombers by daylight or at dawn. The whole strategy of the war turns at this period on this ship, which is holding four times the number of British capital ships paralysed, to say nothing of the two new American battleships retained in the Atlantic. I regard the matter as of the highest urgency and importance. I shall mention it in Cabinet tomorrow, and it must be considered in detail at the Defence Committee on Tuesday night [i.e. 27 January].

Mountbatten's triumph was to link the location for a raid with a compelling and unarguable argument to the Admiralty for carrying it out. The true strategic rationale for the attack on Saint-Nazaire, therefore, was not to deny the port to *Tirpitz*, but merely to raid the French Atlantic coast, in order to remind Hitler of Britain's offensive potential. *Tirpitz* was the excuse used by Mountbatten to elicit Admiralty support for his venture, and was viewed as so compelling an argument that, in both the popular mind and in that of subsequent historians, the two have been erroneously conflated. In this Mountbatten succeeded where Keyes had failed, by winning doubters to his cause through subterfuge, rather than through the blunt logic and brute force of his predecessor – an approach that had been spectacular in its failure. Confirmation that this was the case in a note sent by General Sir Alan Brooke to General George Marshall, the US Army Chief of Staff, on 9 April 1942: 'We were executing a number of raids on the enemy-occupied coastline from Norway to the Bay of Biscay in order to force on the enemy a feeling of insecurity and uncertainty.' That the *Tirpitz* (or any other capital vessel for that matter) might be hindered in its activities was a beneficial end of the strategy, not its goal.

SEVEN

Saint-Nazaire

Saint-Nazaire sits on the northern side of the Loire at the point at which the river opens out into a six-mile-long estuary that gradually widens to meet the waters of the Atlantic as they press up against the French coast through the Bay of Biscay. Before reaching Saint-Nazaire the river Loire meanders its way peacefully through Nantes and the rich countryside, heavy with the vines that for centuries have made it one of the world's best-known wine-growing regions. Saint-Nazaire itself had long been a fishing and shipbuilding port, and though not on the scale of Brest or Lorient to the north, it was and is strategically important in the region. The entrance to the port from the open sea is through a single deep-water channel, the Passe des Charpentiers ('Carpenters' Channel'), which runs close to the northern bank of the estuary. To the south, shallow waters that are revealed as mudflats at low tide extend across most of the estuary, denying access to the Loire to any vessels drawing anything over a few feet. Rear Admiral Adolphe Lepotier, a Free French naval officer who knew the Loire well, described it expressively as full of 'sandbanks that skulked treacherously beneath the expanse of unbroken water'. Knowledgeable local pilots were regarded as indispensable for safe passage through these waters. Access to Saint-Nazaire from the Bay of Biscay via anything but the Passe des Charpentiers was not considered possible for anything larger than a fishing smack or tunny boat. At the mouth of the estuary the river is six and a half miles wide.

Saint-Nazaire grew into a modern shipping centre with the construction of the Old Mole, a breakwater 25 feet above the waterline atop of which perched a lighthouse, in 1835. A wet-dock basin was dug in 1856, followed quickly thereafter by the arrival of the railway and, in 1862, by the installation of the first trans-atlantic telegraph between France and South America. It was in this year that Saint-Nazaire's later reputation as a shipbuilding centre began, with the construction of major shipbuilding facili-ties. A second dock basin was created at Penhoët in 1881, to allow the servicing of larger ships. As a result, the town became an important unloading port for Allied troops during the First World War, and particularly in 1917 for the United States Army.

It was here that the pragmatism of the Old World clashed with the puritanism of the New. A number of the town's obliquely described 'houses of toleration' (*maisons tolérées*: brothels) were placed off limits to US servicemen, which incensed the local Chamber of Commerce and town hall, who were keen to take commercial advantage of the massive influx into the port of American virility. The situation became so strained that President Georges Clemenceau intervened to suggest a compromise, offering to allow the US military medical authorities to control the *maisons tolérées* and setting them apart exclusively for the use of US serv-icemen. This sort of pragmatism proved shocking to sensibilities in Washington, and the offer was rejected, with predictable conse-quences for the incidence of venereal disease amongst American servicemen in France.

After 1918, following the rapid shrinking of the commercial opportunities offered by war, the town and port turned its attention back to major shipbuilding, with the completion in 1921 of the 34,500-ton SS *Paris* and in 1926 of the even larger (43,100-ton) SS *Île de France*. But it was the building of the SS *Normandie* between 1928 and 1934 that placed Saint-Nazaire firmly in the centre of our present narrative, because to accommodate the construction of this 83,000-ton super passenger liner, the largest, fastest and most luxurious of her time, an equally massive dry dock was required. Designed by France's most formidable civil and structural engineer, Albert Caquot, the 'Louis Joubert' dry dock (named after a local official) was completed in 1934. At 350 metres (1,150 feet) long – the length of three football pitches – nearly 50 metres (160 feet) wide and with a depth at high-water mark of 44 feet, it was the largest of its kind in the world at the time. Because of its role in the building of the SS *Normandie* the dry dock was widely known after the name of the vessel. Caquot's genius allowed the dock to have two functions, first as a lock, granting access between the port of Saint-Nazaire and the Loire river; and second, once the water has been drained from it, as a dry dock.

The Normandie Dock was and remains massive, a considerable feat of engineering and the birthplace of the 148,000-ton *Queen Mary II* in 2003. It was enclosed at either end by two massive rolling dock gates ('caissons'), moving transversely and operated by hydraulic winding machinery. It is hard not to be amazed at the size of these enormous caissons: a photograph taken after they were built shows the figure of one of the workers standing dwarfed at its base, as the huge metal box towered 46 feet above him, the height of three double-decker buses. Each gate or caisson, when opened, disappeared into a chamber in the lockside and was 52 metres in length, nearly 9 metres wide and 14 metres high, and weighed 1,250 tons. The two steel rolling caissons were identical in construction except that the inner gate was decked over to form a roadway whilst the outer (i.e. facing into the Loire) had only a footway. When the dock was open to the sea the 'floating' caissons would roll across the entrance (driven by electric motors placed in buildings at the end of each inlet chamber) on rails set in concrete on the lock floor. Each caisson was wound in and out of its chamber by means of two large twin wheels which, with their motors, were situated in winding houses sitting on the western edge of the Normandie Dock.

When in use the compartments of the caissons would be flooded with water to act as ballast, and therefore locked immovably in place, before the water would be pumped from the lock. The pump house was a large building near the outer gate recess, containing four separate pumps with an aggregate capacity of 167,000 gallons per minute, enabling them to empty the dock from low-water level to the sill in seven hours. The motors for the pumping house were at ground level, but its massive pumps sat 40 feet below ground.

The dock area consisted of a forward port (the 'Avant Port'), open to the south directly from the Loire and enclosed to east and west by two convergent jetties 407 feet apart, and two basins northward of the Avant Port accessible only through locks. On the landward side of the Avant Port lay the Old Town of Saint-Nazaire, a closely built rabbit warren of small workers' houses crammed together next to the docks. The entire dock area was substantial. The distance from the light on the seaward end of the west jetty of the Avant Port to the north wall of Penhoët Basin, the northern basin, is 2,890 yards. The Penhoët Basin can be entered via the Avant Port and Saint-Nazaire Basin, the southern basin, by ships up to 10,000 tons, but the main entrance for large vessels was through the Normandie Dock at the south-east corner of the basin. The southern entrance to the Avant Port was crossed by both a swing bridge and a lifting bridge. At the north-eastern corner of the Penhoët Basin were situated a further three, smaller, dry docks. In early 1942 the seaward main lock gate of the Normandie Dock was protected by a double boom against torpedo attack.

The 1936 census recorded the population of Saint-Nazaire as 43,281 (it had reduced to 11,802 by 1945 as a consequence of the attentions paid to it during the war), many of whom lived in the cramped terraces of the Old Town, squeezed between the Loire, the southern entrance and the Place de la Vieille Ville (Old Town Square), all the buildings between the square and the Old Entrance being warehouses and dockyard buildings of various kinds.

Saint-Nazaire played a significant role in British humiliation following the fall of France, as a large proportion of the defeated British Expeditionary Force and its French allies were evacuated from the port in mid-June 1940 following the German invasion that had begun only six weeks before. The popular myth of Dunkirk assumes that the whole of the BEF was evacuated by little ships off the beaches of the Pas de Calais between 26 May and 4 June. In fact, while the 'victory in defeat' of the Dunkirk evacuations saw approximately 198,229 British troops along with 139,997 French and some Belgian troops rescued from the port and adjoining beaches, an additional 191,870 Allied troops (144,171 of them British) and a large quantity of their equipment were rescued from eight major seaports on the Channel and Atlantic coasts in the ten days between 15 to 25 June. Over 57,000 of these troops were evacuated from Saint-Nazaire.

It was during this otherwise successful evacuation that Britain suffered her greatest-ever maritime tragedy, one that for reasons of wartime morale was immediately hushed up by the British authorities. At 3.48 p.m. on 17 June 1940 the RMS *Lancastria*, with as many as 9,000 evacuating soldiers and civilians on board, all of them escaping the rapidly advancing German forces, fell victim to repeated air attack by Junkers 88 bombers while lying stationary on the edge of the estuary awaiting naval escort back to Britain. Three direct hits caused the ship to list first to starboard then to port; she rolled over and sank within twenty minutes. Many drowned, were choked by the oil or were killed by the German fighter-bombers that returned to strafe victims in the water. Estimates of the deaths incurred in the worst single loss of life for British forces in the entire war range from 4,000 to over 7,000.

The loss of the 16,000-ton liner proved to be a metaphor for the wider calamity rapidly engulfing France, for it was on the same day that Marshal Pétain called for an armistice with the invaders, prompting, the following day, the fierce and famous *cri de coeur* by General Charles de Gaulle on the BBC that saw the first, faltering start of the resistance of Free France:

> Must hope disappear? Is defeat final? No! For France is not alone! She is not alone! She is not alone! She has a vast Empire behind her. She can align with the British Empire that holds the sea and continues the fight. She can, like England, use without limit the immense industry of the United States. This war is not limited to the unfortunate territory of our country. This war is not over as a result of the Battle of France. This war is a worldwide war . . . Vanquished today by mechanical force, in the future we will be able to overcome by a superior mechanical force. The fate of the world depends on it.

Driving this desperate rhetoric under the tracks of its advancing panzers, the vanguard of the German forces reached Nantes on 19 June and occupied Saint-Nazaire on 21 June 1940. Almost at once the *Kriegsmarine* began the transformation of the port into one of five secure German bastions along the Atlantic coast (Brest, Lorient, Saint-Nazaire, La Pallice and Bordeaux) from which the maritime war against Britain could be prosecuted. Indeed, within two days of the armistice a train carrying Vice Admiral Karl Dönitz and his HQ staff together with a wide range of submarine equipment, including torpedoes, left Wilhelmshaven for Lorient. The U-boat *U-30* – commanded by Kapitänleutnant Fritz-Julius Lemp, who had earned the dubious privilege of firing Germany's first torpedoes of the war, against the unarmed 13,400-ton liner SS *Athenia* on 3 September 1939 – arrived on 7 July 1940 following a month-long patrol which had resulted in the sinking of five ships in the Bay of Biscay.

The immediate purpose of the French ports was to provide the *Kriegsmarine* with direct access to the Atlantic for its U-boats, which till then had been confined to the narrow space squeezed into the North Sea between Wilhelmshaven, Bremerhaven and the entrance to the Kiel Canal at Brunsbüttel. Construction of gigantic U-boat pens designed to withstand even the heaviest and most sustained aerial bombardment began in March 1941, and in Saint-Nazaire nine of fourteen had been built by February 1942, able when complete to house twenty submarines. Even today the size of the pens is staggering, concrete monsters still dominating the heart of the Saint-Nazaire docks and defying any idea that they might one day be demolished. They occupy an area of some 46,644 square yards. At virtually 330 yards long and 142 yards wide, with a roof nearly 9 yards thick, the entire construction consumed some 627,840 cubic yards of concrete. Construction of the submarine pens in all five French Atlantic ports was to devour 14 million cubic feet of concrete and a million tons of steel. In January 1941 the 7th U-boat Flotilla (7 *Unterseebootsflottille*) moved there from Kiel, with Type-VII U-boats, followed in February 1942 by Type-VIIs of the 6th Flotilla (6 *Unterseebootsflottille*) from Danzig.

Submarine crews operating out of Saint-Nazaire were quartered in conditions of some luxury at hotels in the beautiful peacetime resort of La Baule, along the coast to the west, beside the beautiful white sands of the wide, sweeping beach. It was here, too, that the *Kriegsmarine* HQ for the Loire Estuary (*Kommandantur der Seeverteidigung Loire Mündung*) was situated. In early 1942 it was under the command of Kapitän zur See Adalbert Zuckschwerdt, who during the First World War had been the captain of the armed raider SMS *Comoran II*, a vessel that was involved in the first action between the United States and Germany in 1917.

The arrival of the United States in the Second World War on 11 December 1941, following Hitler's declaration of war, helped initiate a second phase for Saint-Nazaire. If the first related to its role as a secure springboard for the dispatch of U-boats into the Atlantic, the second was a defensive strategy that was to evince itself in the construction of a massive German version of the Maginot Line, called by them for propaganda purposes the Atlantic Wall, stretching some 6,000 miles from the Spanish border to

Norway. Hitler's long, rambling speech to the Reichstag in which he announced the Axis declaration of war on the United States also announced the implementation of this defensive strategy:

> From Kirkenes [in Norway] to the Spanish frontier stretches the most extensive belt of great defence installations and fortresses. Countless airfields have been built, including some in the far north that were blasted out of granite. The number and strength of the protected submarine shelters that defend naval bases are such that they are practically impregnable from both the sea and the air. They are defended by more than one and a half thousand gun battery emplacements, which had to be surveyed, planned and built. A network of roads and rail lines has been laid out so that the connections [to the installations] between the Spanish frontier and Petsamo [in northern Norway] can be defended independently from the sea. The installations built by the Pioneer and construction battalions of the navy, army and air force in cooperation with the Todt Organisation* are not at all inferior to those of the Westwall [along the German frontier with France]. The work to further strengthen all this continues without pause. I am determined to make this European front impregnable against any enemy attack.

The Germans worried that it would be through the French ports that the Allies would one day attempt to force their way into a bridgehead on the Continent of Europe. Their error was to ignore the lessons of France's dependence upon a similar, physical barrier in 1940, one that was defeated with ease because it found itself bypassed and therefore strategically irrelevant. But despite this, in 1942 priority was given to the fortification of prominent seaports, one of which was Saint-Nazaire, and for the

---

* Named after the German Minister for Armaments and Munitions who established a massive labour organisation that undertook large-scale civil engineering projects across Germany and occupied territories during the Second World War.

two years that followed some 1,300 bunkers were constructed by the Todt Organisation over an area that extended from La Vilaine in the north to the town of Pornic in the south. Bunkers were designed in depth stretching from the sand dunes on the coast miles into the countryside, and intended to be mutually supporting, grouped around principal locales and boasting a mixture of weaponry designed for various purposes: to destroy ships off the coast, landing craft on the beaches and tanks and infantry on land.

It is clear from the intelligence summary prepared for Operation *Chariot* that much of the information regarding land defences came from aerial photography. Specifically, no artificial anti-tank obstacle or permanent roadblocks could be seen on the land approaches to Saint-Nazaire, and no pillboxes or barbed wire could be detected. 'In general,' the report concluded, 'it can be said that there are no important land defences, other than the AA batteries, which are probably capable of being used in an anti-tank role, but it must be stressed that the photographs at present available are of such a scale that only major defence works could be seen.' However, it was known that the Germans had gun-laying radar, known as 'Seetakt', and radar that was able to guide aircraft onto moving targets. On 25 June 1940 German Stukas had found and sunk HMS *Delight* in the English Channel (20 miles off Portland Bill) after being guided to her by a 'Freya' radar situated on Cap de la Hague, west-north-west of Cherbourg. In the spring of 1941 the Cherbourg coastal batteries had fired by night on the battleship HMS *Revenge* at a distance of 15 miles, again guided by radar. The presence of coastal radar on the peninsula at Le Croisic due west of La Baule and the possible existence of a similar installation on the northernmost point of the Île de Noirmoutier to the south of the Loire Estuary had been reported.

A mixture of units was involved in this defensive programme in 1941 and 1942. Zuckschwerdt's forces had three main elements; a naval artillery battalion, an anti-aircraft artillery regiment (comprising three battalions), and troops providing harbour defences. Situated on the Pointe de Chémoulin at the place where the Loire Estuary touches the Bay of Biscay on the north side of the estuary, overlooking the entrance to the Passe des Charpentiers, was *Marineartilleriebataillon* (Naval Artillery Battalion) 280, commanded by Kapitän zur See Edo Dieckmann. This unit had at least twenty-eight large-calibre artillery pieces (of 77, 150 and 170 mm calibre) pointing seawards to the south and east, including two massive captured French 240 mm railway guns, which had arrived at Batz-sur-Mer,15 kilometres further west, in September 1941. Twelve of these guns were clustered in three batteries guarding the northern entrance to the estuary. The HQ of 22 *Marineflakregiment* (22nd Naval Anti-Aircraft Regiment), commanded by Kapitän zur See Karl-Conrad Mecke, was situated at Saint-Marc, between the Pointe de Chémoulin and the Pointe de l'Ève, although the guns at the latter position were unmanned during the night of the raid. Mecke had three artillery battalions with forty-three guns, mainly 20 and 37 mm weapons (the 703rd under Korvettenkapitän Thiessen, 705th under Korvettenkapitän Koch and the 809th under Korvettenkapitän Burhenne), and in the heart of Saint-Nazaire itself Korvettenkapitän Kellermann commanded the dock defences.

In addition General Karl Ritter von Prager's 25th Corps garrisoned Western France as part of Army Group D. The 333rd Infantry Division (Lieutenant General Rudolf Pitz), comprised mostly of forcibly conscripted Poles, Czech auxiliaries and Soviet volunteers recruited from German prison camps, occupied this part of the Loire, its 679th Infantry Regiment being located near La Baule. Several hundred well armed and relatively well trained infantrymen could be deployed to any area in a 20-mile radius within half an hour. It is difficult to estimate how many fighting men constituted the defence of the region, although it is clear that the British suggestion that there were ten thousand servicemen and workers in and around Saint-Nazaire in early 1942 was a serious underestimate – Edo Dieckmann told Peter Lucas Phillips that there were 5,000 troops defending the Saint-Nazaire area in 1942. Adolphe Lepotier noted after the war that 'Monsieur Grimaud, who at the time was attached to the mayor of Saint-Nazaire, told him that there were more than a hundred thousand Germans in the region around the Loire Estuary from Pornichet Point to St Gildas.' Many of these would have been workers for the Todt Organisation, building both U-boat facilities and what became known as the Atlantic Wall.

The danger for the Germans posed by these substantial defences, even in their relatively nascent 1942 state, was complacency. When Vice Admiral Dönitz conducted his visit of inspection of the U-boat base on 27 March 1942, with Hitler's recent directive undoubtedly on his mind, he asked Herbert Sohler of his plans for countering a potential British Commando attack. Sohler dismissed the prospect out of hand. Dönitz, presciently, is supposed to have remarked: 'I would not be too sure.'

When, on 23 January 1942, John Hughes-Hallett outlined his plans to Mountbatten COHQ's head of intelligence, Wing Commander The Marquis de Casa Maury (known to his friends as 'Bobby' and something of a playboy who had been part of Mountbatten's pre-war social circle) informed him at once that work had been undertaken in Keyes's time several months before to evaluate a raid against Saint-Nazaire, and a considerable amount of information was readily available in the files. Indeed, part of the material amassed the previous year had been studies undertaken by Royal Engineer officers Captains Bill Pritchard MC and his friend Robert ('Bob') Montgomery, on the subject of how to undertake the demolition of the lock, and its supporting infrastructure.

The fear at the time was that German capital ships could take advantage of the port's dry dock to make repairs following forays on the high seas. In fact, the first written record suggesting an attack on Saint-Nazaire was an Admiralty request to the

Commander-in-Chief Plymouth on 10 August 1941 to consider an operation, after consultation with Keyes, against the massive caissons of the entrance lock leading to the Penhoët Basin and the huge U-boat pens that the Germans had been building since their arrival in 1940. The Admiralty hoped that a raid could be mounted during the next favourable tide and moon conditions, in late October 1941. Indeed, prior to sending this request to the C-in-C Plymouth, Admiral Sir Charles Forbes (operational responsibility for raids at this time resided in the regional Naval HQs), the Admiralty's Department of Navy Plans had undertaken extensive analysis to understand how an attack on Saint-Nazaire might be achieved. It suggested that it might be practicable by MTBs working in conjunction with a small landing and demolition party, and might perhaps be coordinated with an operation of this type that was being planned against Brest. In this, a specially adapted vessel – MTB 74 – was equipped with two bow-mounted torpedo tubes to enable a close-range attack against the German capital ships – the *Scharnhorst*, *Gneisenau* and *Prinz Eugen* – currently holed up in the harbour.

There were two reasons for the Admiralty's interest in an attack on Saint-Nazaire, outlined by the Admiralty in a request from Combined Operations on 23 August 1941. First, as discussed in the previous chapter, the Normandie Dock was the sole location in France capable of receiving the *Tirpitz*, and the destruction of the caisson would deny its use to the Germans. Second, the port was now a U-boat base of the first importance, containing ten submarines as well as tankers and other shipping. When complete there were expected to be fourteen separate submarine pens in place. It was therefore a valuable target for an attack from the sea using Commando-type troops landed from small ships that could infiltrate up the river and its estuary in secret, launching a surprise attack on the hopefully unprepared defenders.

The Admiralty urged the consideration of demolition parties primarily because a torpedo attack alone on the caissons was not considered capable of putting the dock permanently out of commission. The dock gates were of the sliding type, moving into the lock gap on rails before being flooded in position. A torpedo would merely punch a hole in them which, despite the gates' considerable size, would then be comparatively easy to repair. It would be better, the Admiralty suggested, to enter the caisson compartment at the side and blow up the runners on which the gate moved, perhaps by twisting the rails or slide mechanism to make the damage permanent. Likewise, landing parties would be able to get directly at any harboured U-boats in a way that would be impossible for torpedoes. London already knew from intelligence gathered from the port that for reasons of safety the submarine crews were billeted outside the town at La Baule, which meant that a *coup de main* attack during the hours of darkness might have a good chance of success. However, it was acknowledged that a single attack on Saint-Nazaire would be unlikely to destroy both targets, as the resources required to destroy the caissons would be much smaller than required to destroy up to ten harboured U-boats.

Time would be critical in the planning. The raiders could not stay on land for long, as they were not designed for engagements any longer than a couple of hours, or ones that required heavy firepower. They had no artillery, for instance, or heavy mortars, and no air-to-ground support. The largest anti-tank weapon they possessed was the pathetic 0.55-inch Boys anti-tank rifle, useless against heavy armour, which was obsolete even before it first came into service in the British Army in 1937. Success was derived from speed and surprise. What they had to do at Saint-Nazaire – demolishing key dock installations – they must do in the least time possible, before withdrawing fast to fight another day. To try for too much, such as attacking both the U-boat pens and the docks at the same time, would be a mistake.

There was much to consider in planning a raid against Saint-Nazaire. First, it was a long way from Britain. The direct distance from the nearest UK port – Falmouth – was about 263 miles, which, even in fast craft, would necessitate at least a two-night journey (fourteen hours at an average speed of 18 knots) across waters intensively patrolled by German surface, submarine and air forces, and which for the most part was far beyond the range of fighter cover from Britain. It would be critical to arrive at the target during the hours of darkness. Unfortunately the Royal Navy's Coastal Forces did not possess any small vessels of the MTB type able to sustain a 500-mile round trip, unless they were dropped off and collected by a 'mother' ship. And even if long-range MTBs could be used, they were unsuitable for carrying troops. An alternative plan was required if troops were to be deployed on shore.

A host of further questions needed answers. What obstructions and minefields posed hazards to the incoming vessels? Where could troops be landed? Could they achieve surprise if the carrying vessels approached across the shallow water to the south? How could the forces retire without making sitting ducks for the Luftwaffe? What was the best way of destroying the U-boat pens and caissons? An important consideration was the need to mask the noise of the operation with a diversionary bombing raid, to keep the German defenders looking skywards rather than towards the sea.

Keyes signed off a response to the Admiralty on 27 August 1941 regretting that no suitable high-speed ships of the type required to carry the MTBs existed, but suggesting that the vessels could be carried by one or more of the slower carriers in use by the Commandos, such as the ex-Belgian and Dutch cross-channel ferries HMS *Prince Leopold*, *Queen Emma* and *Prinses Beatrix*. On the latter point, the Commandos were not demolition specialists with the skills required to destroy the complex targets identified by the Admiralty, so trained explosive ordnance officers of the Royal Engineers would be called upon.

When Forbes met the Admiralty's planners at 3 p.m. in the Old Upper War Room between Whitehall and Horse Guards on Tuesday 16 September 1941 to discuss the prospect of a foray against Saint-Nazaire, the subject was considered in more than a little detail, but it was reluctantly determined that as no fast boats were available, any plans to mount an attack would remain entirely theoretical. Importantly, these discussions were still based on considerations of attacking both the U-boats in their pens and the caissons of the lock gates. Indeed, it was suggested that the pumping stations should also be destroyed. The return journey also posed significant difficulties, as it would have to take place in daylight, and the vessels provided for the return journey would be subject to intense air and shore attack. One suggestion was that a submarine might wait to take off the survivors in the approaches, given that a T-Class vessel had recently embarked over 130 men in the Mediterranean. It was essential that long-range fighters such as Bristol Blenheims or Bristol Beaufighters should also be made available to cover the withdrawal.

Following these discussions Forbes took the decision, despite the high priority assigned by the naval staff in London to a possible attack on Saint-Nazaire, not to proceed with a raid as currently conceived because of its 'negligible chance of surprise and consequent small chance of success with probability of losses'. The view at the time was that at least three types of covering troops would be required for a raid of this kind, chiefly to protect the demolition teams and to fend off counter-attacks by the defenders, thus increasing the size and scale of the original proposal. But the Admiralty were not to be put off. On 4 November 1941 Commander George Faulkner RN, the Admiralty's adviser on Combined Operations, prepared a comprehensive and well argued brief in which he concluded that because 'success in rendering the dock useless would deter the enemy from sending *Tirpitz* into the Atlantic' the operation was urgent. Despite the objections thrown up by Forbes, the strategic imperative to deny Saint-Nazaire to the Germans for the purposes of repairing and revictualling the *Tirpitz* remained overwhelming.

Faulkner advocated a heavier scale of attack than earlier envisaged, carried out by small craft of the R Boat or 'Eureka' type (an early assault landing craft) approaching over the mudflats in calm weather. Additionally, to allow a withdrawal at night he suggested that the attack be launched at high water between midnight and 4 a.m. A submarine could be positioned at the mouth of the Loire to act as a navigational waypoint for the approaching raiders, and efforts be made to assess the effectiveness of the local German radar facilities known to exist on the northern bank. His view was that planning to attack both targets (the U-boats and the caissons) would allow success to be achieved in at least one of these.

Critically, Faulkner's carefully argued description of the solution suggested that the best way of destroying the caisson to the Normandie Dock was not by torpedo but by means of a shallow-draught vessel, travelling at not less than 15 knots, crashing into the seaward end. He even went so far as to suggest two likely contenders for this sacrificial role, the Thames passenger steamers the 1,500-ton TSMV *Royal Sovereign* or the 1,100-ton MV *Queen of the Channel*, capable of carrying 1,600 passengers. (Clearly he was not aware that both ships had been lost the previous year, one to dive-bomber attack off Dunkirk and the other to a mine in the Bristol Channel.) But the germ of an idea had been sown by Faulkner, namely that of using a sizeable, shallow-draft vessel to drive itself into the gates at speed and thereby to render them inoperable. On receipt of Faulkner's paper Hughes-Hallett noted that, as it was clear that severe losses might be expected, the objective should be a large-scale attack designed not just to destroy the dock gates but the port, port facilities and ships as well. The force should be trained and kept ready for the right window of opportunity provided by a positive weather report.

But given Forbes's resistance to the proposal, Faulkner asked the Special Operations Executive (SOE) on 15 November 1941 whether it could develop a scheme to effect the destruction of the lock. The request was sent to the desk of Major David Wyatt RE, the SOE adviser to COHQ, and his neat handwritten notes in royal blue ink on the subject can be found, carefully preserved, in the National Archives at Kew. SOE had been established in the previous year with the task of taking subversion and sabotage into the heart of enemy-occupied territory. By the end of 1941, however, its offensive capabilities remained nascent and they would not see fuller expression until 1943. Faulkner asked Wyatt to consider an operation run by SOE in which the Admiralty would provide landing facilities on a quiet part of the French coast, explosives and a small number of demolition experts. But whichever way he looked at it, Wyatt could not find a solution to the problem posed by the extensive German security measures around these deeply sensitive installations. The SOE agent Sergeant Joël Letac suggested to him that he could undertake demolitions that would nevertheless be repaired within a week.

In a file note made on 15 November Wyatt concluded: 'SOE's immediate reaction is that they are very unlikely to have the necessary resources for at least two months, and that even then it is very unlikely that they can take on an operation of this magnitude.' The destruction of the docks, therefore, would not be achieved at the hands of SOE. Alternative means were required.

EIGHT

Resistance

It has often been assumed that the intelligence the British were able to amass about Saint-Nazaire prior to 1942 was a product of their military familiarity with the port: it had featured strongly in the history of the BEF between 1939 and 1940. But this is only partly true. While detailed information did exist in Britain concerning the construction of the Normandie Dock (of which more later), a great deal of contemporary intelligence was available through other sources. One was aerial reconnaissance, the role of the RAF's Central [Photographic] Interpretation Unit (CIU) based at Danesfield House, near Marlow at Medmenham on the Berkshire and Buckinghamshire border, a sister organisation to Bletchley Park. Likewise, a significant amount was secured through the work of secret agents.

At this distance in time it is not easy to be precise about the extent and detail of Allied intelligence operations in France in 1941 and early 1942, especially given the nascent state of many formal resistance organisations, or *réseaux*, which did not reach their apogee until 1944. Nevertheless, the intelligence file in the National Archives relating to Saint-Nazaire and the layout of the port from contemporary sources is surprisingly substantial. File DEFE 2/128 includes fifty-four photographs of the base's fourteen submarine pens – both under construction and completed – as well as photographs of the inside of German U-boats in their pens, together with extensive details of the port facilities, including detailed specifications of the Normandie Dock. The staggering fact is that all of this material was obtained by subterfuge under German noses by intelligence officers and extraordinarily brave *résistants*. The astonishing amount of detailed material in the files of the National Archives pays homage to a number of remarkable intelligence coups at a time that is generally considered to have been a relatively unfruitful period in the history of resistance in France. It also points to the fact that this early stage was peopled by men and women of quite outstanding courage, some of whom were in the pay of British, Polish and Free French intelligence services, but many of whom were not, and who carried out their actions for private motives, or simply for no other reason than for *la gloire de la France* at a time when the omens for eventual victory, given the seemingly superhuman powers of both the Nazi state and its war machine, were so few as to seem, to many, non-existent.

Although it is impossible to say exactly who was responsible for each part of the material contained in DEFE 2/128, what is known is that a range of separate agencies were operating at various locations in France at this time, with varying objectives and different results, and that possibly three separate organisations were responsible for sending highly sensitive information out of Saint-Nazaire and the other French Atlantic ports. Few knew of the efforts of others, although occasionally they stumbled across each other. Some of the earliest, most energetic and most successful intelligence-gatherers on the Allied side were the Poles, the residue of the close links between Poland and France in the interwar years; some were sponsored by MI6, some by de Gaulle's Bureau Central des Renseignements et d'Action (BCRA, Central Bureau of Intelligence and Operations) and some by SOE. Others were entirely self-made, the spontaneous eruption of resistance to the occupiers by men and women outraged at their sudden loss of liberty, and the violent repression of their freedoms by a wholly assertive and sometimes (and increasingly) violent Germanic totalitarianism. Whatever its view of perfidious Albion or of pre-war political differences between Left and Right, Church and State, Gallic pride needed very little patriotic motivation when confronted by the sight of polished jackboots strutting disdainfully over ancient French cobbles.

One such *réseau*, begun in Paris in the late summer of 1940, was based around a group of friends who worked at the Musée de l'Homme, housed in the massive Palais de Chaillot on the Rue du Trocadéro overlooking the Seine. The first efforts of this group, led by Anatole Lewitsky (an anthropologist), Boris Vildé (a linguist, who had escaped early German captivity) and Yvonne Oddon (the museum's librarian), were to disseminate anti-German literature, produced on a printing press in the basement of the museum. This became the newspaper *Résistance*. The Germans, of course, had resources of their own in intelligence and counter-intelligence, which made wartime France the focus of considerable, and danger-ous, intrigue.

By the end of 1940 four separate Polish cells had been estab-lished covering all of occupied and Vichy France ('Tudor' in Marseille, 'Panhard' in Lyon, 'Rab' in Toulouse and 'Interallié' in Paris). Within the Tudor network (run by Colonel Wincenty Zarembski, who had been head of Polish Intelligence in Paris at the outbreak of war), but working to MI6 in London, was an agent working under the codename of 'Doctor'. A former Polish naval officer, Lieutenant Tadeusz Witold Jekiel had escaped to Britain, and now operated out of Bordeaux, but specialised in securing intelligence about shipping movements from all five of the French Atlantic ports, eventually leading what became known as the 'Marine' cell. Not much escaped the gaze of this group. Jekiel had attended the Grande École Nationale du Génie Mari-time in Paris in 1937 before working at the shipbuilding control commission in Le Havre between 1938 and 1939: for a foreigner his knowledge of the French Atlantic ports was unrivalled.

Information gathered by these men made its way back to London either by radio or by ship-borne courier. Lysander flights did not start in northern France until early 1942. Lieutenant Colonel Gilbert Renault-Roulier (codenamed Rémy) managed to get three sackfuls of material back to London on one of these flights (Operation *Julie*) on the night of 27 February, from a snow-covered field at Saint-Saëns.˙ Zarembski ran a primitive transmitter from Toulouse, and in July 1941 'Armand' (Captain Roman Czerniawski, later to play a crucial role in the success of the Allied 'Double Cross' system, where his codename was 'Brutus') had established his own radio link with London from Paris. In the French capital information would arrive courtesy of a wagon-lit attendant on the Paris to Marseille express, which was then transmitted to MI6 via agents working for the one-time MI6 agent in Paris, Wilfred ('Biffy') Dunderdale, using a radio set that had arrived from London in August 1940. Lieutenant Benjamin Cowburn of SOE observed that, as time went on, 'some of the finest resistance activities were to be those of railwaymen'.

One of the channels by which reports on naval activity reached London was via the US diplomatic bag, at least until the Allied invasion of North Africa in November 1942, when the embassy was closed down and the Germans occupied the Free Zone. Messages and material were smuggled across the Demarcation Line into the Free Zone, where they were placed in the US diplomatic bag at the relocated embassy at Vichy. The bag would then make its way to the US embassy in Berne, whence the information it contained was transmitted by MI6 to London. In addition, a small boat ran each month from the seaside village of Saint-Raphaël midway between Cannes and Saint-Tropez, making for Gibraltar, carrying contraband, evaders and escapers as well as packages destined for London.

There were two French sections in SIS, one specifically for

---

* See Rémy, *The Silent Company* (London: Arthur Barker, 1948), pp. 262–7.

supporters of de Gaulle (A5), led by Lieutenant Commander Kenneth Cohen, and the other recruiting from sources that were not the natural bedfellows of the Free French, such as Vichyites and monarchists (A4) – the latter section under Biffy Dunderdale. By 1941, led by Cohen, A5 had established loose networks of spies across the French Atlantic ports, many utilising connections between First World War veterans. According to Keith Jeffery's history of MI6, good coverage of the French Atlantic ports had been established by the end of 1941. Likewise, Dunderdale had been instructed by Sir Stewart Menzies (the head of MI6) to concentrate the efforts of A4 on securing intelligence from these ports, especially about U-boats and commerce raiders.

On 20 December 1941 Rémy, a film producer in civilian life, but now leading the *réseau Confrérie Notre-Dame* (CND), was in his apartment in Paris, together with his wife Edith, when one of his agents, Alex, arrived with 'an enormous parcel' that he placed on the kitchen table. He then undid the string. What happened next is related by Renault-Roulier in his book *The Silent Company*, published in Paris in 1945, and in translation three years later in London:

I could hardly believe my eyes. It contained the original German plans of the submarine bases, not only at Lorient, but also at Brest, Saint-Nazaire, La Pallice, and Bordeaux . . .

My wife and I exchanged anxious looks. The value of the dossier was beyond imagination. Almost too good to be true . . .

'It was the six bottles of Sauterne that did the trick' said Alex with a smile. 'My German boss was very pleased. He went on leave to Berlin three days ago.'

We looked at him, awaiting the sequel.

'I had taken a wax impression of the key of the steel cabinet in which he kept the plans and also of the key to his office, which he locked up when he went away. It was no trouble at all to get into the office during lunch hour. And here we are.'

'But when he comes back, he will notice that the plans have gone?'

'Not immediately. There are twelve copies of each plan. I have taken one of each, so it won't be noticed. And then if he did notice, he's not likely to publish the fact. He'll be too worried about his own position.'*

So it was that a matter of days later, this priceless intelligence made its way to London via a courier route Renault had set up through Spain. It very nearly did not get there. On arrival at Montparnasse station in Paris, Alex was fearful that his prominent package would be examined by the ever-vigilant guards at the exits. Seeing an elderly lady struggling with her suitcase, he offered to help. Gratefully accepting, she carried the smaller package in exchange. 'His' suitcase was carefully examined; the old lady with 'her' package was waved through with a nod.

This rich seam of material complemented that which had already found its way to London that year. Earlier in 1941 the 'Kul' *réseau* (later 'Alliance'), which worked to provide intelligence directly for MI6, also managed to send material about Saint-Nazaire to London. Marie-Madeleine Fourcade, the audacious leader of this resistance group, recalled in *Noah's Ark* how one of her agents, Antoine Hugon, arrived one day in the late summer of 1941 at her secret HQ in Pau, in the foothills of the Pyrenees:

He was a garage owner and had the unusual distinction of having been awarded the Iron Cross for having saved the life of a drowning German soldier in the First World War. He made a point of wearing it openly, which presumably made his missions into the less accessible zones that much easier. He proudly unfolded a

---

* By a remarkable coincidence Renault found himself in a Lysander flying from Britain over Brittany to a field near the village of Saint-Léger-de-Montbrillais, 124 miles west of Saint-Nazaire, on the very night of Operation *Chariot*. See Matthew Cobb *The Resistance* (London: Simon & Schuster, 2009), p. 105.

huge plan that he had wrapped round his body and smuggled across the demarcation line. It showed all the U-boat pens recently built at Saint-Nazaire, reproduced to scale, down to the last inch, by the engineer Henri Mouren.*

In another instance the Breton nationalist René-Yves Creston and a member of what became known as the *Musée de l'Homme réseau* under the leadership of Boris Vildé discovered that a childhood friend, Albert Jubineau, a Paris-based lawyer, had established a *réseau* in Saint-Nazaire based on his friends and colleagues in the judiciary: lawyers, magistrates and court staff. Through Creston, Jubineau was able to make contact with Vildé (now codenamed 'Maurice') and Lewitsky ('Chazalle'). Creston undertook at least three trips to Brittany and on one of these brought back secret German documents on the docks, submarine pens and Normandie Dock at Saint-Nazaire for onward passage to London. At the time the safest route was still inside the diplomatic bag at the US embassy, arranged through the auspices of the librarian, Miss Penelope Royall. It was a dangerous business, with torture and death the inevitable consequence for anyone captured.

In February 1941 plans of Saint-Nazaire had arrived at the Musée de l'Homme and were carefully copied. One set was left with Creston and another given to a young female courier, a white Russian émigrée by the name of Madame Erouchkowski, who also worked at the museum. Unbeknownst to the other members of the *réseau*, however, Erouchkowski was in the pay of the Gestapo, and she allowed her copy of the Saint-Nazaire plans into German hands. Soon afterwards Creston was arrested and jailed for five months, but before his capture he had managed to get his copy of the notes to the US embassy, where in due course they were successfully delivered to London. Through the treachery of another of their number, Albert Gaveau, most of the *réseau* were rounded

---

* Hugon was executed at Mont Valerian Prison on 30 November 1942.

up and put on trial in March 1941. Nineteen people were arrested, of whom ten were ultimately sentenced to death. Anatole Lewitzky and Boris Vildé were two of seven executed on 23 February 1942. Yvonne Oddon, Sylvette Leleu and Alice Simmonet, who had also been sentenced to death, were deported instead, along with Agnès Humbert. All four narrowly survived the war.

A third source of intelligence was available to London in 1941 through a *réseau* established by the BCRA and MI6 in Brest. Codenamed 'Johnny', it was run jointly by Lieutenant Philippon and Dr Antoine Vourc'h. Vourc'h, the father of nine children, was demobilised as a doctor in the French Army after the armistice and allowed to return home to the village of Plomodiern in western Brittany, some three miles from the sea, where he was the local doctor. His involvement in resistance activities began with assisting the escape of young Gaullists wanting to reach London – he arranged for fishing boats to take them under cover of darkness from the seaside villages of Douarnenez and Camaret. A number of his sons, together with some of his demobilised friends, escaped by this route to Britain, disguised as fishermen. Francis and Guy joined No. 4 Commando, and Jean trained with the BCRA to return to France armed with a couple of radios.

A significant role in the rapidly growing *réseau* was undertaken by Vourc'h's fourteen-year-old daughter, Marguerite. Returning from her boarding school, the Maison d'éducation de la Légion d'Honneur at Saint-Denis, just outside Paris, in October 1940, she needed no persuading to help her father find information about German defences and shipping. She would spend her holidays cycling along the coast, gathering whatever information she could on German defences, weapon emplacements and shipping. No one took any notice of her. Her travel to and from school at the start and end of each term provided her with perfect cover for carrying messages and parcels between Brittany and Paris. When she returned to Paris, hidden among her books and bags was the secret information garnered along the coast. 'There was no reason to suspect me,' she recalled. 'I was a young girl, travelling to my school. I was never arrested. I would take it to an apartment in Paris. I never wanted to know anything about the lady I gave it to. If the Germans found me with it, they would have tortured me; the less I knew, the better.' On one occasion when she and her parents were taking secret documents to a contact, their car was stopped by French police and German soldiers. While her father attempted to persuade the soldiers to let them on their way, Marguerite was passed the thick file of documents and, kneeling on the floor of the car, she stuffed it inside her corset. Sitting back in her seat, she smiled sweetly at the German soldier, who waved the car on its way. 'Because of my age,' she later observed, 'I seemed to be able to slip through the German security cordons. They just didn't suspect me.'

In March 1941 the sailing boat *L'Émigrant* landed Robert Alaterre, Jean Le Roux, Jean Milon and Daniel Lomenech in the sand dunes near the village of Lampaul-Ploudalmézeau, 15 miles north of Brest. These men constituted the first of what Dunderdale described as 'Johnny's Group', which formalised what Vourc'h had been carrying out since the previous October. Robert Alaterre was the radio operator, and Jean Le Roux was the son of the remarkable Madame Le Roux, who befriended the Brest harbour master and soon gained his trust. Before long, considerable quantities of valuable information regarding shipping movements in and out of the port found their way to London. Reporting to the BCRA, their initial task was to provide information regarding the *Scharnhorst* and *Gneisenau*, which had arrived in Brest on 21 March 1941. Because the coastal seafaring community was small and closed, it is reasonable to assume that organisations like 'Johnny' were also able to receive information relating to all five of the French Atlantic ports, including Saint-Nazaire, and equally it's likely that the activities of young *résistants* like Marguerite Vourc'h were not restricted to Brest.

There is a final tantalising suggestion in the files in the National

Archives that an SOE agent was in Saint-Nazaire in December 1941, or perhaps in the week or months following this date. The assessment written by SOE as to the ability of that organisation to conduct an operation records: 'One agent is due to proceed to the Saint-Nazaire area shortly.' On 16 December Captain V.D.A. Donaldson RN, a staff officer at the Plans Division of the Admiralty, wrote to Major David Wyatt:

> With reference to the matter about which you saw him last Saturday, Rear-Admiral Power (ACNS(H)) has been consulted, and considers that the reconnaissance should go ahead and preparations made in case the reconnaissance indicates that there are reasonable chances of success.

Did the reconnaissance to Saint-Nazaire go ahead as suggested? Was there an SOE agent or agents in Saint-Nazaire in late 1941 or early 1942, as Wyatt had indicated was planned to be the case? The SOE historian, Professor M.R.D. Foot, notes that a Sergeant Joël Letac, who first landed by parachute on 15 March 1941 with four other French soldiers to undertake the assassination of the Luftwaffe pilots of *Kampfgeschwader* 100 in Brittany (Operation *Susannah*), may well have been this agent.* Otherwise, the files remain empty and history silent on SOE's role in penetrating the port and returning with viable intelligence to support the raid. SOE may well have been successful, but there is no evidence to suggest that it was able to contribute to the raid in a meaningful way. There is, nevertheless, plenty of evidence to demonstrate that enough other agencies and individuals were at work to provide better than adequate intelligence to help the planners in Richmond Terrace frame their plans for a raid.

---

*   M.R.D. Foot, *SOE in France* (London: HMSO, 1966).

NINE

The Decision is Made

Lord Louis Mountbatten found that his desire to mount a powerful raid to cement the role of Combined Operations in the otherwise limited array of Britain's offensive capability, together with Churchill's and Pound's keenness to do anything to prevent the *Tirpitz* sallying forth from its Norwegian hideout into the rich pastures of the Atlantic, providentially overlapped. Indeed, this new-found common purpose was to help, in time, to rebuild the relationship between Combined Operations and the Admiralty that had been damaged during Keyes's tenure, though relations during the planning phase remained strained.

From this point on there was no question in COHQ but that the purpose of the Saint-Nazaire raid was to deny the *Tirpitz* a berth on the French Atlantic coast. So it was that on 7 February 1942 Mountbatten was able to send an encouraging memorandum to the Admiralty stating that Combined Operations had come up with a viable plan, and one in which he had confidence. Initially prompted by SOE's estimation that the damage from one of their raids could be repaired by the Germans in only eight to ten days, David Luce and John Hughes-Hallett had sat down together on 21 January and come up with the bare bones of a plan. Hughes-Hallett recalled that they were able to sketch it out in about an hour, chiefly because they were able to revive many of Faulkner's ideas from the previous November.

The physical and geographical characteristics of the challenge had led the two men to build on Faulkner's solution of employing what they described as an 'expendable ship', drawing less than twelve feet to take advantage of the much higher than usual sea levels created by the spring tides (a detail confirmed by the LOTI), which would ram the outer caisson of the Normandie Dock and destroy itself with a large quantity of onboard explosive. This would rip apart the massive outer gate, and open up the lock to an MTB that would enter the now flooded dock to fire its torpedoes at the inner caisson at the far end. It was clear to the two men that the very heavy construction of the outer gate to the dry dock could only be destroyed by a large vessel ramming it. It was also clear that the nine recently completed U-boat pens and the five in the process of construction on the western edge of the Bassin de Saint-Nazaire were of such massive construction that it was unlikely that any effective damage could be carried out by a raid conducted by lightly armed infantry. If, however, the basin could be made tidal by the destruction of the lock gates, it was possible that the Germans would be badly hampered in their use of the docks for U-boats, as the vessels would be able to move in and out only at high tide, and would be damaged by being repeatedly grounded every time the tide went out. The Luce/Hughes-Hallett plan envisaged the vessel sailing from Plymouth or Falmouth, accompanied by four motor launches of the 'Fairmile' class, a small craft used for coastal work, together with an MTB and a Fairmile motor gunboat (MGB) fitted with what Hughes-Hallett described as 'special navigational aids' – a reference to sonar ('ASDIC') and elementary radar.

The route to the Loire, and the precise timing of the arrival of the little fleet, would be calculated using advice from the Royal Navy's Superintendent of Tides, together with intelligence about the habits of German meteorological flights, known as 'Zenits', over the western extremities of the English Channel, the Celtic Sea and the Bay of Biscay. Approaching the Loire from the south-west, the vessels would cross the flats before the expendable ship accelerated to a speed of about 20 knots to embed herself in the lock gates. The men of the ship's company, commandos and demolition experts carried on board would then exit the stricken ship over the fo'c'sle and take cover nearby, while the tons of explosive on board would detonate and destroy both caisson and ship. Water would flood into the dock, after which the MTB would enter and fire its torpedoes at the inner caisson. The engines would have been removed from the MTB's torpedoes and replaced with additional explosive, the weapons being launched by compressed air and propelled by this accelerant power for 150 yards before they hit the water, and travelled to their target. The soldiers and demolitions troops would then swarm over the docks destroying key points, before retiring to board the Fairmiles, in which they would return to Britain, protected at sea by two or three destroyers that would wait off the Loire during the raid.

According to Hughes-Hallett the plan was hatched in a trice and accepted by Mountbatten in principle a few days later. The work undertaken by Luce and Hughes-Hallett to build on the work of the previous summer and develop a robust plan able to be executed by a reinvigorated Combined Operations in the spring of 1942 was opportunely timed in view of the anxiety then being experienced both in No. 10 Downing Street and the Admiralty about the prospect of a foray into the Atlantic by the *Tirpitz*.

Churchill's letter to the Chiefs of Staff Committee on Sunday 25 January has already been noted. The next day Churchill discussed the problem with Sir Dudley Pound, and on the following day – Tuesday 27 January – Mountbatten found himself lunching with his old friend Captain Charles Lambe RN, Deputy Director of the Plans Division at the Admiralty. Among the subjects discussed was the *Tirpitz*. Could not Combined Operations look again at the problem of Saint-Nazaire, asked Lambe. Fresh from his briefing, Mountbatten was able to confirm that work was already well advanced on that very subject.

The first written expression of the work undertaken by Luce and Hughes-Hallett came in Mountbatten's memorandum to the Admiralty on Saturday 7 February. Cunningly, Mountbatten, having identified a solution to the Admiralty's *Tirpitz* problem, now asked the Admiralty itself to commit to the enterprise by identifying the destroyers that could carry out the task, one of which would be sacrificed in the operation. The sacrificial vessel needed to be between 1,000 and 2,000 tons, capable of cruising at 15 knots and sustaining a short burst of 20 knots, have a draught of less than 12 feet and be able to undertake a single journey from Britain of up to 500 miles (assuming that the most direct route, for reasons of security, was not adopted). The memorandum suggested that the best dates to deploy were between 13 and 16 March and 11 and 14 April: in March there would be ten and a half hours of darkness available and nine hours in April. To provide navigational certainty Mountbatten suggested that a submarine be pre-positioned at the mouth of the Loire to act as a light beacon, and that air support be provided as a diversion during the raid. Enough was known of the German radar currently in use to indicate that it could only be used to detect one set of targets, aerial or maritime, at a time. With a bombing raid under way at the same time, it appeared that it would be more likely that the German radar unit known to be on Cap Le Croisic would be pointing skywards, rather than out to sea.

Perhaps anticipating a robust challenge to the outline plan, especially that part relating to the expendable destroyer, Mountbatten insisted that he would not neglect the question of air support. He assured the Admiralty that 'the project is not put forward light heartedly but has been given a lot of thought. I have a complete model, some excellent photographs and first-class intelligence about Saint-Nazaire available in my Headquarters.' In the notes accompanying the letter Mountbatten touched on the paranoia in Whitehall about the German battlefleet, knowing that it was this subject above all others that would guarantee a positive response to his plans for a substantial raid on the French Atlantic coast: 'If we succeed in rendering the dock useless, it might effectively deter the enemy from sending *Tirpitz* into the Atlantic. The operation should therefore be carried out as soon as possible.'

It was not until 11.15 a.m. on 19 February 1942 that the first detailed meeting on the subject was conducted at 1a Richmond Terrace, chaired by Mountbatten, covering the substance of the proposed operation with sixteen interested individuals conscripted from COHQ, the Admiralty and, for the first time, the Special Service Brigade. The COHQ contingent – and primary architects of the plan – included Hughes-Hallett, Luce, Group Captain Fred Willetts RAF, Brigadier Haydon and Captain Peter Young (who was seconded, at the time, to COHQ). There were three officers from the Admiralty, together with Captain Bill Pritchard MC RE.

It was by an extraordinary series of coincidences that Pritchard found himself at the centre of the planning for the raid. An experienced combat engineer, Pritchard had already conducted an extensive analysis of the requirements for disabling dock mechanisms by means of demolition, and it was his experience that enabled Combined Operations to be confident that the tasks set for the Commandos at Saint-Nazaire were achievable. Bill Pritchard's father was the still-serving Master of Cardiff Docks, which meant that the young Bill had grown up steeped in the folklore of the docks, and had known his way around their great machinery from the earliest age. After school he had served an apprenticeship with the engineering branch of the Great Western Railway, based in Cardiff docks, and joined the Territorial Army, being commissioned into the Royal Engineers and joining 246 (Cardiff) Field Company RE. Serving with the BEF, on 16 May 1940, under fierce and accurate enemy fire, the then Lieutenant Pritchard had blown up a pontoon bridge which had been left partly intact by the Belgian Army, for which he was awarded the first Military Cross awarded to an officer of the Territorial Army in the war.

In 1940, with the threat of German invasion looming, Pritchard was given responsibility for drawing up the plans for the demolition of British ports, considering that the French failure to destroy their own ports prior to their surrender had been a grievous blunder, as it gave carte blanche to the Germans for the further prosecution of their war aims. By an extraordinary coincidence the template he was given in order to draw up a demolition plan for the British docks was the blueprint for Saint-Nazaire. Having made a brief study of the effect of German bombing on Cardiff docks, he had also concluded that the best way to destroy dock infrastructure was by means of carefully placed explosives on critical machinery, rather than by aerial bombardment.

Haydon opened the meeting on 19 February by outlining the Luce/Hughes-Hallett plan to drive an obsolete destroyer into the Normandie Dock. He suggested that the demolition work planned for after the destruction of the vessel could be undertaken in an hour by approximately eighty men trained in the art of demolition, guarded by about one hundred commandos of his Special Service Brigade. The meeting accepted the view that the whole operation would be made easier if it were conducted in proximity to a heavy bombing raid, first of all on the dock area as the ships approached their target, and then moving on to the area of the Old Town.

Hughes-Hallett then ran through the naval plan, explaining the role the expendable destroyer would play. The explosion would rip the vessel in half, and obliterate the gate. The great advantage of using a destroyer for this task was that it was armoured, and thus would withstand a good measure of direct enemy fire as it travelled up the Loire, bearing its complement of commandos and demolition troops. The problem was that no promise of such a vessel had yet been received from the Admiralty, although Mountbatten's request had travelled the 528 yards from Richmond Terrace to the Admiralty Building a full eleven days before. Clearly, the prospect of losing one of its precious ships in a suicide raid was, although not unprecedented (especially given the almost mythical status enjoyed in that generation of naval officers by the Zeebrugge Raid), not entirely palatable, and despite the urgency of the requirement to 'do something about the problem of Saint-Nazaire' no positive decision had yet been made about releasing such a vessel. Destroyers were the workhorses of the fleet. They were relatively scarce and required for a multitude of other uses, especially that of convoy protection.

Hughes-Hallett told the meeting that a formal request had been submitted to the Admiralty for a destroyer, either Free French in origin or at least manned by the Free French, in order to be able to give de Gaulle the propaganda benefit of announcing that French troops had engaged German targets in occupied France. Instead of deploying a second destroyer to accompany the explosives-laden suicide vessel and to bring the survivors home, the meeting discussed the almost desperate suggestion that the wooden Fairmile motor launches more commonly used for coastal support activities in the English Channel be employed to recover the men after the raid, and return them home. The Fairmile 'B'-type boat was a mahogany-hulled vessel displacing 85 tons and normally carried a complement of fifteen men. One hundred and twelve feet long, they were powered by two Hall-Scott petrol engines. Designed for coastal support work and anti-submarine duties, they enjoyed only limited range and were not designed for close combat. They were armed with a 3-pounder (47 mm) Hotchkiss quick-firing gun (which had been in Royal Navy service since 1886) and a pair of equally ancient 0.303-inch Lewis machineguns.

A discussion took place about the limited range of these vessels, and it was agreed that two additional 500-gallon fuel tanks would need to be added to each to ensure that they could make their way to the Loire, and return. It was decided that it would be good for the sake of harmonious inter-Allied relationships that some should be manned by the Free French, perhaps four in total. But it was also agreed that the vessels would need to be far better armed than they were to support a foray far beyond their usual sphere of action, especially with the prospect of heavy air attack. Accordingly it was agreed that the old Hotchkiss 3-pounders would be replaced with the newer, rapid-firing single-barrel 20 mm Oerlikon anti-aircraft gun, although the Royal Navy had only a very limited number of these weapons and they would need to be dismounted from their present locations on other ships.

The issue of protection against air attack was also considered, especially on the journey home, when the raid would have stirred up a hornet's nest over north-west France and precipitated a furious response from the Luftwaffe. It was known that there were at least eight airfields in use by the Luftwaffe within one hundred miles of Saint-Nazaire (Nantes, Vannes, Rennes, Kerlin, Dinan, Laval, Dinard and La Rochelle), all of which could produce aircraft capable of attacking vessels entering, or escaping from, the Loire within about 30 minutes, although it was also believed that the air threat had diminished somewhat with the mass transfer of Luftwaffe units to the East following the start of Operation *Barbarossa* the previous June. Since no sustained air cover could be provided for the passage beyond the limited protection offered by Fighter Command off the British coast, specially selected crews would need to receive training on the Oerlikon, and sufficient ammunition made available to provide cover for the journey south, the penetration of the Loire, and the voyage home. It was felt that this would give the small craft an advantage over any air attack to which they might be subject.

The meeting concluded with an evaluation of the proposed timings for a raid. It was already clear that the first set of dates proffered – 13 to 16 March – were too soon to be practicable, but that alternative dates at the end of the month, at a time of unusually high tides, would have to be considered.

It was no surprise that the Admiralty remained loath to commit to the deliberate destruction of one of its precious vessels, whatever the otherwise obvious virtues of the plan. Mountbatten had to work carefully to ensure that he manoeuvred all the decision-makers in this process to a point at which they not only supported the raid in theory, but accompanied it with positive action. It was not until 23 February, four days after this first, crucial planning meeting in Richmond Terrace, and only after receiving clearance from the Admiralty to do so, that Mountbatten wrote formally to the C-in-C Plymouth, Admiral Sir Charles Forbes, asking that such a vessel be made available. 'I have obtained permission from the Admiralty to discuss the matter with you,' wrote Mountbatten, 'and with the other authorities directly concerned with the naval plan.' It appears that the Admiralty believed that the responsibility for sourcing a destroyer to be deliberately expended in a Zeebrugge-type assault was out of its hands, and was instead the job of the operational C-in-C.

Mountbatten, having failed to secure what he needed through his direct channels into the Admiralty, and only belatedly asking Forbes, decided to go straight to the top. If the Chiefs of Staff Committee believed that the raid had a reasonable prospect of success, the First Sea Lord (Admiral of the Fleet Sir Dudley Pound) would be under enormous pressure to deliver what Mountbatten needed. Pound, of course, was aware of Churchill's imperative to do something about Saint-Nazaire'. Unsurprisingly, at their 63rd meeting on 25 February the Committee gave their general approval for Operation *Chariot*, in conjunction with a sister operation against the French coast around Bayonne – *Myrmidon* – and Pound committed himself to considering whether a suitable British ship could be made available.

So it was that at 3 p.m. on 26 February, with Rear Admiral Charles Forbes in attendance for the first time, a further meeting, chaired by Mountbatten, took place in Richmond Terrace. Pound's deputy, the Assistant Chief of the Naval Staff responsible for 'Home Fleet' operations (Rear Admiral Arthur Power), represented the Admiralty. Mountbatten reiterated that the principal bar to success was that a suitable vessel had not yet been identified, the implication being that if the problem of the *Tirpitz* was as serious as the Admiralty claimed, their foot-dragging on the provision of a destroyer was inexplicable.

The Chiefs of Staff were reluctant to use a Free French vessel. The options for a British vessel included a destroyer, submarine or even 'landing ship infantry' or LSI (such as the Commando vessels HMS *Prinses Joséphine Charlotte*, *Prince Charles* or *Prince Leopold*). A submarine offered the best hope of escaping detection, but a destroyer was preferable given the speed with which it could impact against the dock gates and its ability to withstand and return fire during the dangerous approach up the Loire. An assault ship like the Commando-carrier *Prinses Joséphine Charlotte* (universally known by the troops as 'PJC') possessed few of these virtues and, what with its 13-foot draught, too deep for the Loire Estuary, was discounted. In addition, as discovery of the little fleet by the Luftwaffe during the outward journey was considered a certainty, the use of an LSI would tip off any intelligent enemy observer that a raid against the French Atlantic coast was imminent. Instead, it was considered that the use of Fairmiles working closely with destroyers, and in which the travelling commandos were kept strictly out of sight, would suffice to maintain the pretence that the little flotilla was nothing more than an anti-submarine or mining operation.

Mountbatten carefully manoeuvred Admiral Power into publicly committing the Admiralty to finding a suitable vessel. This in turn committed the recently conscripted Rear Admiral Sir Charles Forbes to the operation. Forbes had been – initially at least – unpersuaded. 'So long as you don't mind having every ship in the raiding force sunk and every soldier and sailor killed,' Hughes-Hallett recorded the gloomy Forbes as saying, 'I am sure it will be a great success.' His attitude was hardly surprising. He and his staff had examined the possibility of an attack on Saint-Nazaire in the very recent past, and had concluded that the chance of success was too slim. Would not the vessels be sitting ducks for detection and attack by enemy aircraft? The direct route to the target – some 263 miles – would take the flotilla dangerously close to the enemy coast, well within the range of enemy fighter aircraft, while the more indirect route – some 450 miles – would mean that the ships would be at sea for a long time, and susceptible to aerial reconnaissance.

Mountbatten was not put off by this not unexpected challenge from Forbes. All problems – and there were many still to be overcome – had solutions waiting for them: they merely required men of vision and action to carry them out. At this point he announced the names of the two operational commanders who would be responsible for translating the plan into reality. The naval force commander was to be the well-known Polar Medal holder Commander Robert Ryder RN, commonly known in the Royal Navy as 'Red', and the military commander was to be Lieutenant Colonel Charles Newman, commanding officer of No. 2 Commando.

Newman was to get his long-desired mission at last. The previous day, Ryder, serving as naval liaison officer to the Army's HQ Southern Command, based at the Earl of Pembroke's home at Wilton House on the outskirts of Salisbury, had received instructions to proceed to Richmond Terrace the following day. He had no other information regarding what might be expected of him, and arrived about fifteen minutes late. The room appeared to be awash with a mixture of gold braid and khaki, with an impressively built scale model of an anonymous port as the centrepiece.

As he slipped quietly into the back of the room, Ryder was startled to hear Mountbatten mention his name in conjunction with the command of the naval forces, reporting to the C-in-C Plymouth. 'Is that all right, Ryder?' Mountbatten asked. Still completely unaware for what he had been volunteered, and anyway hopelessly bored with life as a liaison officer in Wilton, Ryder answered in the only way he could. 'Yes sir!' he replied. The historian Brigadier Cecil Lucas Phillips explains that Hughes-Hallett had telephoned the Admiralty the previous week asking for a suitable candidate for the job of naval force commander. He stated specifically that he required a first-class officer. 'Why so?' came the query at the end of the telephone. 'You can count on a VC for him, if that's a guide,' Hughes-Hallett had replied. When, at the conclusion of the meeting, Ryder turned and introduced himself to Newman he pointed to the model and asked: 'What is this place?' Laughing, and unsurprised that the nominated naval force commander had not yet been briefed, Newman told him: 'It's Saint-Nazaire.'

At thirty-four years of age Ryder ('Bob' to his friends and family) had already enjoyed an action-packed career. Joining the Royal Navy in 1926, he was first a midshipman on the battleship HMS *Ramillies* before being promoted to lieutenant for service on HM Submarine *Olympus* in China between 1930 and 1933, responsible for navigating the submarine to its Far Eastern station. On his return to Britain from Hong Kong in 1933 he and some friends spent a year navigating the 16,217 miles home on the ketch *Tai-Mo-Shan*, through the Panama Canal.* This adventure was quickly followed by another, participating in the British Graham Land Expedition to the Antarctic, in command of the three-masted schooner *Penola*, between 1934 and 1937. Returning to more regular service he was appointed lieutenant commander in the battleship HMS *Warspite* before serving with a force of decoy or Q-ships in 1940. It was in the Q-ship HMS *Willamette Valley* that he was torpedoed by *U-51* three hundred miles off the south-west coast of Ireland, spending four subsequent days clinging to debris at sea before being rescued. He then commanded the frigate HMS *Fleetwood* before taking charge of the landing ship infantry HMS *Prince Philippe*, which sank after an unfortunate collision in thick fog in the Firth of Clyde in 1941. It was during a period

* In 2008 this ketch became famous in the film *Mamma Mia*.

of shore duty in Salisbury while languishing at 'Their Lordships' displeasure' for losing his ship that he was picked from the Admiralty's list of active destroyer commanders, and ordered to attend the meeting at Richmond Terrace.

Newman had had a head start over Ryder: he had been in Richmond Terrace since Monday morning, and had spent the previous three days poring over the rich files in COHQ in a fever of keen anticipation. By his own admission both he and the men of No. 2 Commando were deeply frustrated by their lack of involvement in the war effort, with endless training throughout 1941 following on from the role of most of them (as part of the Independent Companies) in the Norwegian campaign in 1940. Now they simply wanted to make use of their intense and extensive training to take the war to the enemy as their commando comrades had done in the Mediterranean and North Africa during 1941. It was true that two troops of No. 2 Commando had been deployed on Operation *Archery* to Vaagso several weeks before in late December 1941, but the men were itching to fight together as a complete Commando. Newman certainly was.

In the unusually calm early weeks of 1942 Newman's men had been enjoying themselves 'mucking about in boats' – the Landing Ship Infantry HMS *Prince Charles* to be precise – practising beach landings in the Outer Hebrides: 'Fed well, navy-priced drinks, hard work all day and are fit as fiddles,' Newman noted in his diary. It was a time, recalled his second-in-command, Major Bill Copland of the South Lancashire Regiment and No. 2 Commando, a veteran of the First World War, of 'lovely calm, warm weather, beautiful scenery, good training and plenty of variety . . . buoyed up with the hope that, perhaps soon, we would be going aboard again for a real operation'.

Returning to the small port of Irvine on the North Ayrshire coast 30 miles south-west of Glasgow on Sunday 22 February 1942, Newman was called to a routine briefing by Haydon. The brigade commander, Newman was told, wanted to explain the

forthcoming summer training programme to each of his commanding officers. Newman was downhearted. Nothing depressed him
more, he admitted, than 'the dismal outlook of yet another long
period of waiting for a Job'. Haydon, however, privy as he was as
Military Adviser to Combined Operations (MACO) to the Luce/
Hughes-Hallett plan, had allocated Newman to be the military
force commander for the raid. At the end of the routine training
meeting he drew Newman aside and calmly told him to get the
overnight train from Glasgow to London, where he would be
briefed on an imminent operation. In his absence Major Bill
Copland was to identify his hundred best men.

After Newman's departure Copland found himself talking to
Haydon. 'Well, sir,' asked Copland, 'what is it going to be?' Was
this to be yet another exercise, or the real thing? For a moment
Haydon did not reply. Then he said: 'For the next three weeks, it
is going to be street fighting, by night.' Copland raised his eye-
brows. 'And then . . . ?' 'This,' Haydon smiled, 'has got to be, no
questions and no answers.' Copland was jubilant. All the infuriat-
ing frustration of the previous two years of war would soon be
over. He tried and failed to disguise his feelings from the other
officers when he gave out his orders for training, and although
they did not indulge in speculation with the men, they knew that
at long last 'something big was up'.

Fresh from the overnight sleeper from Glasgow, but itching with
excitement, Newman reported to Richmond Terrace early the
following morning after first checking into his hotel. Awaiting the
arrival of Haydon (who had travelled south on the same train, but
who had gone home first, before returning to the office), he was
handed the thick file on Saint-Nazaire, the accumulated intelligence
material on the docks and the Luce/Hughes-Hallett plan. 'For the
remainder of the day,' Newman recalled, 'I waded through the file
with photographs of the construction of the dock, working draw-
ings of its gates, pumping stations and winding houses, pictures
of the *Normandie* being launched and many other facts and figures.'

When Haydon arrived later that morning he explained the basic plan. An excited Newman wrote in his diary: 'I was from this moment turned into a being with a one-track mind and a goal as exciting as one could wish for.' The two men then spent the whole of the following day – Tuesday 24 February – talking through the detail of how a raid might be successfully executed. A room was found in Richmond Terrace for Newman to use as a planning centre, and in pride of place on a table in the centre of the room was the scale model of Saint-Nazaire prepared the previous year by the Central Interpretation Unit at Medmenham.

In terms of the role of the RAF, Fred Willetts, who had been appointed to provide liaison with Bomber Command, was able to report that in response to Mountbatten's initial request for diversionary bombing, Bomber Command had suggested a plan that comprised two distinct phases and involved a total of sixty aircraft. In the first phase twenty-four medium bombers would attack the dock area for an hour and three quarters for a period beginning an hour and a half before Z-hour (i.e. 1.30 a.m. BDST). In the second phase, a further thirty-six medium bombers would attack the town for two and one quarter hours beginning 15 minutes before Z-hour, this time with 250-pound incendiary bombs. The latter made more noise compared with high explosive and, it was considered, would cause comparatively fewer casualties on the ground.

Clearly a considerable amount of attention had been paid to various components of the plan, but on first talking things through with Newman, Ryder gained a measure of the work that he needed to complete before the operation could get under way. It was daunting. He 'had neither a staff nor a headquarters, much less a car' he later remarked. Everything, 'including the collection of the force and its training had to be achieved in less than four weeks'. In immediate conversations with Luce and Hughes-Hallett, both Ryder and Newman discussed the lack of an expendable destroyer, without which, Hughes-Hallett insisted, the operation would not proceed. On this issue he remained immovable, and Ryder was later to pay tribute to his single-mindedness. At the time, Ryder suggested increasing the number of Fairmile launches from the twelve that had been allocated, and doing without the destroyer if the Admiralty was not going to provide one. Newman, desperate for the chance of action, destroyer or not, suggested that the Commandos alone could achieve significant damage in and around the port area even if the outer caisson to the Normandie dock remained intact. Hughes-Hallett, however, stood his ground. Without a destroyer the attack would be dangerous, bloody and futile: if the Admiralty could not provide an appropriate vessel the operation was off, and if necessary the Admiralty would be given an ultimatum to that effect.

For his part, and despite his early antagonism, it did not take long for Forbes to support the plan. On Saturday 28 February Mountbatten was able to report to the Chiefs of Staff Committee that the C-in-C Plymouth had examined and approved the operation in principle. Furthermore, the Admiralty told Mountbatten that it was attempting to secure a 'suitable ship' as a matter of urgency. Time was running out to make a decision, prepare the ship and train the men in the four weeks remaining before the spring tides offered one of only two or three opportunities that year to strike decisively at Saint-Nazaire. In a note drafted by Mountbatten he warned that the last safe moment to appoint such a ship was 2 March. If a Royal Navy vessel was not forthcoming, he asked for permission to approach General de Gaulle to use the 1,800-ton Bourrasque-class *Ouragan* ('Hurricane'), a vessel that had been suggested by Charles Lambe as possibly available. Without a destroyer, and using Fairmiles alone, Hughes-Hallett argued it 'would make success less certain, the extent of the damage that can be done less great, and will much increase the risk of heavy casualties'.

Mountbatten and his team need not have worried. In the nick of time, Admiral Pound was able to announce to his colleagues on Monday 2 March that he had arranged to provide a British ship for the operation. It seems fair to suggest that the proposal to approach de Gaulle, together with what amounted to an ultimatum by Mountbatten to Pound – that if the raid did not go ahead, then the balance of maritime power in the northern Atlantic would remain in Germany's favour – forced the Admiralty's hand. Assuming that the operation would be launched at the end of the month, COHQ now had twenty-eight days to turn an idea into reality. The ship? She was a superannuated 1,200-ton American destroyer by the name of USS *Buchanan*, built in 1919, which had become HMS *Campbeltown* on her transfer to the Royal Navy. She had been given to Britain as one of fifty similar vessels provided in exchange for United States use of British bases in the Caribbean. She appeared in Devonport ready for alterations to begin on 10 March 1942.

Preparations for Operation *Chariot* were not the only thing exercising the minds of Combined Operations at the time. The raid on Saint-Nazaire was to take place immediately before a much larger operation, Operation *Myrmidon*, in which three thousand troops of No. 1 and No. 6 Commandos, one and a half battalions of Royal Marines, together with two squadrons of an armoured regiment equipped with Valentine tanks and a motorised infantry battalion, were to be directed against the harbours of Saint-Jean-de-Luz and Bayonne, inside the Adour Estuary in south-west France. The plan – apart from delivering a strong message to Hitler about Britain's determination to continue fighting – was to disrupt road and rail transport between France and Spain before re-embarking for home.

TEN

Planning

On the day following Pound's announcement on 2 March that a sacrificial destroyer had been found, a second meeting took place at Richmond Terrace. As with the first, the primary purpose of the meeting held on 3 March 1942 was to update the principal organisations involved of the planning – Combined Operations, the Special Service Brigade, the Admiralty and Plymouth Command – to identify and resolve any immediate and obvious gaps, and to test any of the core assumptions that made up the Luce/Hughes-Hallett plan. Ryder and Newman began by providing an outline of the idea so far, which was for HMS *Campbeltown*, manned by a reduced crew of seventy-nine (its normal complement was 146) to drive into and destroy the outer caisson of the Normandie Dock, making it unusable for strategic German maritime purposes for a very long time. Newman was later to admit that he was 'more nervous giving the military outline at this meeting than at any other time'. He had every reason to be, having had only a few days to take the Luce/Hughes-Hallett plan and to make it his own.

The *Campbeltown* would be accompanied by 180 commandos carried on twelve Fairmile 'B' motor launches. However, Newman was anxious to avoid, as Hughes-Hallett described it, putting 'all his eggs into one basket' and opposed the original idea of putting all the commandos on the destroyer, arguing for more rather than fewer Fairmiles. If Hughes-Hallett had had his way only the minimum number of launches would have been sent on the operation:

the best solution would have been two destroyers, one to destroy the gates and the other to bring the sailors and commandos safely home. Given the difficulty COHQ had experienced in securing a single destroyer, however, the chance of obtaining two was negligible: COHQ was well used to dealing with realities rather than aspirations, and with the Fairmiles being the last things left in the Royal Navy's armoury, they were adopted without further debate. But Ryder was still concerned that the cumulative firepower of these vessels remained limited, and he argued the case for more rather than fewer launches, some to be deployed in the MGB and MTB role, to protect the vanguard of the little fleet as it approached and travelled up the Loire to its target. In the lively debate that ensued, Hughes-Hallett expressed strong concern about the extreme vulnerability of these thin-skinned, petrol-driven coastal craft with such limited range that they would have to be towed at least part of the way.

A flurry of updates was received from around the table. In respect of the explosive charge for the *Campbeltown*, Commander George Norfolk RN, the Director of Torpedoes and Mining at the Admiralty, advised that he had agreed with the captain of the Torpedo Warfare Establishment at HMS *Vernon* in Portsmouth to release one of his best explosive ordnance officers, Lieutenant Nigel Tibbits RN, to join the operation. Tibbits's primary task would be to design the explosive charge for the *Campbeltown* and to accompany the operation to ensure that it detonated as planned. The torpedo specialists to assist him would be provided from Forbes's Plymouth Command.

Fred Willetts then explained the outline air plan. In response Ryder asked if it would be possible to have at least some low-flying aircraft over the harbour from Z – 15 minutes to Z + 15 minutes to draw the fire of the anti-aircraft artillery, despite the obvious threat of a 'blue-on-blue' engagement in which bombs could fall on the flotilla or the disembarking commandos. Willetts said that he would examine the possibility, but the question demonstrated that Ryder had no idea how inaccurate aerial bombing was at the time.

In respect of the navigational beacon at the mouth of the Loire, David Luce stated that the submarine was required to show a light from a time after nautical twilight. It was expected that the force would pass the submarine at 10.30 p.m. It would flash a series of 'Ms' by Morse code (dash-dash) at ten-minute intervals commencing at 9.30 p.m. The submarine should then withdraw.

The relief all round caused by the allocation of HMS *Campbeltown* the previous day was palpable, and the meeting quickly agreed the principles of her conversion to suicide ship. She was currently berthed in Portsmouth but would sail at once to Plymouth, where alterations would be undertaken at Devonport Dockyard, after which she would join the remainder of the flotilla at Falmouth.

That afternoon, travelling in one of the few staff cars allocated to Combined Operations Headquarters, Ryder and Newman drove the 70 miles down the A3 to Portsmouth, accompanied by an old friend of Ryder's who had been nominated by the Admiralty to oversee the conversion: Constructor Commander John Merrington RN. This was a stroke of good luck, removing any possibility that there might be any practical antagonism between the Dockyards and Admiralty as the work progressed. The list of alterations required, in the main, to lighten *Campbeltown* to ensure a maximum draught of 10½ feet (and certainly no more than 12 feet, down from the ship's existing 14-foot draught), as well as adding armour plate on the deck to provide protection to the accompanying commandos, was concluded, Ryder recalled, in less than an hour.

Fascinatingly, on the journey to Portsmouth Ryder decided not to allow Newman to board the vessel, or indeed to be seen near it. With security in mind, Ryder believed that the presence of a Commando officer on the dock or on board would at once give the game away to the crew. A frustrated Newman was forced to watch proceedings from the back of the car, engaging in desultory conversation with their WRNS driver. Most of the ship's armament, including her three 4-inch guns and her distinctive 2-pounder single-barrelled Rolls Royce 'pom-pom' gun, would be replaced by eight twin-mounted Oerlikon rapid-fire 20 mm cannons, primarily because they were considered much more effective in the anti-aircraft role. HMS *Campbeltown*'s 12-pounder (3-inch) quick-firing gun was transferred to a new position in front of the bridge on the fo'c'sle.

Merrington also had the idea of making her look more 'Germanic' and suggested removing two of her funnels and cutting angles on the remaining two. Making her resemble a German Möwe-type destroyer, he thought, might just give her a few moments' advantage in the Loire while German defenders puzzled at her identity through the night sky. Some months previously HMS *Campbeltown*'s bows had been strengthened in an experiment to see whether it helped to cut through the booms that protected enemy harbours, which would now serve to give the ship more penetrative power when striking the caisson. Steel plates were to be welded along her deck in order to provide some protection to the commandos who would have to be accommodated during the run-in.

For the next two days planning was concentrated in London. Newman described them as 'probably the most momentous ones in my life'.

Planning! What a multitude of thoughts and events are covered by that single word. An office to myself (literally locked in for security reasons), a marvellous model of Saint-Nazaire, a large-scale aerial photograph, the intelligence summary, a general outline of the plan, and there you have my day's work. The many meetings at which the plans were discussed, the number of people growing daily who were let into the know, the continued worry of keeping the plans a secret were a worrying period for me.

Fred Willetts facilitated meetings with the RAF. Thinking of the effective use made by the Germans in Norway of Stukas to support the ground advance, Newman wanted to know whether the RAF could provide close air support to his troops on the docks during the raid itself. Unfortunately not, came the response. The distance from Britain, lack of ground-to-air communication, threat of poor weather and difficulties with attacking ground targets at night while distinguishing between friendly and enemy forces made it a non-starter. What about using French-speaking troops to help with managing the local population during the raid? Could better and more recent aerial photographs be obtained, as it was evident that the Germans were working hard to develop and fortify the port? The Ministry of Information were insistent on sending a group of press representatives, certain that it would be the same sort of jolly jaunt that could describe the Lofoten and Vaasgo raids. Newman believed instinctively that this was wrong, and pressed hard against the imposition on his force of these men, who would also use space essential for commandos. 'In the end it was agreed that one press representative only should accompany us,' he recalled, 'although as it turned out, they sent two and they both sailed!'

During this time of planning and preparation Major David Wyatt introduced both men to SOE's technical development organisation, known as Station IX, based at the Frythe hotel near Welwyn, about an hour's drive north from London. 'Many gadgets were examined and either included in the scheme or turned down,' Newman noted. 'Expanding ladders, grapnels, rockets, special wireless sets, all had to be tried out and decided upon.' Ryder and Newman also observed a demonstration of the experimental 'Lifebuoy' man-portable flame-thrower, but decided not to include it in the plan. It was at Welwyn that Wyatt was to prepare all the plastic explosives – some 1,350 pounds in all – for the raid.

The Special Service Brigade had gathered extensive demolitions experience during 1940 and 1941, and lessons had been learned from the raids on Lofoten and Vaagso about just how ineffective badly laid explosives could be. Although all commandos were introduced to the use of explosives, especially the new malleable 'plastic' type that could be literally wrapped around the object to be demolished, it was clear that there was an art to successful demolitions, requiring specific training on the types of object targeted. One of the first of Newman and Haydon's considerations therefore, was the selection and training of the men who would be required for the demolition tasks. The first realisation was that there were too few men in No. 2 Commando with enough experience of explosives to make up the numbers required, and Haydon requested the names of volunteers from across the Special Service Brigade to receive specific training for, and to accompany, the raid. The expertise of Bill Pritchard had been secured by Hughes-Hallett at the outset of the planning (COHQ had a copy of his and Montgomery's plans to destroy the Saint-Nazaire docks the previous year), and an immediate request was submitted for him to be transferred to COHQ. It was he who took responsibility for preparing and then delivering the training programme for these men.

The first step was to gather at Lochailort some eighty men (the number would eventually reach ninety) drawn from No. 1, 3, 4, 5, 6, 9 and 12 Commandos who were given a week's refresher training in the use of plastic explosives and detonators, learning how to maximise the blast made by an explosion by channelling it directly against a target. The greatest danger in the use of explosives lay in allowing the blast to dissipate in all directions, so the Lochailort instructors ran the men through a series of drills to familiarise them with the art of getting the biggest bang out of the amount of 'plastic' they used. 'We enjoyed blowing up dead trees and large slabs of mountainside,' recalled Stuart Chant, one of seven men from No. 5 Commando attending what he assumed to be just another training course, 'but it did not cross our minds that this portended our being earmarked for duties of a different kind . . .'

The training finished, they returned to Dartmouth only to receive, a few days later, instructions to entrain once more for Scotland. Frustrated with what they considered to be the idiocy of military administration, this time the men detrained at Edinburgh, where they were transported across the Forth road bridge in buses to the tiny port of Burntisland, finding themselves in the company of their colleagues who had been at Lochailort the previous week. It was here that the men were introduced to port installations for the first time, and to Bill Pritchard. None of the men realised that the reason they were at Burntisland was because it boasted a small dock area with two basins where the height of the water was managed with lock gates, ideal for training the men on the rudiments of its destruction. Lieutenant Corran Purdon found himself with two other officers – Gerard Brett and Paul Bassett-Wilson – together with thirteen NCOs: Sergeant Deery and Corporals Blount, Jones, Chetwynd, Johnson, Chung, Hoyle, Callaway, Molloy, Wright, Lemon, Reeves and Ferguson.

Chant was impressed at once with Pritchard, a 'good-looking young captain' who 'had already won an MC in the fighting before Dunkirk' and who 'possessed a profound knowledge of dock installations'. So too was Corran Purdon, who was happy to acknowledge that he and his fellow officers idolised Pritchard, as much for his professional competence and technical expertise as for his relaxed approachability. To allay any suspicions about what they were doing, so as to maintain operational security, Pritchard told the men what Chant thought a plausible reason for their work. They were told that the purpose was 'that if the Germans were to invade Britain and capture our ports, then we . . . would blow up our own dock installations before they could be used by the Germans'. Corporal Bob Wright admitted that this subterfuge worked: 'Nobody had the remotest idea that it was training for a Job,' he confided to his diary.

After a few days at what Chant recalled was the cold and bleak Burntisland, learning the vulnerable points of both docks and ships, the men were exposed to a larger scale of docks, and its four dry docks, at the Rosyth naval shipyards, 8 miles to the west, under the massive shadow of the Forth road bridge. It was at Burntisland

and Rosyth, recalled Lieutenant Corran Purdon, that the men 'learned about caisson and double lock gates, winding houses, opening and closing machinery, steel bridges, cranes, guns, pumping stations and power stations'. They were able to take their newly acquired knowledge of plastic explosives learned at Lochailort, and apply it to the complicated business of dry docks and lock gates.

The large group then divided in two, one party, including Chant, travelling south again to Cardiff, and the other to Southampton. The two groups were to spend ten days in each of the respective docks, before swapping locations. At Cardiff Pritchard took the men through a careful programme to introduce them to the minutiae of dock demolitions, while in Southampton the training was undertaken by the tall, powerfully built sapper Captain Bob Montgomery, 'laying demolition charges on all parts of the docks, day and night' recalled the German-born Sergeant Richard 'Dick' Bradley, 'until we could almost do it blindfold'.* Southampton was home to the massive King George V Dock, which Wing Commander Casa Maury had discovered by chance the previous year had been designed by the same engineer who designed the Normandie Dock in Saint-Nazaire. It was the perfect place to rehearse.

Purdon was impressed with the quality of Pritchard's training. He was a born leader, he observed. 'He won the affection, respect and admiration of everyone from the outset and made every aspect of our training alive, vibrant and vitally important to each one of us.' Pritchard, unknown to the men, had already designed exact explosive charges for each target and had allocated specific jobs to individual teams, and they practised day and night – literally – on the specific jobs they would be required to undertake in Saint-Nazaire. Eight men led by Lieutenant Robert 'Bertie' Burtinshaw would destroy the outer caisson in case *Campbeltown* failed in its

---

* Born in London of German parents, Bradley's birth surname was Goebbels. For three years (aged eleven to fourteen) he attended a Cistercian monastery school near Bregenz, in Austria. He spoke fluent German with, he explained, 'an English accent', and fluent English 'with a German accent'.

primary duty; Lieutenant Chris Smalley was tasked with demolishing the winding house for this caisson and four men under the command of Stuart Chant would climb 40 feet down into the deep bowels of the pumping house to destroy its massive machinery. Lieutenant Gerard Brett would attempt to breach the northern caisson whilst Corran Purdon destroyed the winding house to this gate. Pritchard even had the men practise in blindfolds, to simulate the effect of darkness and disorientation they would experience in combat.

It was while Purdon's group was in Cardiff that the news was released on 28 February of the successful raid by men of Major John Frost's parachute-delivered troops on the German radar station at Bruneval in Normandy. The newspapers on Sunday 1 March 1942 were full of news of this small and daring venture, described by some excited editors somewhat prematurely as an 'invasion'. The Reuters report recorded Frost commenting that his men 'did excellently'. The 22-year-old Lieutenant Peter Young* of the Parachute Regiment, a former Fleet Street journalist, described how he had almost reached his objective before encountering any opposition. A German sentry challenged the approaching troops twice and then fired. The paratroops, who had held their fire as long as possible, 'rubbed him out', said Young. 'After that we hunted them out of cellars, trenches and rooms with hand grenades, automatic weapons, revolvers and knives.' Purdon read this and 'wondered when our turn would come'. He had not long to wait.

With the training complete it was time to catch the train to Southampton, where the men met Bob Montgomery, many for the first time. When he arrived at Southampton railway station Chant noticed at once that the war had banished the normal peacetime hustle and bustle of what had before the war been one of the busiest dock and liner complexes in the world: the close proximity of the Luftwaffe in north-eastern France meant that the docks were

---

* Not to be confused with the now Captain Peter Young of No. 3 Commando, who was working at the time in COHQ.

vulnerable to almost daily attack from the air, and so were now little used. This gave the men virtually the complete freedom of the dockyard, and especially of the giant King George V Dock, then the second-largest in the world, and an almost exact replica of the Normandie Dock in Saint-Nazaire. For the next ten days Montgomery practised the forty-five men constantly, day and night, so that they could identify exactly where they needed to lay their demolitions to create maximum effect. The training resulted in the men becoming expert not just in the use of explosives, but also in the complex workings of dry docks, caissons, winding houses and pumping stations. They concentrated on understanding the workings of the winding stations that controlled the mechanisms to open and close the caissons; the power stations that provided power to the winding stations; the swing bridges that opened and closed to allow for the movement of shipping, as well as the operation of the dockside cranes.

Then, on Saturday 7 March a new set of aerial photographs from Medmenham demonstrated unequivocally that the dock area in Saint-Nazaire boasted very strong air defences. It made sense to assume that German anti-aircraft weapons could quickly be converted into the anti-ship role. 'In studying these on the Saturday we found four Heavy Coastal Defence Battery positions right in the centre of the dock area,' Newman recalled. These were obviously recently constructed. Advice suggested that this would entail at least another sixty enemy personnel to deal with on the raid, and initiated a frantic conversation with Haydon. Unless there were at least two more Fairmiles and an additional thirty commandos Newman judged that the Commando strength as presently constituted was fatally weak. He spent that Saturday evening at the Piccadilly Hotel on Piccadilly Circus 'with a nasty feeling that it might all turn out to be another disappointment. However, Sunday morning brought forth two extra Motor Launches . . . A wire to Bill Copland for a further thirty men to be detailed brought our fighting strength up to more reasonable proportions.'

Ryder finally made his way to Plymouth for a meeting with Forbes on Monday 9 March (in the midst of handing over his previous job in Salisbury, and attempting to help his wife, Hilaré, move house), and was immediately struck by the difference in tone and attitude in the C-in-C Plymouth from that he had first seen in London six days before. Forbes was all attention, and promised to get him what he wanted. 'Not much point in being a commander-in-chief,' he said, 'if you can't get what you need.' On the same day Forbes convened a meeting of his senior staff officers – Commodore Tom Fellowes (his chief of staff) and Commander C.R. McCrum (his chief planner) – to allow them to meet Ryder and Newman, and to confirm the final plans. A workmanlike meeting noted Tibbits's view that the explosive charge in HMS *Campbeltown* should be set in a watertight compartment built about 30 feet back from the bow, which would then hopefully find itself resting against the caisson when the ship came to a halt, in a position to do the greatest damage to the gate when the vessel exploded.

Tibbits's idea was to place a large quantity of readily available explosives, of which Mk VII naval depth charges, each weighing 400 pounds and containing 290 pounds of amatol (a highly explosive material made from a mixture of TNT and ammonium nitrate), seemed the most sensible option, in a position underneath the main gun support and directly above the fuel tanks. The twenty-four depth charges would be carefully secured in a square steel container and covered with concrete, not merely so that the individual charges would not break adrift on impact but because, in line with the principles of explosive behaviour, the power of the blast would be so much greater as a result of their containment. These depth charges, constituting a total quantity of 3.1 tons of amatol, would generate sufficient destructive force, Tibbits believed, to obliterate the destroyer and everything around it.*

Importantly, Tibbits proposed, to universal agreement, to

---

* Some accounts erroneously refer to a charge of 5 tons. This is an error, as it represents the cumulative weight of the 24 depth charges (actually, 4.8 tons), rather than of the amatol contained therein (3.1 tons).

triple-fuse the explosives. Two separate fuses with 2½-hour delays would initiate a set of waterproof cordtex linking each one of the twenty-four depth charges, and Tibbits himself would insert a final acetone-delay fuse with an eight-hour delay after the vessel's impact with the caisson, as a further guarantor of detonation. Forbes had at first been sceptical about allowing commandos to operate in the dock area because he believed that the explosion would cause casualties among them; a delay to allow for evacuation would remove this fear. In addition the ship would also be scuttled (using separate charges in the stern) after she had struck the caisson, to prevent the vessel slipping away from the initial point of contact if she wasn't able to jam herself immovably in the dock, and to prevent the Germans dragging the vessel clear. The meeting agreed to Tibbits's proposals, and the instructions for the additional work to HMS *Campbeltown* were given that evening to the dockyard at Devonport.

Repeating the points made in Richmond Terrace on 3 March, both Ryder and Newman then asked Forbes for additional small craft to join the twelve Fairmile launches already allocated to the operation. Ryder in particular wanted more armed vessels to be able to deal with 'offshore patrols, examination vessels, guard-ships or any chance encounter with minor war vessels' and urged Forbes to allocate whatever MGBs or MTBs were available. An especial concern of both Ryder and Newman was that once the little fleet reached the Loire the headquarters vessel should not be HMS *Campbeltown*: if the destroyer could not traverse the mudflats, for instance, it would leave the two force commanders embarrassingly high and dry, stuck on board what would suddenly become a white elephant and in a position in which they would be unable to control the battle. Unfortunately, only one of each type (MGB 314, commanded by Lieutenant Dunstan Curtis, and MTB 74, commanded by an eccentric Welsh aristocrat, Sub-Lieutenant Micky Wynn*) was available: both were duly allocated to the raid, in

---

* Later Lord Newborough.

addition to four more Fairmiles from the 7th Motor Launch Flotilla based in nearby Dartmouth. The latter were armed with two 18-inch torpedoes that sat on either side of the funnel, but there was no time to arm them with Oerlikons. Curtis's MGB 314 was fast (reaching some 26 knots) but lightly armed, boasting a single 2-pounder gun and four powered 0.50-inch heavy machineguns, and would act as a headquarters ship for Ryder and Newman once the Loire was reached.

To get there both boats would need to be towed behind one of the destroyers, as they did not have the range to make the 900-mile journey there and back, on their own. Ryder and Newman would therefore travel on one of the destroyers, and transfer to the MGB off the Loire. Wynn's MTB 74, with its two 18-inch torpedo tubes (each containing an enhanced quantity of explosives after the motors had been removed – 1,800 pounds, or nearly a ton, designed to cripple a battleship) mounted on the foredeck, rather than amidships as was more usual, would act as a reserve for HMS *Campbeltown* if the latter failed to strike the outer caisson. MTB 74's heavy torpedoes would be ejected from their tubes by compressed air, travel over any torpedo net barrier before striking the water and exhaust themselves after a few hundred feet at the inner caisson of the lock (or the outer caisson, if the destroyer failed in her mission), where they would settle to the bottom and explode later on a delayed fuse. The additional petrol tanks being fitted to the other Fairmiles would also be required for both MGB 314 and MTB 74.

Wynn's MTB 74 was a unique vessel, a Vosper Thorneycroft design adapted specifically to attack the *Scharnhorst* and *Gneisenau* while they were holed up in Brest. Now that they, along with *Prinz Eugen*, had successfully executed their 'Channel Dash' and to the embarrassment of the Admiralty escaped the British blockade, MTB 74 had become available. Hughes-Hallett had always envisaged MTB 74 playing a role in the raid, but Ryder had equivocated. Wynn conducted his own vociferous lobbying to join the raid and was eventually rewarded for his perseverance by being added to Ryder's little fleet. But for all its incredible speed (up to 45 knots) his vessel seemed only to have two speeds – slow or very fast – with nothing in between, which made it a very poor boat for convoy work. It also had a minuscule range, and to be used at Saint-Nazaire it would need to be towed all the way out, and some of the way back, necessitating the addition to her decks of extra fuel tanks.

The meeting also discussed the relative advantages of a short and a long route to Saint-Nazaire. The former would take the Force 70 miles from the French coast at dawn. The problem was that at the speed of the slowest vessel (two, of course, were being towed) – some 12 to 13 knots – the journey would in any case take a long time to get to the Loire (at least thirty-five hours), and extending the route far from the coast in order to minimise the chances of detection from the air would keep the fleet much longer at sea, and therefore as vulnerable arguably to detection as a shorter journey undertaken closer to the coast. Avoiding detection was paramount: if the Germans got wind of the arrival of a flotilla off the Loire it would be slaughtered long before it closed on its target. So the aim had to be to arrive off the Loire in darkness.

As far as Ryder was concerned the meeting was a success. He had secured six additional vessels from Forbes, four more torpedo-carrying Fairmiles from the 7th ML Flotilla, together with MGB 314 and MTB 74, bringing his flotilla up to a total of eighteen vessels – nineteen if HMS *Campbeltown* was counted. Planning was moving strongly, arrangements slotting together day by day. Hopes were high.

ELEVEN

Falmouth

On the afternoon of 10 March, following the meeting with Forbes, both Ryder and Luce visited HMS *Campbeltown*. The elderly vessel had swept into Plymouth harbour that morning ready for the final conversion works, which began the moment she docked at Devonport dockyard. The 'Constructor in charge of conversion was confident that it would be completed on time' Ryder noted. It appears that Ryder relented sufficiently on the security front to take Newman on board the destroyer on this occasion.

Britain at the time harboured an exaggerated fear of the extent of Nazi espionage, although this paranoia paled into insignificance compared with the spy mania that raged during the First World War. Nevertheless, in the popular mind at least, a well-developed spy network provided at least some rationale for repeated German military successes against Britain since the beginning of the war, and the exhortation among other things that 'Careless Talk Costs Lives' chimed with a strong public fear of how far the country had been penetrated by Fifth Columnists preparing for the parachutists or beach landings that would trigger an invasion. There was especial concern that the Germans had eyes in British ports, watching the comings and goings of its precious maritime traffic. Even Ryder mentioned the widespread belief in 1942 that there was a spy in Falmouth, a factor that was taken into consideration when determining where the jumping-off point for the operation should be, and in his post-action report Newman (in 1946) raised the possibility that the strength of the German response in Saint-Nazaire was in part due to warning received through their intelligence services.

Fuelled by this fear, MI5 and organisations involved in military counter-intelligence spent a considerable amount of time attempting to flush out what Winston Churchill described in 1940 as 'this malignancy in our midst'. Great pains were taken to keep secrets secret, down to the tiniest details relating to military operations and exercises. Operation *Chariot* was no different, and the files in the National Archives bulge with security-related concerns to a level that might be seen as paranoid, including extensive telephone-intercept material detailing otherwise innocent conversations among members of the general public who seemed to indicate a knowledge of or an interest in the raid, both before and after its execution.

At the meeting in Richmond Terrace on 26 February a strong concern was voiced about operational security: stressing that the fewest possible people must know about it. The cover story for concentrating all the Fairmiles in one place would be an extended patrol to intercept U-boats returning through the Bay of Biscay to their French Atlantic ports, and Casa Maury was to maintain a master register of everyone with knowledge of the raid. In due course Ryder was to invent the '10th Anti-Submarine Striking Force' as the title of his burgeoning organisation, and he found that when he started using the title in his formal communications the relevant authorities in Plymouth and elsewhere quickly got behind the subterfuge. Then, on 5 March, further security arrangements were agreed, the most crucial being that all servicemen allocated to the operation be confined to ship or barracks with effect from 15 March, with no shore leave allowed. Only after that would they be briefed on the coming operation. Men were allowed ashore only in groups, and under the control of an officer. All mail was to be censored, and there was to be no disclosure of the location or date of the operation until the fleet had actually sailed.

The most important element of security, however, remained that of deception. It was impossible to hide the build-up of the Fairmiles in Falmouth. Even though when the Commandos arrived HMS *Prinses Joséphine Charlotte* was berthed in a different part of the harbour, there was a risk that in the absence of confirmed information tongues would wag, especially in a port like Falmouth, where ship-watching ran in the blood and was a common topic of conversation. So rumours were started regarding the mission of the 10th Anti-Submarine Striking Force, tropical helmets were delivered with much fanfare to the dock supply area for the motor launches, and faked signals were sent providing instructions aimed at satisfying even the most persistent speculators.

Extensive work went on to confirm the most suitable climatic conditions for the raid, both in terms of the tides and the weather. The LOTI analysis indicated that the conditions of moon and tide were suitable only on the nights of 28/29 March, 29/30 March and 30/31 March; the best night in terms of the highest point of the spring tide was the night of Sunday 29 March. The raiders would have an accurate forecast at least twenty-four hours in advance, but if the raid could not be executed on any of these nights, and unless the winds were light, it could not be executed at all.

By Monday 9 March Ryder issued his training programme for the three weeks remaining before the raid. It was a period of intensive practice for the Fairmile crews when they arrived at Falmouth on 12 and 13 March. Many of them had only limited experience of operating closely with other vessels, and virtually none had operated with other vessels at night. None had done so with heavily armed passengers who needed practice with repeated embarkation and disembarkation procedures in full kit, or engaging shore targets with unmounted Bren guns. Forbes had offered Ryder a planning room and 'sleeping berth' in the conservatory of the Tregwynt Hotel overlooking the sea front, which he gratefully accepted and where he moved in on Thursday 12 March.

For the Navy, the plan for the weeks to come revolved around assembling the Fairmiles and drilling them relentlessly, beginning

on the afternoon following their arrival, under the orders of Lieutenant Commander William 'Billie' Stephens RNVR, who was the
commanding officer of the 20th Motor Launch Flotilla and skipper
of ML 192. Ryder remarked: 'I am afraid they must have thought
I was the most exacting sort of person to serve under, as I kept
making them do it again, or producing all sorts of trivial reasons
for their having to shift berth or refuel during the night.' MTB 74
arrived in Plymouth on 14 March and was then towed some of
the distance to Falmouth to test the towing mechanism to be used
on the outward voyage. In his book *The Colditz Story* Major Pat
Reid described Stephens as something of a daredevil: 'He was
handsome, fair-haired, with piercing blue eyes and Nelsonian nose.
He walked as if he was permanently on the deck of a ship.'

Stephens's leading telegraphist was the 22-year-old James Laurie,
an experienced sailor who had joined the Royal Navy in 1936. After
many months of active service in the English Channel with the
'little ships' of the coastal flotillas, in January 1942 he found himself
posted to Brixham in Devon to join Billie Stephens's ML 192. This
vessel was due to be handed over to Free French crews in early
March, but on 28 February orders were received to proceed to
Southampton for new orders. 'On arrival work was begun, fitting
new guns and two upper-deck fuel tanks, an indication that some
fairly lengthy journeys lay ahead of us,' Laurie noted. 'But to where?'
He was not to know the answer for another two weeks. The demolition teams, having completed their familiarisation training in the
Cardiff Docks, also made their way to Falmouth that Friday by
train, changing at Truro to take the branch line the final 11 miles
on to Falmouth.

It was on this day also – Friday 13 March – that Newman finally
left London for Falmouth in a large car borrowed from the Combined
Operations pool. Without the assistance of Stanley Day he was
forced to drive himself, the vehicle crammed full, as his diary notes,
with 'maps, models, wireless sets and all sorts of impedimenta'. As
he was leaving the front steps of Richmond Terrace he bumped

into Lord Louis Mountbatten, who was returning to the building from the street. In a snatched conversation Mountbatten encouraged him to think of the strategic aspect of the operation. 'This is not an ordinary raid,' he told Newman, 'it is an operation of war.'

Making his way out through West London Newman headed first to Marlow on the Thames to visit the CIU at Medmenham in order to examine the latest aerial photographs. Every time he looked at these he seemed to find something new, and sometimes worrying. This time the photographs showed not just that a large merchant vessel was in the dry dock, but that German defensive arrangements were developing fast, with one or two extra gun positions that had not been found before, on buildings within the dock area. A further two hundred miles and nearly six hours later brought Newman to Tavistock, where he spent the night in a hotel. For security reasons he was forced to transfer the entire contents of his car ('the large model of Saint-Nazaire, all the latest aerial photos, four of the very latest wireless sets, and the orders in embryo for the raid') into his bedroom, only then to discover that the room had a poorly functioning lock. Desperate that he should not be the cause of a major security breach by leaving his room in an insecure state to visit the bar or restaurant downstairs (the hotel's services evidently did not extend to room service), he was forced to endure a very uncomfortable and hungry evening 'spent almost entirely in my bedroom', guarding against the loss of any of the highly secret material in his possession. He arrived in Falmouth on Saturday 14 March, much to his relief, and was able to meet up with Day and Copland on the newly arrived HMS *Prinses Joséphine Charlotte*, noting that the troops were 'all in fine fettle and bursting to know what it was all about'.

Lance Sergeant Don Randall recalled that the journey from Ayr to Falmouth on the *Prinses Joséphine Charlotte* 'was swift, despite a choppy sea, and the vessel steamed into the sheltered waters of the River Fal soon after midday the next day, and anchored in Carrick Roads'. During the two-day journey south from Ayr, Private

Bob Bishop recalled, everyone's 'morale was sky-high, the food was good, duty-free cigarettes abounded, and all was right in the Commando world, as we knew we were at last on our way to somewhere to actually do something!' The men in Ayr had had an inkling weeks before when it was noticed that 'Uncle Charlie' had been missing for some time from his HQ in No. 2, Wellington Square. Sergeant Blattner observed to Bishop that this state of affairs was 'a bit weird'. He noted that:

Mrs Newman had been seen that day, so the Colonel was obviously not on leave, and concluded that maybe, just maybe, something might be coming up. Meanwhile, the second-in-command, Major Bill Copland, continued to control the Commando giving no clues as to the reason for the absence of Charlie Newman . . . All our wonderings ceased when Captain Mike Barling, our medical officer, was joined by a second doctor, Captain David Paton RAMC. We knew then that we were not being given two MOs for nothing. Something was in the wind for sure!

On Sunday 15 March, the day on which shore leave was banned and security clamped down, the Fairmile crews were introduced for the first time to 'their' commandos. On ML 306 (commanded by Lieutenant Ian Henderson RN and supported by sub-lieutenants Philip Dark – nicknamed 'Jimmy-the-One' by his men – and the Australian Pat Landy), Ordinary Seaman Ralph Batteson was immediately impressed by the bearing of his new guests. 'They were tough and resolute,' he observed, 'and showed lightning-swift reactions when required. True, they were dressed in a motley assortment of clothing that could hardly be called standard issue, but I knew that they had been specially trained and selected for this mission, and were to be relied upon.' Fourteen were assigned to his Fairmile, including the experienced raider Lieutenant Ronnie Swayne, Sergeant Thomas Durrant and Lieutenant John Vanderwerve. Ryder himself took charge during that Sunday, exercising the motor launches in groups, packed to the gunwales with heavily laden commandos, practising coming alongside, depositing the troops in the dock area, before re-embarking them again.

By now none but the least inquisitive soldier or sailor could fail to grasp the tempo of events. On Stephens's ML 192 Ordinary Seaman George Davidson recalled: 'We became suspicious about the whole business because we knew there was something afoot and when the ferry with the troops on board arrived [HMS *Prinses Joséphine Charlotte*] we were all making wild guesses as to what was the next move.' 'We practised going alongside jetties at night,' remembered Sub-Lieutenant Hugh Arnold on ML 446, 'which made us suspicious that we had nothing to do with Anti-Submarine operations.' The injunctions regarding security were variably observed. Corporal Bob Wright noted in his diary for 21 March how he and six of his fellows were taken sailing by three naval officers. It was a beautiful spring day. Once out of sight of the PJC they 'soon put in at a village and had four pint tankards of good English bitter'.

After a final burst of training the men from Southampton travelled to Cardiff to join the team there and enjoy a meal with Pritchard at the Angel Hotel on the evening of 12 March before travelling on to Falmouth next morning. On the platform at Cardiff Pritchard overheard one of the commandos guessing aloud that they were bound for Saint-Nazaire. Rumours were rife, and difficult to squelch altogether, although Pritchard was alarmed at what he feared might be a breach of security. He promptly had the man arrested, although happily, on investigation, the context proved to be rumour, and nothing more. The man was released and joined his fellows, slightly shaken, the following day.

This first stage of the planning process was complete by Monday 16 March, when Ryder and Newman's outline operational plan was submitted to Forbes by Mountbatten. Attached to this were the draft orders for the submarine that had been chosen to act as a navigational beacon, which had received the approval of the Admiralty. The submarine (at Position Z – 46° 48' North, 2° 50' West) would be passed by the attacking force at 10.30 p.m. approaching on a course 45 degrees. The arrival time of HMS *Campbeltown* at the Normandie Dock was to be 1.30 a.m. BDST. With the explosives due to detonate 1½ hours later (the charges would be armed an hour before impact) the re-embarkation must be completed by 3 a.m. That gave the Commandos 90 minutes to carry out their demolitions and move clear before the destroyer exploded.

Likewise, the objective of the raid was confirmed: it was, in priority order, to destroy the lock gates and mechanism of the Normandie Dock, the smaller lock gates and their installation, and other key points such as pumping machinery to the basins. Final targets, if any happened to be accessible on the night of the raid, were any U-boats and shipping in the line of fire.

It was clear from the start that getting *Campbeltown* into the outer caisson of the Normandie Dock was essential: all other tasks associated with the Fairmiles and the demolitions were secondary, designed to support the achievement of the primary task and not to detract from it. Just before the task force sailed a letter from Brigadier Haydon made it clear to Newman that the destruction of the Normandie Dock was the absolute priority of the mission; its accomplishment would rate as success, whether or not the Commandos were also able to land and carry out their demolitions.

Ryder's basic plan was for a single, cohesive force to travel in formation (and so provide the strongest possible anti-aircraft protection through the massing of the combined Oerlikons), but thereafter to divide into separate roles on arrival at Saint-Nazaire. The formation adopted was to be two parallel columns, which would be collapsed from the arrowhead formation adopted at sea, led at its apex by MGB 314, with HMS *Campbeltown* in the forward centre. Groups 1 and 2, the port or left-hand column and the starboard or right-hand column, would each comprise six Fairmiles, provisionally listed as follows (although operational necessity would change some of these arrangements during the raid):

Group 1

ML 447 (F.N. Woods)
ML 457 (Tom Collier)
ML 307 (Norman Wallis)
ML 443 (Kenneth Horlock)
ML 306 (Ian Henderson)
ML 341 (Douglas Briault)

Group 2

ML 192 (Billie Stephens)
ML 262 (Edward Burt)
ML 267 (Eric Beart)
ML 268 (Bill Tillie)
ML 156 (Leslie Fenton)
ML 177 (Mark Rodier)

Both columns would be protected forward and rear by four torpedo carriers (MLs 160 – Boyd; 270 – Irwin; 298 – Nock and 446 – Falconer). Because of their role in providing protection to the force they would not themselves transport commandos. While HMS *Campbeltown* made directly for the Normandie Dock the six Fairmiles of Group 1, the port column, would pass close to the end of the Old Mole engaging the shore defences before rounding up sharply to go alongside the north side at the steps. After the Commandos had landed, the vessels were to secure alongside, bows facing outward, under the orders of Lieutenant Reginald Verity RNVR, the beach master.

It was a crucial assumption of planning by both Ryder and Newman that any and all German defences along the external harbour wall, and especially the two large concrete pillboxes on the Old Mole, would be completely subdued during the initial assault. No contingency plan was devised in the event that the Germans managed to prevent a landing along the harbour wall. This was a fundamental flaw. Meanwhile the six Fairmiles of Group 2, the starboard column, would trail HMS *Campbeltown* during the approach and then proceed alongside both sides of the Old Entrance, just west of the Normandie Dock. Three launches were to be detailed to remain alongside the north side of the Old Entrance to embark *Campbeltown*'s crew and any casualties. When fully loaded these boats were to proceed out of the Loire. If not fully loaded they were to lie off within hailing distance of the Old Mole awaiting returning Commandos, whom they would then run in to collect when the next batch were ready to depart.

There was a chance that when *Campbeltown* arrived off the Normandie Dock both caissons would be open, which would make it impossible to destroy the target as planned. If this should happen the *Campbeltown* was to disembark her Commandos as near the prearranged landing place as possible, make her way into the Normandie Dock and self-destruct against the inner gate.

As for Newman, his plan had three complementary components. Assault parties would attack and destroy known defences across the dock area and secure the area to prevent interference by German counter-attack. Demolition parties would destroy selected targets with explosives, all the while defended by protection parties to keep them undisturbed by the enemy.

In concert with Ryder, Newman had allocated his troops into three groups, totalling 246 men. Group 1, with eighty-six men under Captain Bertie Hodgson, carried in the port column, would land and secure the Old Mole. Its role was to ensure the retention of the Old Mole as the embarkation point, as well as to destroy the power station and blow up the gates and bridges of the South-ern Entrance. Group 2, totalling eighty-seven men under Captain Micky Burn, would travel in the starboard column and would land within the Old Entrance. Its role was to clear the warehouse area between the Normandie Dock and the Bassin de Saint-Nazaire (i.e. the submarine basin). In the extreme north the bridge crossing the entrance to the Bassin (the Pont de la Douane) was to be destroyed to prevent the Germans from using it as a route to attack the re-embarkation of the Commandos at the end of the raid. The final group of seventy-nine men was to be carried in HMS *Campbeltown* herself. Their tasks included destroying the southern caisson (if the *Campbeltown* should fail), the northern caisson, the pumping station and the two winding houses. Commanded by Major Bill Copland, the various teams would be led by Etches, Brett, Denison, Purdon, Roderick, Burtinshaw, Chant, Hopwood and Smalley.

Close attention focused on the withdrawal, for which very detailed instructions were to be developed and the outline sketched out in the operational plan of 16 March. The limit of 90 minutes on shore meant that the force must complete all its tasks and re-embark by 3 a.m., so as to be safely out of range when the charge on the *Campbeltown* exploded. Only with key demolitions uncompleted could this order be ignored. All men – commandos and sailors from the destroyer alike – were to proceed to the Old Mole, where the Fairmiles would push off after each had been loaded with forty men. They were then to proceed independently to a predetermined point (Position Y some 25 miles south-west of Saint-Nazaire).

During the first approach into the Loire vessels were specifically instructed to ignore the damage incurred by other boats as it would imperil the remainder of the operation. All were to fend for themselves. However, on the withdrawal these orders were reversed: every effort must be made 'to get damaged boats out to sea, assisting each other as necessary'. The two escorting destroyers (HMS *Atherstone* and HMS *Tynedale*) would pass through Position Y at 5 a.m. in order to pick up craft that might be in difficulties, take on board personnel from the retiring Fairmiles and generally rally the force.

Despite their familiarity with larger vessels, Newman was keen for his men to gain their sea legs in the Fairmiles, which handled vastly differently from the old ex-Channel ferries such as HMS *Prince Charles* and the *Joséphine Charlotte*, and so Ryder arranged an 'extended cruise' to the Scilly Isles for those commandos who would travel to Saint-Nazaire in one of the 'little ships'. This journey of some 60 miles began at 9 a.m. on Monday 16 March, with the return planned for 2 a.m. the following morning. It proved to be a testing time for all but the hardiest of sailors, and a useful exercise for the Fairmile crews in keeping station in rough seas. The Atlantic swell got up, and although the vessels coped well Ryder decided to shelter in the Scillies overnight, to allow the sea to die down before the return journey. By all accounts the commandos were grateful to him for this indulgence as, despite their now considerable familiarity with ships, being thrown about in a Fairmile was an unhappy experience for many, most finding themselves lying wretchedly prostrate in the vessels with seasickness. Clearly the raid was dependent on calm weather.

Those lucky enough to be travelling on *Campbeltown*, like Stuart Chant, were excused this ordeal, confining their 'energies to a gentle march in the lovely countryside of Cornwall, then bathing in an early spring sun'. Corran Purdon also enjoyed a leisurely swim in the clear waters of the Fal with his comrades on 16 March. Drying off in the warm sunshine afterwards, whilst lying in the grass, the 'very tough rugger Blue, Harry Pennington, said to me that England was worth dying for and I wondered afterwards if he had had a premonition of his death'. Thinking this over, Purdon also concluded that even if the raid for which they were preparing 'got sticky' he agreed with Pennington, and would gladly die for his country. He was twenty.

For Private Bob Bishop, a member of Lieutenant Ronnie Swayne's protection team, the period in Falmouth was nothing different 'from the usual regimen of long, forced marches in daylight and darkness, weapons drills, and the usual emphasis on maintaining top physical condition' except for the fact that all the men now knew that a 'show' was imminent. No one guessed what it was, however. 'Rumours as usual, were flying round the mess tables,' noted Bob Wright in his diary. 'Nobody knew, but everyone had a rumour of his own.' At least the weather was calm. Sub-Lieutenant Richard Collinson RNVR, assigned to ML 192, was greeted on his arrival in Falmouth on Wednesday 18 March by 'the trees showing the early signs of spring and birds singing in the woods bordering the creeks of Falmouth Harbour'. It was hard to believe that there was a war on.

On the evening of 17 March, following the return from their excursion to the Scilly Isles, a comprehensive security blanket was placed on the Commandos (who had all rejoined HMS *Prinses Joséphine Charlotte*) and the men of the Royal Navy allocated to the raid. The next day – Wednesday 18 March – Newman gathered all his thirty-nine officers together in the wardroom of HMS *Prinses Joséphine Charlotte* and, using the scale model as his reference point, together with a chalk board, yet without revealing the actual location (this would only be disclosed after the force had sailed), he and Ryder briefed them on the overall plan for the raid. It was the first time that those not in No. 2 Commando had met Newman, and the first time that most men had met Ryder. Chant was especially impressed by Ryder's three stripes on each sleeve and the rare white ribbon of the Polar Medal on his jacket.

Many put two and two together and assumed that the presence of a naval officer with a Polar Medal suggested a further foray to Norway. This suspicion was instantly quelled. As the briefing began Newman introduced Ryder, who stood up and told the assembled gathering that their target was a strategic port on the coast of France. Captain Micky Burn heard Second Lieutenant Tom Peyton give a gasp of excitement at the news. Burn was considerably impressed with the quality of the intelligence Combined Operations had been able to bring together, the thoroughness of the plan and the well-executed and skilful briefing. This was not simply another raid, Newman informed them, but an important part of Allied strategy. For Corran Purdon the emotions were mixed: relief that a show was at last under way; uncertainty because the raid could yet be cancelled. There was no doubt in his mind nevertheless that he would not only survive, but be back a day or two later in time to enjoy a massive party in London.

Also present at the briefing was Robin Jenks, a career naval officer, well-known son of a former Lord Mayor of London and commanding officer of HMS *Atherstone*. He considered 'there were two things which might prove fatal or might not, weather and enemy air reconnaissance'. Bob Montgomery had worked with Bill Pritchard the previous year to design a plan to destroy the Saint-Nazaire docks. He recognised the exquisite wooden model at once, but kept his mouth shut. Lieutenant Stuart Chant heard that he would be assigned to HMS *Campbeltown*. The ship, he realised, 'was expendable and those of us on board knew that. We also realised that when the German defences fired on us . . . we would be in grave danger of being damaged to the point of losing mobility, and in danger of sinking before we reached our objective.' Purdon could barely contain his excitement when Newman began the briefing: 'We were to study and discuss the model and the accompanying maps and diagrams until we could visualize localities and routes almost as if we had already visited the place.'

Next day came Newman's briefing to the men, this time on the mess deck of the ship, with all his officers present. The assembled group listened eagerly and silently to what Newman proudly declared would be 'the sauciest thing since Drake!' He explained to them that because the 'raid had a high element of risk . . . we could not expect any guarantee of a safe return,' Chant remembered: 'If there were those who were married, or who had reservations about going on the raid, now was the time to say so, with no reason to be ashamed or fear of being criticised. No one said a word.'

Corporal Bob Wright thought the plan so audacious that it 'almost takes one's breath away'. Private Bob Bishop was struck by

Newman's telling them that while Mountbatten was confident that the Commandos would do the job, it would be a close-run thing and that there was no guarantee of returning alive. He, too, was impressed with the clarity of Newman's presentation. When he had finished explaining the detail of the raid Newman asked: 'Well, what do you think of that?' Bishop recalled that he 'was answered by a roar of approval that shook the closed room where we had been assembled'. Bill Copland considered that confidence 'lay behind that cheer: we had trained hard, we knew our jobs and we felt equal to any demand.' 'This is Commando stuff,' thought Wright, who considered that it would go some way to avenging the recent loss of Hong Kong.

Not all men reacted in the same way, however. Micky Burn, watching each of his twelve men, saw Lance Sergeant Bill Gibson blanch: 'I knew that he knew that he was going to be killed. It was a kind of instinct. He was quite white, but not frightened. It was a horrible feeling.' To Lance Sergeant Don Randall the task Newman and Ryder described seemed enormous, perhaps impossibly so. The success of the operation, he considered, would depend upon meticulous planning and preparation, on complete security, training, and navigation and seamanship of the highest order; on surprise and on the drive, discipline, training, determination and swiftness of the small commando force once it had landed. Considerable risks remained that could not be quantified. One sighting by any number of sources – aircraft, U-boats, a fishing boat equipped with radio, a German naval patrol vessel – might give the game away. The *Campbeltown* might not manage to get over the mudflats. The entire raid would be launched with just over six hundred men.

For his part, however, the 21-year-old Private George Stevenson gave no thought to the risks and was 'quite pleased to be getting on with something'. Corporal Bob Wright agreed. The conversation in the mess that night, he observed, was about the two weeks' leave they would all receive when they returned.

Their target stayed secret, of course, which had the men

scratching their heads and trying to recall long-ago geography lessons. Was it to be Cherbourg, Lorient, Brest, or maybe Le Havre? Stevenson too could only guess, although he noticed a distinct change to the normally vigorous training, as an emphasis on street fighting appeared. He joined Captain Richard Hooper's party on Lieutenant Leslie Fenton's Fairmile, ML 156. 'We were thoroughly briefed,' he recalled. 'I was impressed with the meticulous detail that went into the plan and the care that went into ensuring that every commando knew and understood what was expected of him.'

On the afternoon of Saturday 21 March Exercise *Vivid* – the dress rehearsal for the raid – got under way, with all vessels but *Campbeltown* sailing to Plymouth in time to arrive half an hour after sunset. Advertised widely amongst the defence community of the area as a test of Devonport's defences, it put the Home Guard, Civil Defence, harbour patrol and local fishing fleet on high alert. Believing that it was a test of local harbour defences, the men of the 10th Anti-Submarine Striking Force and their accompanying commandos had no idea that it was they, rather than the defenders on land, who were being rehearsed.

As Ryder was to admit, the exercise was a hopeless failure, though a number of crucial lessons were quickly learned and acted upon. A guard ship at the entrance to the harbour area gave the alert as soon as the massed Fairmiles approached out of the evening gloom, initiating the switching on of the town's anti-aircraft searchlight array over the harbour, bathing the oncoming vessels in light for the twenty minutes or so before they were able to draw alongside the docks, and deposit their commandos among the Home Guard, who had seen the Fairmiles coming and were itching for a good old-fashioned scrap to show off their prowess.

On Ian Henderson's ML 306 Ralph Batteson recalled: 'The orders were to make our attack as realistic as possible without permanently disabling any of the opposition. I was into the spirit of the exercise by now, and really looked forward to the action.'

Our craft glided towards its target under cover of darkness, hardly leaving a ripple on the smooth, glassy surface of the water. We seemed to move in total silence, giving no hint of our arrival. Tonight there was no moon, but before long we had grown accustomed to the enveloping darkness, and with the advantage of our 'night eyes' we would be able to pick out any likely targets with ease. As ML 306 edged ever closer to the shore I almost felt sorry for our unsuspecting victims, who were about to be caught with their trousers down.

I was still enjoying this rather complacent feeling of superiority when the night around us was blasted into a blinding glare of light. Our attack force had not been unexpected after all and now we were taken by surprise. For a moment I was too shocked to react at all as the blaze of searchlights trapped us like hypnotised rabbits. Shock gave way to a feeling of anger and dejection that we had failed to catch our opponents unaware, but this sensation quickly faded as the attack force made for the shore, and I realised that the raid was still to go ahead.

ML306 reached the jetty, and was made fast as the commandos poured ashore in search of their victims. After the humiliation of being discovered so easily by the land forces, it gave me a certain amount of pleasure to watch our friends flashing around the dock area and taking as many prisoners as possible. The commandos went about their task with frightening efficiency, and, I suspect, with sadistic delight. Anyone foolish enough to resist them had a bloody nose to remember them by, and the noise of battle rapidly changed to yells of outrage from the collared enemy, who were often trussed helpless as lambs to nearby cranes and lamp posts as the commandos went after those who remained.

To those of us looking on it had become a scene reminiscent of comic silent films as the commandos rampaged around the docks, leaving chaos behind them. Those enemies unlucky enough not to be tied up were grabbed and flung with contemptuous ease into the waters of the harbour, floundering and swearing as they flailed their way back to land . . .

For some reason, observed a confused Corporal Arthur Woodi-wiss of No. 2 Commando, who considered the evening a disaster, 'everyone regarded this as most encouraging'. He could not see why. The exercise let the cat out of the bag so far as Batteson was concerned (the Royal Naval crews had yet to learn of their destina-tion). 'Wherever we were going,' he thought, 'it was to be a combined naval and commando raid on a land objective, and we were under no illusions that it would be infinitely more dangerous than the expedition to Devonport had been.' The searchlights had shown up the inadequacy of some of the motor launches' paint scheme, which according to Lieutenant Frank Arkle of ML 177 'shone like diamonds' against the dark sea. Only the previous month they had painted them in a novel new striped pattern which worked well in early morning mist. At night, and in the full glare of searchlights, it proclaimed their presence. A programme of repainting began that carried on, in some vessels, right until the point of departure for the raid.

Given the likelihood that they would be spotted long before the fleet reached its target, Ryder sought every opportunity to bluff and confuse the enemy during the run-in up the Loire. He decided to display *Kriegsmarine* battle ensigns (the *Reich-skriegsflagge*) on each of his destroyers as a legitimate *ruse de guerre*, before hostilities opened, in order to persuade inquisitive eyes on the enemy's side that these were friendly vessels. John Merrington's advice to remove two of *Campbeltown*'s stacks and reshape the remaining two would also help, as would subterfuge associated with German fleet signals and challenges. To make the raid a success, Ryder needed all the help he could get.

TWELVE

Ryder and Willetts's Plans

On the evening of Monday 23 March Ryder gathered all the Fairmile commanding officers and their first lieutenants on HMS *Prinses Joséphine Charlotte*. Each CO was handed a large sealed envelope containing his orders for the operation, which they were only to open when they were five miles off shore. The men were not to be told until after they had set sail. The Royal Navy crews had no choice as to whether they went on the operation, unlike the commandos, all of whom were volunteers for 'hazardous duty', and had been especially trained for raiding operations of this kind. They were even offered an 'opt-out' if they were married and did not wish to go. No such opt-out was offered by Ryder to his men. Listening to Ryder, Sub-Lieutenant Richard Collinson on Stephens's ML 192 was filled with apprehension on learning that he was to be part of an attack on such a formidable target. Having experienced sea action against the *Kriegsmarine* before, he was filled with fear, but knew that he had to hide it from the men:

> You just had to keep up an optimistic front, but I felt a complete fraud, when I overheard some of our ratings saying cheerfully among themselves, 'Mr Collinson says its going to be alright!' after I had tried to be upbeat, when they asked about the operation . . .
>
> The rest of the time passed very slowly for me, with the possibility of being killed or wounded seeming very real: I never

seriously considered the alternative of being captured unhurt. I kept hoping ignobly, but in vain, that bad weather would blow up and cause the cancellation of the operation.

The plan was that at 8 a.m. on the morning of 27 March, if the weather conditions were suitable, Forbes would issue the order 'Preparative Chariot', placing all vessels at 30 minutes' notice for sea. HMS *Prinses Joséphine Charlotte* was to dispatch all the troops to their respective vessels by Eureka boat, where the men were to remain below. If the weather continued favourable, at 11 a.m. Forbes's HQ would order 'Carry out Chariot', at which point Ryder was to sail at a time of his choosing. The chosen route took the 10th Anti-Submarine Striking Force far out from land, to evade observation by reconnaissance planes and, if sighted, to present a view of a force making its way to Gibraltar, with no landward intentions. The five waypoints (see Map 1) were:

A. 49° 40' North 05° 47' West
B. 48° 35' North 06° 07' West
C. 46° 32' North 05° 47' West
D. 46° 39' North 05° 00' West
E. 46° 26' North 03° 18' West, which was to be reached not before 8 p.m. on the evening of 28 March.

Once at Point E, the force was to make for Point Z, where HMS *Sturgeon* would be stationed to show its navigational light. To ensure that the flotilla as a whole was not held up by stragglers, Ryder built in a relatively slow speed – 12 knots – that he hoped would ensure that all the Fairmiles could manage. At this pace the journey was expected to take thirty-five hours. Radio silence was to be maintained until past the distinctive pepper-pot shape of the Les Morées lighthouse.

During the voyage and the approach to the Loire some basic rules were to be observed. First, as they were travelling under a *ruse de guerre*, the three destroyers (although not the Fairmiles) would fly the *Reichskriegsflagge*; all vessels would hoist the White Ensign just before they opened fire on the enemy. Enemy aircraft were not to be fired at unless they specifically targeted the force. Finally, all soldiers were to keep a low profile on deck, showing themselves only if they were wearing duffel coats or oilskins, with steel helmets or woollen caps to distinguish them as sailors rather than soldiers.

Once Point Z was reached, MGB 314 would be released from its tow from HMS *Atherstone* (Newman and Ryder would now travel on this escort destroyer rather than the *Campbeltown*, which instead would tow Micky Wynn's MTB 74), come alongside the destroyer and receive both Ryder and Newman and the men of their respective headquarters staff. Then, while *Atherstone* and *Tynedale* moved off to patrol some 30 miles to seaward of Saint-Nazaire the attacking force would head into the Loire. The course they were to follow would take them east of Les Morées tower, which they were to reach at about 12.30 a.m., and thence on to their respective targets in the harbour via the Passe des Charpentiers exactly an hour later.

As the run-in was expected to be 'hot', Ryder laid down explicit instructions about opening fire designed to preserve the element of surprise for as long as possible:

It is vitally important that fire should not be opened prematurely. Unless unforeseen circumstances occur the MLs are to wait till the Senior Officer opened fire. Do not fire wildly all over the place but watch their tracer and aim at the source of it. Do not endanger our own craft: the Starboard column in particular should not fire through the Port column without making quite sure the range is clear. Fire control at each gun should be a special task of the junior officers; miscellaneous Lewis and Bren guns must also be controlled most carefully on the Starboard column otherwise they will only hit our own side. MLs in rear should concentrate on the Flak positions on the South Mole.

Getting HMS *Campbeltown* onto the lock gate at night was no easy matter and would call for split-second timing and exact navigational judgement. Individual vessels were to adjust their position and their speed on their own initiative, to match the way the battle was developing. Despite the size of the dock, the gate would not be obvious in the harbour wall and would only rise a few metres above the grey waters of the harbour: hitting it dead-on was going to be extremely difficult to achieve. The exact positioning of the destroyer on the outer caisson was specified for the first time in the operation plan, underlined below:

> *Campbeltown*'s immediate object is to force her way past the anti-torpedo net protecting the outer lock gate and ram the latter <u>in such a way that the fo'c'sle projects over the lock gate</u>. The military units in the ship are then to disembark. As soon as they have done so, *Campbeltown* is to be scuttled, the fuses for the demolition charges are to be fired and *Campbeltown*'s crew evacuated in M.L.s detailed by [Ryder].
>
> Note: The demolition charges in *Campbeltown* have a delayed action of two hours [*sic*].
>
> If the outer lock gate is open, *Campbeltown* is to go alongside port side to abreast the outer caisson. The troops are then to disembark and the ship is to be scuttled so that the demolition charges are fired in such a position that the maximum damage will be done to the entrance of the lock.

Contingency plans had been made in case of HMS *Campbeltown* grounding on the mudflats. If it proved impossible to shift her in time to take her part in the operation, the four torpedo-armed Fairmiles were to proceed alongside her, two to take off her commandos and two to embark the ship's crew. The destroyer was then to be scuttled and the main demolition charge fired with a delayed-action fuse set to ensure that no craft joining or leaving the assault would be endangered, specifically to prevent examination of the vessel by the enemy.

The force would re-embark from the Old Mole under the direction of Lieutenant Reginald Verity RN. Fairmiles would pick up the troops on a first-come-first-served basis, then put out to sea independently to rendezvous at Position Y. *Atherstone* and *Tynedale*, spread 5 miles apart, would sweep through this location at 6 a.m. aiming to pick up the crews of any craft in difficulty and rally the remaining force before starting the journey home. Any coastal craft deemed unfit to reach land was to be scuttled after rescuing its crew. The entire force would then proceed home via another waypoint (Position T, at 46° 32' North 04° 16' West), passing Ushant on their right-hand side in darkness.

For the first time consideration was given to the possibility that men might be left behind on enemy soil owing to damage inflicted on the Fairmiles during the raid. Any men who found themselves stranded were 'to endeavour to escape by seizing an enemy vessel and proceeding to Gibraltar or a neutral port'. Captain Antony Terry of MI19, nominated to accompany the raid on 23 March, was scheduled to talk to the men on 26 March on 'aids to escape', and Squadron Leader A.J. Evans MC, a well-known escaper from the First World War, likewise spoke to the men on board the PJC, over the ship's tannoy system, of his experiences. By all accounts this was a bore – reminiscences rather than practical advice. For his part Terry spoke fluent German, having lived in Berlin, where his father had been a member of the British embassy, until 1927. In 1928 he began work in London as a junior reporter with *The Sunday Dispatch* and almost certainly became involved with MI6 during this period. In 1939 he joined the Army and received a wartime commission in 1940 onto the General List (its rather nondescript badge of a Lion and Unicorn being

Corporal Bert Shipton (No 9 Commando) on the left, helping Sergeant 'Dai' Davis (No 2 Commando), after their capture on the morning of 28 March. Davis was wounded in the furious exchange of fire on the *Campbeltown* during the run-in up the Loire. *Bundesarchiv, Bild 101II-MW-3721-19 / photographer: Kramer*

A group of wounded commandos lying in front of the Café Moderne after their capture. From front, Lieutenant Gerard Brett (No 12 Cdo), Lieutenant 'Tiger' Watson (No 2 Cdo), the mortally wounded Private Thomas McCormack (No 2 Cdo), and Lieutenant Stuart Chant (No 5 Cdo), fearful of the soon-to-explode HMS *Campbeltown*, and so still wearing his helmet. Behind Chant can be seen, lying, the German-born Sergeant Richard Bradley. His original surname was Goebbels. *Bundesarchiv, Bild 101I-065-2302-25 / photographer: Koch*

A German photograph of one of the many smouldering Fairmiles in the Loire on the morning after the raid. *Bundesarchiv, Bild 101II-MW-3717-11A / photographer: Kramer*

The human cost of the raid. The lone body of a Commando lying in an area near the railway, which from similar photographs indicates that it was in the vicinity of the Pont de La Douane (Bridge M). The likelihood is that this is the body of Corporal Blount, a member of Lieutenant Gerard Brett's Demolition Party. *Bundesarchiv, Bild 101II-MW-3721-26 / photographer: Kramer*

German servicemen on the deck of HMS *Campbeltown*, blissfully unaware that they are standing on top of several tons of amatol. *Bundesarchiv, Bild 101II-MW-3722-20 / photographer: Kramer*

A photograph of the *Campbeltown*, deeply embedded in the southern caisson, in a photograph looking east, towards the town. *Bundesarchiv, Bild 101II-MW-3724-03 / photographer: Kramer*

Survivors of ML 306 just after being landed ashore by the *Jaguar*. HMS *Campbeltown* had exploded as they disembarked, showering them with debris. Sub-Lieutenant Pat Landy RANVR is wearing the white jumper and hat. Private Eckmann is standing to the right of Landy, looking directly at the camera. Lieutenant Ronnie Swayne is talking to Landy, with his back to the camera. *Bundesarchiv, Bild 101II-MW-3720-17 / photographer: Kramer*

Captain Micky Burn (No 2 Cdo) and Rifleman Paddy Bushe being escorted into captivity from their hiding place on a German vessel in the Bassin de Saint-Nazaire. *Bundesarchiv, Bild 101II-MW-3723-34 / photographer: Kramer*

HMS *Campbeltown* in Devonport dockyard converting to its role for the raid. Note the steel sheeting erected to protect the commandos lying on the deck.

In a photograph taken directly from the Intelligence Files in the National Archives, the SS Normandie in the giant dock which gave it its name, before the war. *The National Archives, ref. DEFE2/128*

MTB 74, a phenomenally fast but temperamental vessel designed to take on the *Scharnhorst* and *Gneisenau* in Brest Harbour, but which saw her own demise in the River Loire. *Imperial War Museum*

A photograph of a mahogany-hulled Fairmile Motor Launch, similar to those that sailed into the jaws of death on the night of 27 March 1942. *Imperial War Museum*

A photograph of Saint-Nazaire port and docks from due south. All the essential detail of the docks can be seen clearly, with the east and west jetties and New Entrance in the foreground, the Old Mole to the right and, behind it, the great Normandie Dock. *The National Archives, ref. DEFE2/128*

Lieutenant Colonel Charles Newman VC *Imperial War Museum*

Commander Robert Ryder RN, VC *Photograph in the possession of the Revd Lisle Ryder*

Lieutenant Commander Sam Beattie RN, VC *Imperial War Museum*

Able Seaman Bill Savage, VC

Sergeant Tommy Durrant VC *The Durrant family archive & Commando Veterans Association*

dismissed by officers of more socially respectable regiments as the 'Crosse and Blackwell'), before being attached to MI19, responsible for interrogating POWs. His role in *Chariot* was to interrogate captured enemy personnel, and he was given the right, on the successful return of the raiders, 'to take away any prisoners, booty and loot'.

If the weather allowed, fighter cover would be provided out to 40 miles from the English coast in daylight, while long-range aircraft from Coastal Command's 19 Group would conduct anti-submarine sweeps in the Bay of Biscay. On 19 March 1942 Forbes requested a squadron of Beaufighters to be placed under the command of Air Vice Marshal Geoffrey Bromet, the Air Officer Commanding 19 Group, for the operation. These aircraft would also provide some protection against attack on the raiding force by enemy aircraft and surface vessels.

From the outset Fred Willetts had been working with Bomber Command to create a viable plan for an air attack that would complement the sea and land assault, and act to divert the Germans from what was happening on the ground. The first iteration of what was known as the Air Support Plan acknowledged that the critical time for this diversion was while the raiders were approaching Saint-Nazaire, and when the Commandos first gained the shore. The first cut of the plan envisaged heavy bombing between 11.30 p.m. and 12.45 a.m., with a Mean Point of Impact (MPI) on the Old Town, and the maximum number of sorties flown during the period between 1 a.m. and 3 a.m. Thereafter for the remaining hours of darkness smaller raids would take place to prevent the sounding of the All Clear, with an MPI in the dock area.

In reality, MPIs in 1942 were largely aspirational: the accuracy of bombing at night was abysmal. Only a very small percentage of bombs at this time of the war fell anywhere near their targets. In 1941, during the ten months when *Scharnhorst* and *Gneisenau* were skulking in Brest, 3,300 bomber sorties dropped 4,000 tons of bombs without doing any irreparable damage to the ships in the harbour, or to the port facilities, instead causing enormous and unintended damage to the town. Likewise, on the night of 12 March 1942 a raid by twenty Wellingtons and twenty Whitleys on the small north-western German city of Emden was considered a success by the pilots until subsequent photographic intelligence demonstrated that the closest strikes were more than 5 miles from the target. Even United States Army Air Force 'precision bombing' by day as late as 1944 was such in name only: the United States Strategic Bombing Survey of 1946 calculated that only about 20 per cent of the bombs aimed at precision targets fell within a thousand feet of their aiming point. In 1942, without the technological advances a further twelve months would bring (primarily through the use of radar target plotting, a technique the Germans were using sucessfully in 1940 at a time when the ostrich-headed authorities in the British Air Ministry were refusing to believe that the Germans even possessed this technology), the figures were a fraction of these.*

A final consideration to be noted in respect of the Air Support Plan was the prohibition against bombing French civilian targets, an explicit instruction from the British Cabinet designed to minimise French civilian casualties, and thus avoid playing into the hands of Nazi and Vichy propagandists. Put simply, if the specific military targets could not be visually observed during the bombing run, bombs were not to be dropped. So, if the pilot and bomb aimer were in any way doubtful about the target, or indeed the target area was obscured for any reason, such as by smoke or cloud, the attack was not to be prosecuted. The only person who could overturn this ruling was the Prime Minister himself.

On 22 March Bomber Command duly presented their updated plan. The outcome came as something of a shock for the COHQ

---

* The story of the battle to identify German radar technology is told in Professor R.V. Jones's *Most Secret War*, first published in 1979 and updated in 1990.

planners, however, as it entailed a reduction from the sixty aircraft allocated in their original proposals to a maximum of thirty-five Wellington and Whitley twin-engined medium bombers allocated to the target over three sequential phases of the raid. To avoid confusion in the air, there would be no overlap between each phase. The first attack would start with bombers repeatedly crossing the target to drop a single bomb on each run. The idea behind this was, first, to maximise the chances of each bomb aimer finding and hitting a suitable target, and second, to extend the attack over the longest period possible. The downside, however, was the much-increased vulnerability of the aircraft to anti-aircraft fire due to the repeated overrunning of the target. The first bomb from each of fifteen Wellingtons would fall on the dock area an hour and a half before the *Campbeltown* was due to strike the outer caisson, and finish fifteen minutes before she was due to strike.

Then, from 1.30 a.m. through to 3 a.m., the second phase would comprise ten newly arrived Whitleys undertaking repeated runs over the northern end of the Penhoët Basin and the building-slips adjoining to the north-east, again dropping a single bomb per aircraft on each run. The maximum Whitley load was twelve 250-pound bombs and two 500-pounders, constituting a total bomb load of 4,000 pounds (two tons) per aircraft and allowing, if required, fourteen separate runs over the target. A Wellington could carry 4,500 pounds of bombs, all of which could be 500-pounders, allowing it to conduct nine separate runs over the target area. In the third and final phase a further ten Whitleys would bomb the dock area between 3 and 4 a.m. to prevent the All Clear being sounded, and to cover the journey down the Loire of the departing Fairmiles.

The plan at this stage therefore entailed a total of thirty-five aircraft undertaking up to 275 individual bombing runs (i.e. one bomb dropped on each run) to drop a total of 147,500 pounds (73 tons) of high explosive on the two main target areas over a period of four hours. Ryder and Newman were disappointed that the new plan had nearly halved the number of aircraft involved, from an original sixty to thirty-five. They were not to know of the strenuous plans that Bomber Command were making to pull aircraft together for the attack on Lübeck planned for the night after Operation *Chariot*, but through Fred Willetts's intervention the RAF reverted to the original plan, such that by the following day Newman was able to include them in his final orders.

All aircraft were now to be armed only with 500-pound high-explosive bombs, with the prospect therefore of sixty aircraft carrying a total of 505 bombs, allowing a combined 252,500 pounds of explosive (over 126 tons) to be dropped on the two target areas over a period of four and a half hours. This represented a major increase in bomb load over the first plan. If all went well it would be a very significant diversion indeed.

One notable change from the draft orders presented here and on 22 March from those originally made on 16 March was that the Old Town was no longer to be a target. The idea was that, as the only men remaining in the open on the ground during air raids would be the anti-aircraft gunners, all other troops retiring to their air-raid bunkers, the commandos would therefore enjoy an uninterrupted and unopposed period going about their business in the docks. The aircrews were carefully briefed only to attack the targets that they had been detailed and, critically, only to drop their bombs when they had visual contact with their target. For reasons of operational security, however, the crews were not told that they were accompanying a seaborne raid. Accuracy was paramount, but to avoid damage caused by anti-aircraft fire the aircraft were instructed not to fly below 6,000 feet, which was the ceiling for low-calibre anti-aircraft shells. Larger-calibre weapons, like the famous 'eighty-eight' (8.8 cm flak guns), could reach a greater altitude (11,900 feet), but the higher the shells were set to detonate the less accurate they became.

The fact that never before had a significant aerial bombardment of this kind been coordinated with a land force was a concern for Newman, who was never confident that the two would work together as the plan required. There was not, for instance, any means by which the troops could communicate with the aircraft, or vice versa.

With the bomber diversion such a critical component of the plan, great concern was expressed about the impact of its possible cancellation in the event of bad weather over the target area. On 24 March Mountbatten expressed these fears at one of the regular meetings of the Chiefs of Staff Committee. The minutes of the 94th meeting of the Committee stated the following (my italics):

> Lord Louis Mountbatten said that the success of Operation *Chariot* depended very largely on the success of the diversion created by air bombing. He was anxious for a ruling as to whether or not the operation should be postponed if the force had sailed and it was then found that air action was impossible on account of adverse weather ... The Committee agreed that Operation *Chariot* *should not be undertaken unless the diversionary air bombing could be carried out.*

Mountbatten discussed the problem at the meeting with the head of Bomber Command, Air Vice Marshal 'Jack' Baldwin ('Bomber' Harris's predecessor). They agreed that in the event of bad weather over the target (fog was the greatest threat at this time of year) at least part of the force would bomb the Luftwaffe aerodromes along the north-west coast of France, but that the final decision to continue the raid would be left to Ryder and Newman. They were to be told of the cancellation or continuance of the bomber diversion no later than 6 p.m. on the night of the attack.

THIRTEEN

Newman's Orders

On Monday 23 March Charles Newman completed his plan in his cabin on board HMS *Prinses Joséphine Charlotte*. A thick copy resides today in a file in the National Archives: it is difficult not to agree with Bill Copland's description of it as perhaps the most fantastic Operation Order ever issued:

> The Army side of the Operation alone had (a) an Operations Order of 14 pages of foolscap (b) an Operations Instructions No 1 of nine pages of foolscap, and (c) Appendices, lettered A to J, covering no less than an extra 38 pages. So that eventually, every Officer was expected to know, and to help his men to understand, the contents of some 61 pages of foolscap.

Newman recorded the numbers of participating personnel to be 156 men from No. 2 Commando with 90 demolitions-trained commando soldiers selected from across the whole of the Special Service Brigade, with two medical officers from the Royal Army Medical Corps (Captains Barling and Paton) and a journalist, a total of 249. Between this date and the start of the operation up to a further twenty men joined the operation.*

---

* It is impossible to be completely precise about the exact numbers at this distance in time. The files in the National Archives list 266; Robert Ryder's account, published in 1947, listed 277; James Dorrian's comprehensive account published in 1998 calculated a total (including intelligence, medical staff and SOE agents, as well as two journalists) of 268, while detailed research by Luc Braeuer and Bernard Petitjean in 2003 listed by name a total of 269.

The distinction between the three types of parties – demolition, protection and assault – had not changed since his original orders on 16 March. Because of the need to attack thirteen separate targets Newman concluded that each group had to be commanded by an officer. The demolition parties varied in strength according to their task, for which they were to carry 1,350 pounds of specially prepared charges (made up by Major David Wyatt of SOE) that could be placed, connected and detonated in a very few minutes. They were then to withdraw to the point of re-embarkation. As these parties had to manhandle their charges, their only personal armament consisted of Colt automatic pistols, newly arrived from the USA. On the other hand the protection parties, comprising an officer and four other ranks, were heavily armed with Bren guns, Thompson sub-machineguns and grenades. Their task was to provide close protection to their allocated demolition party whilst the explosives were being laid, after which they were to cover the party's withdrawal back to the point of re-embarkation.

Finally, each assault party had at least two officers and twelve men, armed similarly to the protection parties. Their tasks were to begin during the journey up the Loire, when they were to assist the Royal Navy to engage targets as the landings drew near. Thereafter their responsibilities included the destruction of enemy gun positions, the formation of perimeters and bridgeheads and the blocking of lines of approach by the enemy from the town, by which the enemy might enter the demolition area. Newman felt it necessary in his preamble to this section in the orders to warn:

It must be definitely understood by parties detailed that the task to which they are allotted is of first priority and must be carried out before any other task is attempted. Furthermore it is not the function of a Demolition Party to entertain the idea of killing Huns until their main tasks and any subsequent allotted tasks have been successfully completed.

He particularly emphasised the subjection of all other activities to the prime importance of achieving successful demolitions. Likewise, Newman explicitly ruled that the imperative of the task overrode that of looking after casualties. Officers were to 'proceed with their tasks with the utmost determination and speed irrespective of casualties to other craft or units' he insisted. There would, presumably, be time to collect and manage casualties afterwards.

Newman outlined the four primary tasks as:

1. To ensure the complete destruction of the Normandie Dock's outer caisson following the ramming by the destroyer, sieving charges were to be placed below water level to cut holes through the gate.
2. To destroy the main pumping station, including the destruction of electrical motors and gear, and the blowing up of the main pumps in the sump well.
3. To demolish both winding houses and dock gate operating gear.
4. To destroy the inner caisson at the northern end of the Normandie Dock.

The completion of these four tasks, together with the successful ramming by the destroyer, would put the dry dock completely out of action for many months. The remaining nine demolition tasks, while important, were peripheral to the achievement of the first four:

The Pont de la Douane, connecting the dock area and the mainland, dividing the Bassin de Saint-Nazaire from the Bassin de Penhoët, was to be destroyed to prevent enemy reinforcements from entering the dock area by this route and threatening the Demolition Parties.

After the completion of [these tasks] and the withdrawal of

the troops to the Old Mole, the bridge and dock gates connecting the Old Entrance to the Bassin de Saint-Nazaire to close this route off to the enemy as a means of feeding in reinforcements, and by the destruction of the lock gates making the Inner Basin tidal and preventing U-boats from entering via this lock.

The two bridges and the three sets of lock gates in the long lock connecting the Avant Port with the Bassin de Saint-Nazaire (also known as the New or Southern Entrance).

The Pumping Station, engines, pumps close by the Avant Port were to be destroyed, in order to prevent any manipulation of the lock gates or water pumping into the Inner Basin.

The plan was that the six Fairmiles would land all eighty-nine men (eighty-six commandos plus two medics and a journalist) of Group 1 at the Old Mole. The aim was to land each of the vessels sequentially on the slipway on the northern and landward side of the Old Mole, through which the troops would disembark to capture the East Jetty and move through the Old Town to cut off the swing bridges and lock gate of the New Entrance, thus isolating the raiders from any German counter-attack from this direction. The slipway on the Old Mole was immediately below a gun position and the landing place was presumed to be out of the line of direct fire from this bunker, although vulnerable from grenades or small-arms fire. All other landing places along the Old Mole or wharf at the landward end of the Mole could be accessed only by the use of scaling ladders, as the level of the Fairmile deck would be at least twenty feet below the Mole. It was hoped that a rapid *coup de main* assault, all the while under the cover of the diversionary bombing raid, would enable the commandos quickly to overpower any defenders who were on duty on the Old Mole at the time of the attack.

Group 1 was under the overall command of the 23-year-old Captain Eric ('Bertie') Hodgson of the Bedfordshire and Hertfordshire Regiment and No. 2 Commando, and comprised two separate assault teams. The first to land – Group 1F, under the command of Captain David Birney – would land from the first Fairmile, Lieutenant Thomas Platt's ML 447 (No. 9), and secure the bridgehead on the Old Mole, making it safe for the arrival of the remaining five vessels. In particular, Birney's assault party was to destroy the enemy positions on the Old Mole, including the gun positions encased in a prominent pillbox on the landward end of the Old Mole itself. This was a critical objective. If for any reason Birney failed to land first and knock out this gun emplacement, which would otherwise jeopardise the entire landing, the next troops on station were to complete this task as a priority, before they went off to complete their own mission.

The assault party was then to secure the landing point at the slipway; clear the routes of any enemy that might impede the demolition parties getting to their targets; clear the small built-up area between the Old Mole and the New Entrance; with the assistance of the French SOE officer Raymond Couraud (whose alias was 'Lieutenant Jack Lee') to deal with any French civilians found in the area, and then form a bridgehead around the Old Mole through which the force would withdraw at the end of the raid to the point of re-embarkation. This Group would also provide close protection to MGB 314, which was expected to be moored alongside the Old Entrance during the operation, as well as clear a house close to the jetty for use by the Regimental Aid Post, whose medical staff would land with Group 1E.

As well as being in command of Group 1, Bertie Hodgson had specific responsibilities with regard to Group 1E, which was to follow Birney's assault team onto the slipway (carried on ML 341 – No. 10, Douglas Briault) before moving through the bridgehead and sweeping down the East Jetty. They were to clear the enemy and small buildings as they proceeded, destroying the enemy guns located there because of the danger they would continue to present to vessels in the river if they were not silenced. After clearing the southern part of the Old Town, and the East Jetty, Group 1E were then to provide a protective cordon at the neck of the area to prevent enemy from craft in the Avant Port leaving and entering the area of the Old Mole.

Once the two assault parties in Group 1 were ashore and securing the area, the three demolition groups (Groups 1A, 1B and 1C) would land. Under the command of Bill Pritchard they would make their way to the targets at the New Entrance, placing demolitions on the lock gate and swing bridges at Points B, C and D, which would then be blown simultaneously. The detail of the demolition parties and their specific responsibilities were as follows:

Group 1A. A demolition party of eight men under the command of Lieutenant Ronnie Swayne of No. 1 Commando together with a protection party of four under the command of Lieutenant John Vanderwerve would be landed from ML 306 (No. 14, Ian Henderson) and would destroy the two lock gates and operating mechanisms and the swing bridge at Point B, on the southern end of the New Entrance.

Group 1B. A demolition party of six men under the command of Captain William ('Bill') Bradley* of the Royal Inniskilling Fusiliers and of No. 3 Commando would be landed from ML 307 (No. 12, Norman Wallis) and would destroy the lock gate and operating mechanism (Point C) in the centre of the New Entrance. Because there were protection parties to the south and north of him, Bradley was required to complete the demolitions under his own steam.

Group 1C. A demolition party of four men under the command of Lieutenant Philip Walton of No. 2 Commando and a protection party of four men commanded by Second Lieutenant Bill

---

* The announcement in the *London Gazette* for the award of his MC from the Vaagso raid was made on 3 April 1942, along with that of Lieutenant Bill Etches, just days after Operation *Chariot*.

('Tiger') Watson of the Black Watch would be landed from ML 457 (No. 11, Thomas Collier) and would destroy the lock gate and operating mechanism and lifting bridge at Point D, linking the New Entrance with the Bassin de Saint-Nazaire.

The Group 1E assault parties down on the East Jetty and the bottom of the Old Town were also instructed to keep a watch on possible enemy fire being brought to bear from the anti-aircraft post at the end of the West Jetty. In case the explosive charges did not completely demolish the bridges and the lock gates at the New Entrance, leaving passage across as a possible line of enemy approach, the protection parties in Groups 1A (John Vanderwerve) and 1C (Tiger Watson) were to remain until the final withdrawal. Newman's instructions continued:

Group 1D. Three demolition parties of fifteen men in total would destroy the boiler house, impounding station and hydraulic power station (Point Z). Four men in Group 1D1 under the command of Lieutenant A.D. Wilson of No. 9 Commando would attack the boiler house; four men in Group 1D2 under the command of Second Lieutenant Paul Bassett-Wilson of No. 12 Commando would attack the impounding station; and four men in Group 1D3 under the command of Lieutenant John Bonvin of No. 6 Commando would be responsible for attacking the hydraulic power station. Their four-man protection team was commanded by Lieutenant Joe Houghton. The three demolition parties would all be carried on ML 443 (No. 13, Kenneth Horlock) while Houghton's protection party was to land from ML 307 (No. 12, Norman Wallis).

Group 1G. The demolition control party led by Bill Pritchard and supported by four commandos was to be landed by ML 457 (No. 11, Thomas Collier). Pritchard was responsible for coordinating the detonation of all the demolitions, and for reporting to Headquarters the results.

The plan for Group 2 was that the starboard group of Fairmiles would land eighty-seven commandos at the Old Entrance. It was feared that a torpedo boom might obstruct the entrance to the lock, so the commanding officers of each Fairmile were instructed to make for any suitable landing site in the vicinity, such as the steps and jetty on the south wall of the Old Entrance and the steps on the north wall of the Old Entrance.

A primary concern was that two enemy anti-aircraft guns at the entrance to the Normandie Dock (Nos 64 and 65) would cause devastation if they were not put out of action. Accordingly, the first assault group (2D), commanded by Captain Micky Burn, carried in ML 192 (No. 1, Billie Stephens), was tasked first with ensuring that HMS *Campbeltown* had made a safe landing before moving on to its main task, which was the destruction of the two flak towers at the northern end of the Normandie Dock. If *Campbeltown* was having difficulties in getting to the caisson because of fire from these guns, Burn was to destroy them before moving north, completing their second task and forming a block against enemy infiltration into the area via the bridge at the northern end of the Bassin de Saint-Nazaire, the Pont de la Douane, until this was blown up.

Newman's instructions for Group 2 were as follows:

Group 2A. A demolition party of eight men under the command of Lieutenant Mark Woodcock of No. 3 Commando together with a protection party of four men commanded by Lieutenant Dick Morgan carried in ML 262 (No. 2, Edward ('Ted') Burt) were to destroy the two gates and operating mechanism and the swing bridge (Point G) at the Old Entrance. The swing bridge was one of the evacuation routes for the withdrawal, men from the *Campbeltown* and the Normandie Dock area needing to come south to the embarkation point at the Old Mole once their tasks were complete. Woodcock was therefore instructed to prepare the swing bridge for demolition and then destroy the lock gates.

If the swing bridge was closed (and therefore not passable by troops) Woodcock was to attempt to open it: if successful the explosive charges were to be placed on the lock gates and detonated. If, however, he was unsuccessful he was to damage the bridge and lay the demolition at the lock gates, but not detonate them until the withdrawal was complete from the north.

Group 2B. The Military Headquarters of eight men including Lieutenant Colonel Charles Newman, together with a reserve of eleven men, would (when not otherwise committed) under RSM Alan Moss engage enemy vessels and submarines in the Bassin by anti-tank rifle fire (Boys rifle) and 2-inch mortars. This reserve was to be landed at the Old Entrance on ML 267 (No. 3, Eric Beart), its main role to be ready at once to move to and fight in any part of the battle area. If and whilst they were not thus employed they were to take up position just south of the swing bridge (at Point G).

Group 2C. A demolition party of four men commanded by Second Lieutenant Harold Pennington of No. 4 Commando and a protection party of four men (commanded by Lieutenant Morgan Jenkins) would destroy the Pont de la Douane at the extreme north of the Normandie Dock (Point M). By this stage Micky Burn's Group 2D should have destroyed the two flak towers, and would help Jenkins to suppress any fire that might come from the top of the flat-roofed customs building on the western side of the Bassin where it was known that a number of guns were situated. If Pennington's group was unable to destroy the bridge they were to create a barricade to prevent the enemy using it to infiltrate into the area.

Finally, ML 156 (No. 5, Leslie Fenton) and ML 177 (No. 6, Mark Rodier) would bring in Group 2E, the 'Special Task Party', twenty-six men commanded by Captain Richard Hooper, supported by

Troop Sergeant Major George Haines. Their task was to move south over the Old Entrance and destroy the two guns on the harbour wall just north of the Old Mole. Once they had done this they were to retrace their steps and engage any vessel in the Normandie Dock that might be providing resistance, doing as much damage as they could to those vessels. They were then to return to the HQ at Point G (i.e. the south side of the Old Entrance) and contribute to Newman's reserve.

Group 3 comprised 79 men to disembark from HMS *Campbeltown*. When the vessel struck, Major Bill Copland would be responsible for organising the disembarkation, after which he was to proceed to the Old Mole to prepare for the evacuation. The first to leave the vessel were the two assault parties, Group 3C under Lieutenant Johnny Roderick and Group 3D under Captain Donald Roy, nicknamed by his men 'The Laird'. During the approach up the Loire these twenty-eight commandos in Groups 3C and 3D were to assist the Royal Navy gunners to engage enemy targets along the banks of the river. Just prior to the ramming of the caisson the men were instructed to lie down and take what precautions they could to withstand the shock of impact, the real effect of which remained unknown. It was thought that the height of the *Campbeltown*'s fo'c'sle would be level with that of the footway over the caisson, requiring the simple expedient of running out gangways from the ship to facilitate quick disembarkation. When the destroyer had finally come to a halt, hopefully wedged in the outer caisson of the Normandie Dock, the two assault groups were to disembark by all available means such as gangways, planks and ladders.

Roderick's assault party (Group 3C) of fourteen commandos were to disembark on the right-hand side of the stricken destroyer and eliminate the gun position on the side of the main Dry Dock entrance (No. 66); move on to destroy the gun positions in the storage unit area on the right-hand side (Nos M70, M10 and 67); and to form a block to prevent the enemy from entering the area from the storage unit area. It was critical that the assault parties gained good fire positions for themselves sufficient to fight off any counter-attack while the demolition groups were carrying out their tasks. If they had time, they were to destroy as many of the storage units and pipelines by fire and/or explosive charges as they could (they carried incendiary devices for this purpose), before withdrawing to the Old Mole through the bridgehead held by Captain Roy and his men at the Old Entrance.

Captain Donald Roy's Group 3D assault party of fourteen men would clamber down the left-hand side of the destroyer's fo'c'sle onto the top of the outer caisson and destroy the anti-aircraft post on the south-west corner of the dock, together with the two gun positions on the roof of the pumping station (Nos 64 and 65). Firemen's ladders had been supplied for the purpose of gaining access to the roof, a dangerous task which Roy had determined he would undertake personally. It was essential that these guns were silenced quickly, although of course there was always the chance that if they did keep on firing, and the demolitions inside the building were successful, they would be destroyed in the subsequent blast. These tasks successfully accomplished, Roy's group would then move to the Old Entrance to form a bridgehead covering the northern approaches to the swing bridge in order to facilitate the withdrawal of the men from the northern sector, on their way to the evacuation point on the Old Mole. Whilst there, they would engage any possible enemy action from escort vessels in the Bassin.

Newman's specific instructions for Group 3 were:

Group 3A. A demolition party of eighteen men and a protection party of five men would destroy the caisson gate, operating machinery and pumping house at Point H. Seven men in Group 3A1 commanded by Lieutenant Robert 'Bertie' Burtinshaw of No. 5 Commando would destroy the outer caisson if it had not already been destroyed, or looked unlikely to be destroyed because of a failure by HMS *Campbeltown*. Four men in Group 3A2 commanded by Lieutenant Chris Smalley of No. 5 Commando would demolish the operating machinery for this gate in the winding house and four men in Group 3A3 under the command of Lieutenant Stuart Chant of No. 5 Commando would destroy the pumping house for the dry dock. They would be guarded by a four-man protection party commanded by Lieutenant 'Hoppy' Hopwood. The explosive charges in the pumping station and the operating machinery and outer caisson would be set off independently under the orders of Bob Montgomery.

Group 3B. A demolition party of thirteen men and a protection party of five men would move quickly to the northern end of the Normandie Dock where they would destroy the inner caisson and its associated operating machinery in the northernmost winding house. Seven men in Group 3B1 under the command of Lieutenant Gerard Brett of No. 12 Commando would place sieving charges against this inner caisson while four men in Group 3B2 under the command of Lieutenant Corran Purdon of No. 12 Commando would destroy the operating machinery in the winding house. They would be protected by a four-man protection party commanded by Lieutenant 'Bung' Denison.

Group 3E. This was the second-in-command group of six men, including Major Bill Copland, which, together with a demolition control comprising Bob Montgomery and Lieutenant Bill Etches and two commandos, were to locate themselves at the raiders' HQ at Point G, just south of the swing bridge at the Old Entrance, forming the basis of a block that would be built up over time by the arrival of other fighting parties. Montgomery (Group 3E) was responsible for the overall demolitions in the Group 3 area, while Bill Etches was principally responsible for those in Group 3B. Thereafter all other commandos would disembark and head for their respective targets. Montgomery was responsible for giving the order to set off the explosive charges and for reporting to Newman their outcome, after which both demolition and protection parties were to withdraw immediately and independently to the point of re-embarkation at the Old Mole.* Newman ordered that if either Pritchard or Montgomery became casualties they were to be replaced by the OIC of the demolition party with whom they were then working.

Newman's orders emphasised that at night, and in the noise and confusion of battle, with raiding parties of all kinds rushing through the battle area, the need for quick recognition of friendly and enemy troops was essential. It was for this reason that the otherwise unusual step was taken of wearing highly visible white scrubbed webbing, together with torches on weapons giving out blue pinpricks of light. Troops in concealed positions, observing the approach of other troops, were especially ordered to wait until they could ascertain from the advancing silhouettes whether they were friend or foe, and only then to shout the recognition password, after which, and only then, they could open fire. Groups were to be known by the surname of the group commander. Likewise, naval personnel were to use the recognition code 'Ryder'. Newman enjoyed establishing the password as 'War Weapons Week', with the reply 'Weymouth', observing drily: 'I defy any German to say that correctly.'

Newman was concerned at the outset about the danger of the Command Party being wiped out in one blow during the journey up the Loire and the landing, so he divided it into three separate groups to provide some contingency should one group be destroyed. In the first group ('Ops HQ') were himself, Captain Stanley Day, his signaller Sergeant Ronald Steele, Captain Antony Terry of MI19 and two commandos with Thompson sub-machineguns (Newman's runner, and Peter Nagel, alias Private Peter Walker, Newman's

---

*   In reality the commanders of the demolition teams, such as Corran Purdon, made their own decisions to initiate their demolitions.

German- and French-speaking interrogator*), together with the journalist Gordon Holman, all of whom were to travel to the Old Entrance in MGB 314 with Ryder. Once it had been confirmed that *Campbeltown* was successfully wedged in the outer caisson, Newman's group were to be landed, where they would establish their HQ at Point G, the south side of the swing bridge at the Old Entrance. From this point they would check the passing through of all troops from the dock area on their way to the Old Mole for re-embarkation. When this was complete, with only Captain Roy's assault party left covering the bridge, the orders for the second stage of withdrawal would be given.

The second HQ group – consisting of Warrant Officer Class 1 Alan Moss (the Regimental Sergeant Major) and a reserve totalling eleven men – were to travel on ML 267 (No. 3, Eric Beart) to secure the HQ at the Old Entrance bridge and to await the arrival of Ops HQ. The third HQ party of ten men (Group 3F), including Major Bill Copland, Captain Bob Montgomery and Lieutenant Bill Etches, were on board HMS *Campbeltown*.

The orders for the withdrawal were extraordinarily detailed, covering every step of the journey for every subgroup from their appointed tasks back to the assembly point at the Old Mole, in proper sequence. The clear expectation was that the raid would follow the pattern of all others: a sharp thrust into the enemy's underbelly, decisive though limited combat against the unprepared and unsuspecting defenders, demolitions, and then a clean withdrawal, all within 90 minutes. The signals for the withdrawal were to be in two stages, the first from the area of the stricken HMS *Campbeltown* – a red-starred rocket – and the final stage at the Old Mole, which was to be a green-starred rocket. Once the withdrawal had been ordered it was imperative that all troops moved as quickly as possible to the disembarkation point, passing through

---

* On 12 March COHQ asked for three 'Sudeten Germans' to accompany the operation. On 17 March it was noted that Private Peter Nagel of SOE would accompany the force as personal assistant to Newman.

the defensive bridgeheads that would pull back only at the last minute. At the Old Mole Lieutenant Reginald Verity, the beach master, would muster successive Fairmiles into the slip, fill them with returning commandos and order them on their way. As each vessel bore away it was to engage enemy defences on both banks of the Loire with the maximum fire possible, and to use smoke to disguise its withdrawal.

Confidence was high. All previous raids had brought back their flock of sullen German prisoners, and Operation *Chariot* was intended to be no different, although men were cautioned not to take too many prisoners, as there would be limited space on the withdrawing Fairmiles for any more than a handful of captives.

Consideration was also given to managing the handful of French inhabitants who would inevitably be encountered. For their own safety they were to be ordered to stay indoors or herded into cover. Learning the lesson from Vaasgo and the Lofoten raids, commanders were instructed to treat with great reserve any apparently friendly offers of assistance: the reality was that the commandos would soon be on their way, and any popular uprising by the local population, or any evidence of French support for the raiders, would bring down hard reprisals against them by an angry and vengeful occupier. To help manage any of the local population encountered all commandos were provided with a list of helpful phrases, in both French and German, which they were encouraged to learn during the short voyage to the Loire. In one of the Wehrmacht photos taken in the immediate aftermath of the raid a German soldier is shown holding a copy of this list of phrases to the camera. They were carefully chosen to be useful for most anticipated situations:

French

Get inside quickly	Dedans vite
Stay inside	Restez dedans
Shut the doors	Fermez les portes

Shut the windows	Fermez les fenêtres
You'll be killed	Vous serez tué
Obey and you'll be OK	Obéissez et tout via [sic] bien
Disobey and you'll be killed	N'obéissez pas et vous serez tué
Where are the Germans?	Où sont les Allemands?
How many are here?	Combien y-a-t'il ici?
Get out	Allez vous en
Shut up	Fermez les bouches

German

Come on	Kommen Sie mit
Shut up	Halt's Maul
You'll be killed	Oder Sie sterben
Scum	Schweinerei
What's up?	Was ist los?
No one here	Niemand Hier?[sic]
Nothing doing	Nichts zu machen
We're sunk	Wir sind kaput
The English are in the town	Die Engländer sind in der Stadt
Back	Zurück
Quickly, for God's sake	Schnell Gott Schnell
Who goes there?	Wer da?
You're surounded	Sie sind umgegangen
We're 2 battalions	Wir sind zwei Bataillonen
Prisoners	Gefangener
It's a whole army	Es ist eine ganze Armee
Back to barracks	Zurück nach die Kaserne
Come down	Herunter
Come out	Heraus
Hands up	Hände auf

In addition, at least two soldiers were brought along on the raid because of their French-speaking credentials, one of whom was the adventurer Raymond Couraud, now an SOE officer under the pseudonym of Second-Lieutenant Jack Lee, and the other a Belgian aristocrat, the Vicomte Arthur de Jonghe, who had been forced to flee Belgium in 1940.

Still only twenty-two years of age, Couraud had lied about his age to join the French Foreign Legion in 1938, fighting in Norway in 1940, for which he won the Croix de Guerre. Taken prisoner by the Germans in 1940, he was released by the Vichy government in December, after which he promptly joined an early *réseau*, organising the flight to safety of several thousand Jews to Spain. In April 1941 with the Gestapo on his tail he crossed the Pyrenees and after several months hospitality in the notorious internment camp at Miranda as a guest of Franco's unfriendly fascist regime he finally arrived in England on 12 October 1941. His journey to SOE was thereafter a brief one, beginning first with the Free French Forces, then the *Action Militaire* section of the BCRA, before finally finding himself in Colonel Maurice Buckmaster's F Section of SOE in early 1942.

The presence of the French-speaking Captain Vicomte Arthur de Jonghe with Bertie Hodgson would likewise deal, it was hoped, with any Frenchmen encountered in the Old Town. De Jonghe proved to be one of the war's more colourful characters. A Belgian patriot, he had early resisted the Germans but was forced to flee to England in 1940 when he was told that the Gestapo had discovered his identity and were seeking his arrest. Commissioned into the British (rather than Belgian) Army, he worked with the Belgian Government-in-Exile and SOE to train Belgian agents for operations in their occupied homeland. At his request he joined No. 4 (Belgian) Troop of 10 (Inter-Allied) Commando in mid-1941 and because of his obvious language skills was allocated to Operation *Chariot*.

Newman's impressively extensive orders testify to the care he and Stanley Day were determined to take in planning the operation, and in ensuring that their troops were prepared for every conceivable eventuality. They contain all the important though mundane aspects of the soldier's existence, directing every detail from dress ('Boots – Special Issue'; 'Battle Dress – Oldest' etc) to radio frequencies, rations, medical and so on. Inflated lifebelts were to be worn during the voyage; periods of fresh air and exercise as far as possible were to be given to all ranks to prevent them from growing lethargic; all ranks were to memorise the silhouettes of the Lockheed Hudson, Hurricane, Whitley, Beaufighter, Spitfire and Sunderland; and officers were to make sure that their men had been to the toilet before landing. Six newly designed BSA foldable bicycles were to be used by 'runners' between the various headquarters during the operation, to speed communications.

FOURTEEN

Final Preparations

The point between Ryder's brief to his commanders on 23 March and the start of Operation *Chariot* was a period of intense but purposeful activity. The process of transhipping all the stores from HMS *Prinses Joséphine Charlotte* to the Fairmiles (and to the *Campbeltown*) began the following night, the vessels topping up with fuel and water before anchoring out in the roads before dawn so that darkness would hide the relationship between the commando ship and the Fairmiles from inquisitive eyes.

For the commandos, the immediate tasks were to assimilate the detail of the precise orders, examining the model and aerial photographs, and memorising orders, routes, timetables and all manner of detail listed in Newman's instructions. 'By squinting at the model from eye-level we were able to build up a picture of this port and what we would have to do when we landed there,' recalled Chant. Newman wrote:

It was thus possible for each little group to discuss their particular task, memorise their routes to their objectives, cross question each other on the detail, and to make certain during the next few days that every man made himself acquainted with his particular job so that he could almost have carried out his task blind-folded. On board, there was a hive of activity preparing the weapons, checking over all the stores, building the equipment to the man, the latter being particularly important as so much individual ammunition had to be carried by each man that it was necessary to make special magazine holders for Bren and Tommy Gun clips.

Bertie Hodgson scribbled in his diary for 24 March: 'Busy after dinner, orders, demolition charges to be made up. Slept like a log and dreams not too horrible for a change – I've reached the excitement stage at the moment. I wonder how long it will last!' The following day was one he described as of 'Great Activity'. Dumps of stores were made up for moving to his allocated Fairmile, and he 'completed Operations Orders for the group. I do hope they will work out OK, there's a lot to think about . . . jobs in the afternoon, such as checking ammunition, stores, food, etc. for the journey.'

On at least two occasions in the early hours of the night men from the assault and protection teams were sent ashore from the PJC to practise tactical movement through Falmouth, carrying out night recognition at varying distances by silhouette, blue-flash torches and passwords, and at firing ranges in the area they practised night firing. Strenuous activity took place in which men racked their brains for anything they might have forgotten. As late as 20 March urgent instructions were dispatched to strip twelve rapid-firing single-barrel 20 mm Oerlikon anti-aircraft guns from their mounts on merchant ships to place on the Fairmiles, and a further six weapons destined for HMS *Campbeltown* were taken off HMS *Prince Charles*, then refitting in the Prince Albert Dock, London. During this time the PJC was so crowded that men were forced to sleep on her decks, a problem made easier, recalled Stuart Chant, by the unusually balmy weather.

On 24 March the two escort destroyers allocated to the operation arrived at Falmouth. HMS *Atherstone* and HMS *Tynedale* anchored together close to the harbour. Destroyers coming and going were a common feature of the port, and a couple of escorts, perhaps arriving from or departing on convoy duty, aroused no suspicion. Ryder immediately vacated the Tregynt Hotel to place his HQ in the *Atherstone*.

The arrival of HMS *Campbeltown* the following day, however, was a different matter. When she arrived she anchored some distance out in the Carrick Roads, away from *Atherstone* and *Tynedale*, and far from the docked *Prinses Joséphine Charlotte*, to prevent any interested and knowledgeable onlooker creating an association between the vessels. The fear of a German spy lurking in Falmouth, radioing back the news of an imminent departure of a raiding force, remained strong. The little flotilla of Fairmiles lay grouped elsewhere in the Cross Roads. To informed observers the *Campbeltown* looked very unlike a British destroyer. Its two raked funnels added a distinctly Germanic air to the vessel, which had been made even more unusual by the armour plating that had been added to the bridge and the deck area. The Oerlikons had been placed on raised platforms that looked akin to band-stands in a park, and caused no end of mirth amongst the professional sailors who watched her arrival. It made sense to park her offshore rather than berth her alongside in the harbour: her appearance was simply too unusual to escape comment.

Her commander was Lieutenant Commander Sam Beattie RN. Forbes had insisted on his prerogative to appoint his own opera-tional commander, but Ryder was content with the decision, as he knew Beattie well. In fact, the previous commanding officer – Lieutenant Commander Christopher Roper-Curzon (Lord Teyn-ham) – was equally competent, but was unknown to Forbes. His lack of experience also played against him. At forty-six he had been commissioned in 1917 and retired from the Royal Navy many years before, being recalled to the colours at the outbreak of war.*

Sam Beattie was, by contrast, thirty-three, and a long-service professional. 'I was overjoyed at the idea of getting Beattie, whom

---

* Roper-Curzon in fact proved to be a first-rate operational commander. He continued to serve with distinction in the Royal Navy, and was awarded the DSC in June 1944 and the DSO in 1945.

I knew well,' Ryder recalled. 'I could wish for no one better.' When the *Campbeltown* had anchored Ryder travelled out to the destroyer by motor launch and formally welcomed Beattie and his stripped-down crew. The young Lieutenant Corran Purdon recalls being 'immensely impressed' with Beattie. He certainly looked the part, he thought. 'Sam Beattie had great dignity and was a tall, good-looking man with an Elizabethan beard and a friendly and calm manner.'

Everything seemed to be coming together well. There were some exceptions. One problem lay with Wynn's temperamental MTB 74. On 23 March it was decided that one of the vessel's three Packard engines would have to be replaced. Without anywhere near the proper facilities, the replacement arrived later that evening, and the mechanics worked all night to have it ready for testing the following day. There was no time for the fuses for Wynn's torpedoes to be tested before they arrived in Falmouth, and so they had to be fitted during the journey out, with Wynn keeping his fingers crossed that the delays would work as expected.

Another problem was Ryder's discovery that the newly fitted Oerlikons on the Fairmiles did not come with their allocated quantity of ammunition: nor could Forbes's HQ seem to be able to squeeze any more out of the Admiralty, despite Ryder's nagging suspicion that ammunition lockers across the Navy were hiding precious supplies that were now urgently needed in Falmouth. Unfortunately, there seemed no way of persuading individual commanders-in-chief to relinquish their stocks, even on the basis of a temporary loan. Ryder was aghast: how could such a critical operation be allowed to proceed with such a dramatic shortage? Robin Jenks was fully stocked and redistributed eight hundred rounds from HMS *Atherstone*, and Beattie was able to release small amounts from HMS *Campbeltown*.

Ryder was later to voice strident criticism of this deficit in his post-operation report. 'How many of our countrymen,' he asked himself, 'realised that we were setting out to make a frontal attack on one of the most heavily defended enemy bases with only half our allowance of ammunition?'

Likewise, Ryder had laboured for weeks without an HQ staff to assist him: everything he was able to achieve he delivered through the force of his own abundant personality, and the good will of friends. This was hardly a professional way to prepare for an operation of such magnitude, and it was only with the arrival of HMS *Atherstone* and HMS *Tynedale* in Falmouth on 24 March that sufficient numbers of qualified men were made available to complete all the administrative and technical tasks involved. By comparison Newman was able to enjoy the full-time support of his adjutant (Captain Stan Day) and a relatively well-staffed HQ. 'A force such as this requires something in the nature of a flotilla leader's staff,' Ryder was later to note for the benefit of future raiders.

Wednesday 25 March dawned warm and sunny, the fifth day in a run of unusually settled weather. As plans stood the force would depart Falmouth for France on Friday 27, landing at their respective targets at Saint-Nazaire in the early morning of Sunday 29 March. On HMS *Prinses Joséphine Charlotte* Ryder gathered his officers, coxswains and gunners together, told them that they were about to embark on a raid, and that they would leave Falmouth in two days' time. Ralph Batteson from ML 306 was one of those listening:

We were invited to gather round a table in the centre of the room. Here, we saw, was a large scale model of an undesignated dock area. I studied it carefully, but couldn't make out any distinguishing feature that identified it to me. Nor were we told what the objective was during the briefing. What we were given was detailed technical instructions as to the positions of the defence guns in this area, and exactly where our ML's were expected to make their landings. All of us were strictly warned not to discuss what we had learned with anyone, not even our fellow shipmates still aboard our own boats.

Would the weather last, or was it tempting fate to assume that conditions would stay calm and clear for another forty-eight hours? Ryder decided not to risk the wait, and although the spring tide would not be at its height until the night of 29 March he asked Forbes by telephone if the operation could depart one day earlier than planned. Permission was granted at once.

At about the same time Ryder was confronted with a new problem. The RAF's No. 1 Photographic Reconnaissance Unit (PRU) based at Heston aerodrome in West London flew regular sorties over the French Atlantic ports, but in order not to excite German suspicion only one additional flight had been planned to overfly Saint-Nazaire before the raid was due to commence. This duly took place on 24 March. On the return of the high-speed (400 miles per hour) photographic reconnaissance Spitfires to Heston the photographs were immediately dispatched the 30 miles to Medmenham, where they were interpreted, and then sent by motorcycle courier directly to Falmouth.*

When he gathered with Ryder, Newman, Beattie and Tweedie, Robin Jenks of the *Atherstone* was delighted to see on the photos two large merchant ships in the Normandie Dock (the *Passat* and the *Schledstadt*), which would also be destroyed when the *Campbeltown* exploded, together with a number of smaller vessels. 'What a prize!' he recalled. 'All of us were full of excited anticipation over these beautiful pictures.' But what gave them all a shock was the sight, with the aid of stereoscopes, of the distinctive shapes of five vessels berthed in the Bassin, which the interpreters at the CIU had identified as Möwe-type torpedo boats, ships of a similar size to British Hunt-class destroyers.

---

* The extraordinary story of the development of RAF photo reconnaissance and its role in eventual Allied success is told by Constance Babington Smith in *Evidence in Camera* (London: Chatto & Windus, 1958) and by Ralph Barker in *Aviator Extraordinaire: The Sidney Cotton Story* (London: Chatto & Windus, 1969). Taylor Downing has comprehensively covered the subject from a more modern perspective in *Spies In the Sky: The Secret Battle for Aerial Intelligence during World War II* (London: Little Brown, 2011)

Ryder recalled looking at these photographs with horror. It had been known for some weeks that an enemy flotilla of five such vessels was in a French Atlantic port, although it was not known precisely where. The PRU's aerial photograph now made their location clear. Newman, lacking his colleague's naval experience, asked Ryder how many commandos he would need to capture them. Ryder paused, and then asked in reply: 'Well, how many men have you got in reserve?' 'Twelve,' Newman responded. Ryder suggested quietly that he would probably need all of them for the job. According to Jenks, Newman 'didn't care a bit and made a plan to cripple them where they lay by fixing "limpets" to their plates and generally to add them to the "bag" by blowing the gates and draining the basin.'

The situation called for a quick decision. There was every chance that the enemy boats would have departed the port by Saturday night. If they decided to cancel the mission because of the threat of anchored enemy vessels, a similar chance to attack Saint-Nazaire might never return. Should they just rely on the plan they had developed, and trust to their luck? Ryder called McCrum at Plymouth Command to seek his opinion. The conversation concluded that Operation *Chariot* should not be cancelled or delayed, but that to redress the destroyer balance McCrum would ask Forbes if two further Hunt-class destroyers might be dispatched to assist in the withdrawal. 'With that,' Ryder wrote, 'I returned to the *Atherstone* and we sailed; the MLs first, followed by the destroyers an hour later.'

What Ryder had neglected to say in his account was that Lieutenant Commander F.N. Woods, commanding officer of ML 447, fell ill only minutes before the Fairmiles set sail and was sufficiently incapacitated for Ryder to determine that he would need to be replaced. He and Woods had collaborated closely in the development of the Naval Plan, and his loss was a serious blow. But the operation could not be delayed, so Woods was shipped off to Falmouth Hospital and, once the flotilla got under way, Lieutenant

Tom Platt of ML 443 was promoted to command the port column in ML 447, with Lieutenant Kenneth Horlock promoted to command ML 443.

Bringing the start date forward by twenty-four hours also required a flurry of last-minute changes to plans, to ensure that Bomber Command were alerted, for instance, that they would now be required a day before planned, and that HMS *Sturgeon* departed at once, so as to turn up on station at Point Z well in advance of the arrival of Ryder's flotilla. 'Before we set sail,' remembered Ordinary Seaman Henry Scott on HMS *Atherstone*, 'there were a terrific number of signals going from one ship to another and a sense of excitement and also a certain amount of nervous anticipation of just how successful the raid would turn out to be and how many of us would be coming back in one piece.' It was considered that carrying the two force commanders and their HQ staffs on *Campbeltown* was too much of a risk if she found herself grounded on the mud banks of the estuary, so Ryder and Newman now decided to remain on HMS *Atherstone* for the journey to the Loire, transferring to MGB 314 once Point Y had been reached on the evening of the landing.

Last-minute tweaks were also being made to Newman's plans. Captain David Paton asked Newman for a pound of sulphanila-mide powder and was amazed when it arrived on the next train from London. Copland noted that every train into Falmouth seemed to bring more stores, of varied kinds. Captain Mike Barling, one of Newman's two medical officers, told him that the casualty reception arrangements were weak, and that he needed more trained medical assistants given the number of casualties that might be expected. In Ayr, therefore, on the afternoon of 24 March Lance Corporal Jack Webb RAMC and three of his comrades were asked whether they would like to join the other half of the Commando. They accepted with alacrity and joined the Glasgow–London train the following morning (25 March), reaching Falmouth on the morning of 26 March with only an hour or two to spare before the little fleet sailed.

Exchanging his .38 Webley for one of the new Colt automatic pistols, Webb found himself on ML 446 along with his medical colleague, Private Tom Everitt and Captain Mike Barling. They were to support Captain Bertie Hodgson's assault team (Group 1E). With no time for any previous briefings, Webb had to pick up the gist of the plan from Everitt. He learned that the three-man medical team of which he was now part would remain on the Fairmile during the action, moored alongside the Old Mole, acting as a medical reception station for casualties brought back on board. When he had been briefed by Barling, Webb 'formed the opinion that this was a suicide job. As it turned out I was not far wrong.'

One of the things most soldiers also found time to do was to complete their final letters home, which their loved ones would receive if they were killed. Major Bill Copland wrote to his wife, Ethel:

> My dearest, I have to write this letter although God knows I hope you never receive it – which you will if I don't come back. We sail in a day or two on a somewhat desperate venture, but one of high purpose. If we succeed, and only the worst of ill-luck will stop us, then we shall have struck a great blow for the cause of freedom. Remember too that if I do get blotted out I shall die in good company, for never did a finer crowd set out on a doughtier task.

The 29-year-old Captain David Paton was well aware of the dangers he was facing. In his farewell letter to his wife he wrote matter-of-factly of facing 'an ordeal from which I might never return'. He went on: 'It may be of some comfort to you to know that if I go down, at least I go down in an attack, and I want you to hold your head high as I am managing to do despite my forebodings.'

Lance Sergeant Bill Gibson, a Glaswegian in the London Scottish and No. 6 Troop, 2 Commando, whom Micky Burn had seen turn white at the briefing, wrote thus to his father on the evening of 25 March, addressing him as 'My dearest Dad':

By the time you get this I shall be one of the many who have sacrificed their unimportant lives for what little ideals we may have – my own ideals I can thank you for.

The job we have been on has been something worthwhile – it has virtually been suicide but the repercussions after we will have finished our task will be very far reaching . . .

[His close friend, Lance Sergeant] Peter [Harkness] and I will be together – our task is very important and just a wee bit dangerous but if we can hold Jerry off it will mean the saving of the lives of a lot of our pals.

Last night [Lieutenant] Micky [Burn] had a talk with us all – he is a really good man – and has promised all of us that you will be notified if the worst has happened to us. So if he is still alive you will probably hear from him.

We have been on this boat for a fortnight now, and we are all determined to see this through – I salute you all No 2 Commando – they are a great lot of lads. Tomorrow morning I am going to Holy Communion – the first communion I have ever been at – but I know God will help us all he can and I pray, Dad, that he will help you and bless Betty for all she has been to us . . .

The morning of 26 March dawned bright and clear, a slight mist lying over the tranquil sea under a low cloud, providing perfect conditions for the start of the long, slow sea journey to Saint-Nazaire. Bertie Hodgson's diary recalled the service of Holy Communion mentioned by Bill Gibson, on the foredeck of HMS *Prinses Joséphine Charlotte* before breakfast, attended by most of the men, regardless of their religious convictions. He observed that the ritual was most comforting, even though he held no strong Christian beliefs. The hours that followed comprised much rushing around completing final packing before what he described as a final 'rousing speech by Charles Newman which put morale up to 100%'. Contemplating his commanding officer Hodgson scribbled: 'He really is a fine chap and all of us realise how much he has done to make the job a success. If anyone has been patient, helpful and charming the whole time, it was he.'

At 9.30 a.m. the signal 'Preparative Chariot' came through from Plymouth, initiating the final flurry of preparations. The previous day the Chiefs of Staff Committee had given their final approval, Mountbatten considering it hazardous but with a considerable prize if Ryder and Newman could pull it off, while Churchill considered the raid fully justified. By noon, the PJC's Eureka boats had worked quickly to distribute her entire complement of heavily laden commandos to their respective Fairmiles. Everybody, remembered Corran Purdon, was 'in tremendous form, everyone very excited at the prospect of the raid'.

Finally, at 12.30 p.m. the signal 'Carry Out Chariot' was received. Hodgson boarded Lieutenant Douglas Briault's ML 341 (No. 10) and wrote in his diary as the flotilla sailed out of Falmouth in glorious sunshine at 1 p.m:

> Well, here it is – the day we've been waiting for for two years for most of us. Busy in the afternoon handing out grenades, ammunition, etc. Everyone in high spirits all the time. I feel more confident now than I have ever felt during the last fortnight, but I still pray that we are allowed to touch land and have a scrap – if we don't the men will go crazy, poor devils.
>
> Very smooth water, good dinner, sardines and bully beef stew. Clear moon and sky and, after talking to Lieutenant Briault went to sleep at about 11 o'clock.

Keen to maintain the pretence of an anti-submarine sweep, the Fairmiles left first, followed an hour later by *Campbeltown* (towing

MTB 74), *Atherstone* (towing MGB 314) and *Tynedale*. Meeting later in the afternoon far from shore, marked by the D Buoy, and sailing for Position A, the vessels adopted their sailing formation, which Ryder described as 'Cruising Order No 1', a wide arrowhead formation at a speed of 13 knots. A light breeze blew from east-north-east, and despite the otherwise calmness of the day the warmth of the afternoon produced considerable haze. They were under way at last. Just over three weeks since Operation *Chariot* had received the go-ahead and had been allocated its 'expendable vessel', the 621 men were en route for Saint-Nazaire.

Many, however, still had no idea of where they were heading, or why. On board Billie Stephens's ML 192, Ordinary Seaman George Davidson knew absolutely nothing of where they were going, or what was expected of his boat. He and his fellow sailors spent the first hours of the journey arranging accommodation for the troops and finding suitable stowage for the large quantities of additional men and material on board. He observed that their guests seemed to have plenty to do, repeatedly stripping and cleaning weapons and ammunition, and checking and packing kit and explosives. With the land well behind them Lieutenant Mark Rodier RN on ML 177 opened his brown envelope. When he saw that his destination and target was Saint-Nazaire he asked Sub-Lieutenant Frank Arkle RNVR, his First Lieutenant: 'Where the hell is that?' 'After some searching of the charts,' said Arkle, 'we found it tucked up a river in the north-east corner of the Bay of Biscay.'

Crammed on board ML 457 were thirty men, fifteen sailors and fifteen commandos, the latter including Lieutenant Philip Walton, Sergeants Dick Bradley and Alf Searson, Corporal George Wheeler and Lance Corporal Homer, together with Captain Bill Pritchard and his demolition control team of four corporals, Maclagan, Deans, Shipton and Chetwynd. The Fairmile was commanded by the well-known yachtsman Tom Collier, who looked, according to Lieutenant Bill 'Tiger' Watson, like 'an average-sized, typical Englishman. It would have been hard to find a more tolerant and hospitable man and, as it turned out, a braver one. This highly competent and experienced young sailor made us as comfortable as his overcrowded little ship allowed.' Major Bill Copland on HMS *Campbeltown*, the hectic flurry of recent hours now behind him, had a chance to relax:

> All that afternoon and evening we sailed under perfect weather conditions, calm with a sunshine haze which helped to reduce enemy visibility. Aboard *Campbeltown* all was ship-shape and comfortable – I had sent [Lieutenant] John Proctor aboard early in the day to fix and allocate quarters – and soon everyone was snugly settled in. There was little to do, all our preparations had been made on PJC and it only remained to arrange our tours of duty for AA Defence, rehearse 'Action Stations' and wait.

On HMS *Atherstone*, Ryder spent his time attempting to keep the Fairmiles on station. Many vessels were struggling to do so – this was the first time that the entire fleet had come together as a single flotilla. The south-east swell made things tricky for some of the less experienced skippers, and took its toll among some of the commandos with seasickness. If they were spotted by the enemy Ryder was hopeful that they would assume the force was Gibraltar-bound. It was only to be at Point C, south of latitude 47° (and thus considerably south of Saint-Nazaire), that the little fleet would change course and angle in towards the French coast. Even then, however, the route would point towards La Rochelle, not Saint-Nazaire, this direction only being changed at Point E, some 80 miles from their target, when the flotilla would finally change direction north-east and head directly towards its target.

Charles Newman likewise was taken up with what he described as the 'thrill of the voyage' and the imminent prospect of action after waiting so long. Bob Montgomery was on the *Campbeltown*, and when visiting his men in the Petty Officers' Mess was offered a large glass of Pussers rum by the Bosun: 'Have this, sir, it'll give you your sea legs,' he was told.

The men, confined below decks unless they were wearing clothes that disguised them as sailors, made themselves at home. Very quickly they discovered that the ship was stocked with plentiful supplies of commodities in scarce supply in Britain, such as eggs, chocolate, bacon, sausages and butter, and it was not long before semi-condoned looting was rife in the kitchens, storerooms and NAAFI shop. Copland insisted on only one rule: a rum ration was allowable today, but not tomorrow. 'We drank endless cups of "Kai", sweet, thick naval cocoa,' Corran Purdon remembers, 'and munched huge bully beef sandwiches, delighting in the scrumptious hot, soft, ship baked bread, a real treat.'

High spirits helped break the pre-battle tension. On *Campbeltown* Lieutenant Robert 'Bertie' Burtinshaw of the Cheshire Regiment and 5 Commando, an extrovert known to his men as 'Bertie Bagwash' because he wore a monocle, unearthed various items of naval uniform in a cupboard, which led to what Stuart Chant described as a 'mad fancy-dress party' during which Burtinshaw put on Sam Beattie's naval cap and 'took over command of the ship and parodied the Senior Service to the delight of everyone on board'.

After this diversion Chant busied himself with the preparations for his demolition task, breaking down his 60 pounds of plastic explosive into small parcels wrapped in brown waterproof paper, each about 2 pounds in weight. They were easier to carry, and to mould around the target when the time came. He remembered:

We were curiously relaxed, light-hearted even, glad to get away from the hustle of preparation and planning and knowing that we were involved in a total commitment of our own making and with no going back. Further than that we did not dare conjecture and during that voyage in the calm of the early spring weather I, for one, did a lot of quiet praying.

Above the little fleet droned a lone Hurricane of No. 247 Squadron from the nearby RAF station at Predannock, staying low and conducting repeated sweeps of the flotilla's perimeter for a short while, leaving the little formation of ships steaming out to the open seas after an hour, the limit of the plane's endurance. Ryder watched the last link with land disappear fast back from whence they had but recently come. In a few minutes, he thought, the pilot would be safely back at his base near Mullion on the Lizard Peninsula, while for them, destiny awaited.

At 7.11 p.m. that evening Point A was reached 25 miles southeast of the Scilly Isles, and without pause the direction was adjusted to take the ships south-south-west, at the same time adopting Cruising Order No. 2, in which the three destroyers were in line ahead separated by a distance of 360 yards (led by *Campbeltown*), with the port and starboard columns of Fairmiles in two parallel lines on either side. 'The signalling of the altered sailing instructions was flagged from the *Atherstone*, picked up and answered by the MLs,' Newman recorded, watching with a soldier's interest from *Atherstone*'s bridge, 'and then, when the last had answered and the signal flags struck, the fine sight of each vessel changing speed and direction to take up its new position is imprinted on my memory.' Sunset came only fourteen minutes later, and they steamed on their new course at 14 knots in the rapidly growing darkness, bringing them to Point B at 11 p.m. They were now a mere 40 miles off the island of Ushant, and well within range of the enemy. But at least the darkness would hide them as they made their way south-south-east to Point C, 160 miles due west of Saint-Nazaire.

FIFTEEN

The Bay of Biscay

The night passed quietly, the flotilla moving purposefully and steadily south through the darkness. 'Everything around me seemed unnaturally calm and silent,' recalled Ralph Batteson. 'It gave me an eerie sensation as I watched the other crewmen move about the boat in this strange, uncanny atmosphere. I felt that I was in a state of suspended animation, moving relentlessly forward into the unknown.' The only excitement of the night came when, at 2.14 a.m., Lieutenant Thomas Platt, the new CO on No. 9 (ML 447), reported what he believed to be a submarine on his port bow. Almost at once, however, he cancelled the report, acknowledging that the unusually large patch of phosphorescence they had seen was probably caused by a large shoal of fish over three hundred feet long.

Lance Sergeant Don Randall recalled that not many men slept peacefully that night. Men going into battle, some for the first time, deal with the prospect of combat in different ways. Randall was struck by how one of his fellow NCOs opened up to him, apologising for not being better company:

He was a man of many more years than the average commando. He had rejoined from the Reserve, after serving his time with the Colours in a Highland regiment. On the Reserve, as a family man, he had experienced many difficult years in Canada earning some means to support his wife and children. I admired his soldierly qualities and steadfastness, and right now through his open and matter-of-fact acceptance of his situation, he bolstered my own confidence.

Much to Ryder's annoyance the following morning started bright and clear – this was a boon to the enemy, and not to him. The surface haze had begun clearing during the night, such that when sunrise came at 6.46 a.m. visibility was excellent. The first act of the morning on the destroyers (but not the Fairmiles) was to hoist the *Reichskriegsflagge*: the White Ensign would only be hoisted the moment that firing began. This *ruse de guerre* was one small element in Ryder's armoury. He was acutely aware of the fact that, since the raid 'constituted a frontal attack by a small force of unarmoured vessels on the heavily defended port of Saint-Nazaire', he was heavily reliant on surprise for success. If the force could get in undetected, and carry out the raid quickly, they would be on their way well before the hornet's nest was fully disturbed. Stuart Chant watched the ensigns being changed, thinking that it 'was an eerie feeling to look up at our masthead and see that sinister and frightening enemy flag fluttering in the light sea breeze, which ruffled its deadly design – a black swastika on a red background.'

Late the previous night Newman, much against his inclination and in spite of his heightened sense of expectation, had turned in for a few hours' sleep. He was back on the open bridge of the destroyer with Bob Ryder and Robin Jenks in time to watch the dawn sun rise quickly above the eastern horizon. Fourteen minutes later, Position C was reached, and with time in hand the speed was reduced to 8 knots as the course was adjusted to the southeast and Cruising Order No. 1 readopted. The slower speed would make the flotilla less conspicuous from the air as the vessels' wake – and the ubiquitous tell-tale phosphorescence – would thereby be minimised, as well as timing the flotilla to arrive off the Loire in darkness that night.

As the little fleet changed direction and settled into its new route, HMS *Tynedale* signalled at 7.20 a.m. that its director tower lookout situated above the bridge had sighted what might be a U-boat on the horizon, which in a Hunt-class destroyer was 11,792 yards (6.7 miles). A few minutes later it confirmed the sighting, made by the eagle eyes of Mr S.W.J. Ford, who was second officer of the watch. On hearing the call from the signaller on *Atherstone*'s bridge (the vessels were on radio silence, communicating with each other solely by means of signalling flags), Newman recorded that immediately: 'I and all eyes and glasses searched the silvery horizon for her. There she was, surfaced and stationary, and as far as we could see, thoroughly unsuspecting.' It appeared to be heading north-east, in the direction of Brest.

The time was now 7.36 a.m. Ryder ordered HMS *Tynedale* to give chase, and told Robin Jenks to take HMS *Atherstone* (slipping the tow on MGB 314) in pursuit as well, leaving HMS *Campbeltown* with the Fairmiles. If the U-boat had seen the flotilla, and suspected it to be British, the game would be up, and before long the skies would be full of enemy attack aircraft and the seas with the enemy torpedo boats out of Saint-Nazaire. It was essential that she be destroyed before she could send any warning radio messages. Equally, *not* to have attacked would have given the lie to the deception that they were an anti-submarine force.

If Ryder's flotilla had not turned to the left at Point C to head south-east on their new route it is likely that both parties would have entirely missed each other. A few minutes later, with both of the escort destroyers heading at full speed towards the target, two French fishing trawlers were sighted to the right of the submarine. This looked to Ryder too much of a coincidence: if the vessels were indeed rendezvousing with the U-boat the presence of the flotilla would be quickly made known by radio. It was critical therefore that not just the U-boat but the trawlers, if necessary, be destroyed.

U-593, commanded by Kapitänleutnant Gerd Kelbling, was reporting to Saint-Nazaire at the conclusion of its first patrol, which had taken it between north-eastern Ireland and the Western Isles of Scotland, leaving Wilhelmshaven on 2 March. During that time it had had one hundred depth charges dropped on it, and although seaworthy was in need of repair: the vessel's trim was so badly out of kilter that Kelbling could only dive or surface by sending the crew forward or aft.

At a distance that Ryder estimated to be 5 miles *U-593* fired a recognition signal, which burst a pattern of silver stars into the sky, spreading out in an umbrella shape, but the submarine held its course, on the surface, apparently convinced that the bow wave coming towards it flying the *Reichskriegsflagge* was in fact a German vessel. When the *Tynedale* had closed to about 5,600 yards (3.18 miles) she hoisted the White Ensign and opened fire. The time was 7.45 a.m.

Below decks on the *Campbeltown* Lance Sergeant Don Randall and his fellow commandos could hear the unmistakable thump of naval gunfire ahead. Newman watched the action from the bridge of the *Atherstone*, driving fast through the quiet sea towards the trawlers. 'Every gun on the *Tynedale* spoke and the sea all round the fast disappearing U-boat was a mass of large columns of water. Whether she scored a hit or not I cannot say, but within a very few seconds the U-boat was completely submerged and not very long afterwards the *Tynedale* was depth-charging the area.'

Fast asleep on ML 192, Richard Collinson was awoken by the concussion of the depth charges, which felt like hammer blows against the thin mahogany hull of the Fairmile. The submarine crash-dived. *Tynedale* at once fired a pattern of depth charges. After the detonation of the first charge the submarine's conning tower briefly broke surface before plunging back into the depths, giving the eager men on the destroyer the opportunity of some twenty seconds to open up on her with their 4-inch gun, Oerlikons and quick-firing quadruple-mounted 2-inch 'pom-poms', before she disappeared. Lieutenant Commander Hugo Tweedie was convinced that he had destroyed her – one of his depth charges had exploded within 70 feet of the submarine – but no more sight or sound was to be had of her. Tellingly, no debris or oil was found on the surface, and at 9.20 a.m., after nearly two further hours in which no definitive sonar signals (using the ASDIC equipment) were detected, the hunt was discontinued.

Part of the problem at the time was that the use of depth charges nullified the effectiveness of sonar, allowing the submarine commander to take evasive action for a period of time after each explosion in which the ASDIC was effectively blind. Ryder tried to put the U-boat off the scent, if it was still watching, by steering south-west for 7 miles, before returning in a wide loop to the north, to the flotilla. Kelbling was in fact having enormous difficulty controlling his submarine, and instead of staying to attempt to fire torpedoes at the attacking destroyers he determined that the best policy was to avoid pursuit by going deep, and in due course return to the surface to report the action by radio. This he managed to do at 2.20 p.m., signalling the Navy Group West in Paris (*Oberbefehlshaber des Marinegruppenkommando West*) that he had encountered three destroyers and ten motor torpedo boats heading west.*

Because of the time spent chasing the U-boat the French trawlers were left to their own entirely innocent devices. Once the submarine chase had ended, however, and the flotilla was back on its original course, further French trawlers were encountered, the first at 11.35 a.m. The number of fishing vessels at sea, and especially so far from shore, came as something of a surprise to Ryder and his destroyer commanders. They were not to know of the considerable pressure in occupied France for food, given the

---

* By an extraordinary coincidence, HMS *Tynedale* and *U-593* met once again off Algeria on 12 December 1943, the destroyer being sunk by a torpedo. After a long chase the U-boat was itself sunk and Kelbling and his surviving crew spent the rest of the war as POWs.

mass detention in Germany of a significant proportion of the French agricultural labour force, either as POWs or forced labourers. This pushed many towards the sea, and fishing vessels, if they had the appropriate licence from the German port authorities, travelled further out into the Bay of Biscay than was usual in peacetime.

The British feared that German observers were on some of the numerous vessels at sea, providing forward eyes and ears for the coastal defences. The first vessel encountered late that morning, the *Nungesser et Coli* out of Saint-Nazaire, was therefore considered a threat to the force, and *Tynedale* was ordered to take off her crew and sink her. A second trawler, the *La Slack*, was stopped by Ryder on *Atherstone* at 12 noon. In his book *The Battle of the Narrow Seas*, which tells the extraordinary story of the 'little ships' of the Royal Navy's Coastal Forces during the war, Lieutenant Commander Peter Scott RNVR, son of Captain Robert Scott RN of Antarctic fame and later the founder of the World Wide Fund for Nature, interviewed Lieutenant Dunstan Curtis RNVR of MGB 314, who was instructed to go alongside the second one, board her and take off the crew and all their papers and charts.

According to Curtis:

the French crew on deck threw their hats into the air [when they saw the White Ensign] and shouted for joy. I said to the captain, 'Je regrette, monsieur le Patron, mais il va falloir vous embarquer et couler votre bateau.' He replied, 'Eh bien, si est necessaire. Pouvons nous apporter nos biens?' (Well, if that is necessary. Can we bring our property?) I said, 'Yes,' and they came on board with a strange collection of 'biens.' There were old blankets, half-cooked fish, a large fishing-net which got in everybody's way and a basin of potatoes which had been simmering over the fire.

Watching from HMS *Atherstone*, Ordinary Seaman Henry Scott was surprised to see one of the fishermen coming out of the hold with a suit on a hanger. Curtis's apologies, more than once expressed, for having to sink his ship were met by the captain with the reply, 'C'est la guerre.'

With the crew removed, the ship was attacked with gunfire. This was less effective than had been hoped, as Newman observed. 'After taking off the crew, very nearly a ship's broadside failed to sink the wretched thing at a very few yards range,' he recalled, 'the shells going in one side and coming out the other, but nothing would sink her. We had to leave her ablaze with holes through her like a colander.' The thirty-two crew of both vessels, Ryder reported, were friendly and quite happy to be taken to Britain. By 2 April twenty-four had joined the Free French forces.

Ryder had by now determined that fishing trawlers were not a threat, as none of them appeared to carry radios or German observers, so for the rest of the day none of the large number that were subsequently seen were stopped or checked.

The day was perfect, with low cloud preventing close observation of the force from the air. Most of the Commando officers conducted last-minute briefings and rehearsals with their men. Corran Purdon went through his plan several times:

> I had the utmost confidence in my four splendid corporals, each of whom could well have had a commission before the war ended had they returned safely from Saint-Nazaire. They all exuded cheerfulness and confidence and were physically as hard as nails. I knew that with them we could not fail unless we were all knocked out before we got there. I think we could all have found our way blindfolded to our winding house and have laid our demolition charges likewise.

On ML 306 Ralph Batteson even thought, at odd moments 'that I was on some kind of holiday cruise as I gazed on the far, sunlit horizon, and ML 306 glided through the placid water.' Stuart Chant and his colleagues on *Campbeltown* made the most of the balmy conditions. When not reorganising and repacking their equipment, they rested, and 'lay out on deck in the warm sun of that beautiful March weather'. On Curtis's MGB large saucers of raisins on the bridge staved off hunger during the long day, while on Kenneth Horlock's vessel a large ham achieved the same purpose.

On board HMS *Campbeltown* after the excitement of the trawlers Sam Beattie invited the officers to the bridge for a glass of the ship's Spanish dry La Ina sherry. A treat the men had forgotten in war-constrained Britain, it was a shame to waste it, he reasoned. Ryder was not able to enjoy such luxuries. At 12.40 p.m. he received a message from Portsmouth reporting that the five German torpedo boats which had, two days before, been sighted docked in Saint-Nazaire had moved upriver to Nantes. Later that afternoon, however, a further message was received informing him that the vessels had again been reported as returning to Saint-Nazaire and might be encountered, either in the estuary or docked in the port. The journey upriver to Nantes had clearly been only a brief one, possibly to demonstrate their presence to the local population.

Back in Plymouth Forbes had decided, belatedly in Ryder's view, to send two further Hunt-class destroyers as reinforcements, HMS *Brocklesby* and HMS *Cleveland*. Ryder was not unduly concerned by this turn of events, and did not believe that the presence of the German ships constituted a reason for changing his plans, though it vexed him to think that these two additional Hunts should have been part of the original plan.

As the day developed the entire fleet were astonished that no enemy reconnaissance had yet spotted them. Robin Jenks observed that during the journey into the mouth of the Loire Newman tactfully made it clear to Ryder that come what may the naval forces were there to take him and his men to Saint-Nazaire. The only disruption to the plans was caused by the faulty port engine of Lieutenant Douglas Briault's ML 341. With little chance of the vessel being repaired in time for it to keep up with the attack flotilla, Ryder ordered Henry Falconer to come alongside the stricken vessel in ML 446, take off Briault's complement of commandos, and then take her place in the order of battle.

Bertie Hodgson was desperately concerned lest he be left behind and miss out on the excitement altogether:

> Awful scramble to get stores, etc, transferred. We lost some distance but attempted to catch up. We spent about one and three quarter hours looking for them vainly (the rest of the flotilla) – it has been one of the most horrible occasions in my life. Watching till the eyes ached, somehow I couldn't believe I could be cheated of this job at the crucial moment. We have at last sighted the MLs and hope to get back in position for the attack. Lovely moon and conditions perfect . . . I feel so relieved now that most of my apprehensions and fears have gone . . .

Briault and his engineer struggled to get the engine going, struggling to follow as Falconer faded gradually into the increasing darkness ahead. Then Falconer's Fairmile disappeared altogether. 'For an hour more he crawled along,' recorded Peter Scott, 'unsure of his position and with no apparent prospect of his engine being repaired. He realised that he had very little chance of finding the river mouth on his own, and he realised, too, that, even if he did find it, he would not be able, at his present speed, to reach it until the operation was all over.' The only option was to turn around, and head back on an emergency course for Cornwall, as he had been instructed to do as a last resort, at a steady 11 knots. This he reluctantly determined to do. The only excitement during the return journey was sighting a Focke-Wulfe about 100 miles west of Ushant, but the aircraft left them alone.

At 8 p.m. that evening *Atherstone* slowed, MGB 314 was released from its tow, came alongside and took off both Ryder and Newman, together with their small staffs. Day nearly ended up in the water, missing the jump from the destroyer to the MGB, and getting his foot squashed between them. Fortunately all he suffered was a twisted leg. The move from the relatively large, armoured destroyer to the tiny wooden gunboat suddenly made the forthcoming battle very real to Newman. One 'felt very much nearer the fighting, and one's nerves instinctively became just that little bit tighter,' he recalled.

They had reached Point E, and were now only 65 miles from the Loire. This was the signal for the adoption of Cruising Order No. 3, the flotilla effortlessly beginning the final journey to Point Z, and the planned rendezvous with HMS *Sturgeon*, at a steady speed of 12 knots, with *Atherstone* and *Tynedale* escorting *Campbeltown*. The escorts were only to leave the flotilla once the rendezvous with *Sturgeon* had been satisfactorily achieved. Cruising Order No. 3 was their attack formation, led by MGB 314 with its radar set and ASDIC sonar equipment, which was to be used for depth sounding across the shallow waters far from the dredged Passe des Charpentiers. 'I was much stirred,' Dunstan Curtis told Peter Scott, 'as I took my MGB to the head of the line.'

The port and starboard columns were protected at the front by two of the torpedo-armed Fairmiles (ML 270 and ML 160 respectively), with HMS *Campbeltown* in the middle, protected on all sides by the motor launches. The port column carried the men of Group 1 heading for the Old Mole; Group 2 in the starboard column headed for the Old Entrance; *Campbeltown* carried Group 3. The two other torpedo-carrying Fairmiles (ML 446, now carrying Briault's troops, and ML 298) protected the rear, along with Wynn's idiosyncratic MTB 74, now released from its tow behind *Campbeltown*.

The men now made their final preparations for battle. On the order to go to action stations on Norman Wallis's ML 307 David Paton 'went forward and found two of my chaps changing their uniforms from trousers to kilts'. They explained to him that as they were likely to die they preferred to do so dressed properly. On ML 192 Richard Collinson now felt much calmer than he did when first briefed on the plan, and after coming off watch and eating a plate of bacon and eggs, fell into a deep, dreamy sleep.

The sun finally disappeared at 8.41 p.m. On ML 306 Ralph Batteson was struck by the huge quantities of jellyfish in the water.

Their number amazed me: there must have been millions of them crowding the surface. From them came a strange, fluorescent glow that shone in the bow waves of our boats as they moved through the shoal. It lit up the gloom and played around us, its eerie glow falling on the craft and their crews. Caught in that strange light, we seemed a ghostly fleet, moving silently through another world.

By now visibility had reduced to about two miles due to low cloud, which seemed to wrap the vessels in a protective blanket as they steamed towards the Loire Estuary. This suited Ryder perfectly, although it was important for Bomber Command that good visibility should prevail over the docks when their attack began at midnight.

Then, precisely at 10 p.m., the flashing light (showing the letter 'M' in Morse code) from the conning tower of the half-submerged HMS *Sturgeon* could be seen out of the darkness directly ahead. Lieutenant Bill Green, the navigation officer, had brought them across 450 miles of enemy-controlled ocean to the exact location, the nautical equivalent of finding a needle in a haystack. It was an extraordinary achievement, and a demonstration of the finest seamanship by both Green and Lieutenant Commander Mervyn Wingfield RN, commander of HM Submarine *Sturgeon*. MGB 314 passed within hailing distance of the submarine at 10.14 p.m., Newman hearing a voice calling 'Goodbye and good luck'.

Wingfield had departed Plymouth immediately on receiving the news that the operation was being brought forward by a day, and found himself in his allotted position by noon on 27 March. He then spent the afternoon nervously checking and rechecking his exact position by means of periscope bearings from prominent though distant shore positions, worried also by the irritating presence of large numbers of French fishing vessels which, he thought, could not fail to spot him just under the surface of the calm, glassy sea. Indeed he was convinced that he had been seen, as the trawlers almost politely kept their distance. Fortunately those that saw him ignored him. Few French fishermen would have been able to tell the difference between a U-boat and a British submarine (and in any case, U-boats were now an especially common sight in these waters), so they wisely left these oversized and dangerous tin fish (at 1,300 tons, *Sturgeon* was considerably heavier than the *Campbeltown*) to their own devices. With the onset of darkness Wingfield surfaced his vessel to recharge his batteries, and within a minute or two of initiating the signal lamp at 10 p.m. the flotilla appeared out of the gloom. He recalled Sam Beattie on the *Campbeltown* giving him a cheery wave, and Robin Jenks calling him by loudhailer in his well-known stentorian tones: 'Hullo, Mervyn. Are you in the right place?' 'Yes,' he replied, 'within a hundred yards, but don't make so much noise!'

The rendezvous with *Sturgeon* was the signal for both HMS *Tynedale* and *Atherstone* to leave their comrades, departing northwards to patrol beyond Point Y, 40 miles beyond, and to await the results of the dawn. Wingfield departed also, travelling on the surface during the hours of darkness, to patrol an area off Brest to the north. Ryder's force, meanwhile, steamed steadily onwards towards the Loire, and their appointment with history.

SIXTEEN

Into the Loire

The adoption of the attack formation by the flotilla was the signal for all the men in the raiding force to go to their designated action stations. The flotilla had shaken itself into its final battle shape by 10.30 p.m., steaming north-east into the mouth of the Loire on the final leg of their journey at a slightly increased speed of 15 knots. The men were tense, expectant. The last rehearsals, packing and repacking had been completed, and only action now waited. It would be a further two hours before the ships were to pass the entrance buoy, at 12.30 a.m., and, at 12 miles (and 60 minutes' sailing time) from Saint-Nazaire, this was the first sight they would catch of the planned air attack.

'On we sailed in that hushed river,' recalled Bill Copland on *Campbeltown*, 'no sound save the steady beat of our engines and our own murmured conversation.' At 11.30 p.m. he gathered his assault, protection and demolition commanders together in the wardroom for a final briefing to check that the men were ready. His officers, he remarked later, were calm, confident and cheerful. At the end of the briefing he dismissed the men with the instruction 'Action Stations, please Gentlemen.'

Those, like Stuart Chant, designated to leave the ship first went to their positions on deck. Corran Purdon and Gerard Brett with their respective demolition parties moved to the wardroom, where they sat with their backs against the bulkheads to try to lessen the anticipated impact of ramming. Nigel Tibbits went below at

12.30 p.m. to set the fuses in their specially designed steel basin underneath the forward gun, including those with the eight-hour delay. If all went to plan the 2½-hour fuses would detonate the *Campbeltown* against the caisson at 3 a.m. If, however, these failed, the eight-hour-delay fuses would initiate the required explosion at 8.30 a.m. BDST. There was now no going back for the destroyer.

Meanwhile, on MGB 314 Charles Newman's mind was working overtime with the 'What ifs?' that always occupy commanders in the hours and minutes before combat. Will the plan work? Have I done enough preparation? But his primary concern at this stage was whether the little flotilla would actually be able to penetrate into the mouth of the Loire, and get through the German defences:

> How far could we proceed up the river before we were spotted? Would we pass over the mudflats without mishaps? When seen, would our German Very lights and efforts to look like a German convoy delay the shooting? Would the air raid keep the flak busy?

We 'were all tense but eager to get this job done' recalled Sergeant 'Dai' Davis on the *Campbeltown*. The men dealt with the tension in different ways. On ML 446 Sub-Lieutenant Hugh Arnold admitted that: 'We were all nervous. One of the sailors was "ill" and showing signs of strain. The first aid kits were pretty rudimentary, so I gave the man aspirin.' On *Campbeltown* the 23-year-old Lieutenant John Roderick and his men 'got into our positions on the starboard side lying on the deck between the protective steel plating specially fitted for us. Behind me I had Corporal Finch while about half way down the line came John Stutchbury bringing up his part of the Assault Party.' Roderick was relieved that at long last they were embarking on an operation, but he had no illusions about what he and his men were about to face. 'My main concern,' he recalled, with the honesty of a young man about to face combat for the first time, 'was that I hoped I would behave myself throughout the action and not through my inadequacy, let the party down.'

Elsewhere on *Campbeltown* Stuart Chant's men lay down on the deck feet first, so as to cushion the shock of eventual impact against the caisson. He observed that Bertie Burtinshaw remained cheerful, almost irrepressible, while Chris Smalley was quiet, alone with his thoughts. Lying on the deck, facing the sky, he breathed in a new 'exciting smell – a whiff of a country, France, a smell distinctive as garlic and Gauloise cigarettes'. Lance Sergeant Don Randall, also lying on the deck, looked upwards at one of the Oerlikon gunners on their 'bandstands', standing to their guns. He was suddenly struck by their professionalism and bravery. The sailors were not volunteers, but were in the same metaphorical boat as the commandos, who were. 'I could see one of them above and in front of my position, leaning on his harness, waiting, patient and disciplined, elevated, exposed and alone.'

On Kenneth Horlock's ML 443 (No. 13) Lance Corporal Joe Rogers of 5 Troop, No. 2 Commando, a member of Paul Bassett-Wilson's demolition team, collapsed with laughter when 'one of the sailors – Leading Seaman Patrick Brady – began putting on a football jersey, I think it was Newcastle United, and saying that he always wore this when he went into action. I remember laughing and feeling a lot better inside, and I have always remembered him as their Number 1 supporter.'

Some of the Fairmile commanders kept their men occupied. Lieutenant Thomas Boyd of ML 160 (No. 8), on the starboard bow of the *Campbeltown*, was one such. 'I had the deck petrol tanks emptied of the last dregs and filled with water, the hand tiller rigged and the medical gear all laid out in the wheelhouse. This kept all hands busy, which I thought to be a good thing.' On ML 177 (No. 6) at the rear of the starboard column Lieutenant Mark Rodier told Lieutenant Frank Arkle 'about making provision for letting his mother and father have his belongings back when we got back from St Nazaire'. Rodier was convinced that he was not going to get out alive.

With almost uncanny precision the first buoy was found by Dunstan Curtis on MGB 314 at 12.29 a.m., a minute before the time that Ryder's naval plan had stipulated. Shortly afterwards the site of the *Lancastria*'s lonely grave was passed on the left-hand side, its jagged steel superstructure just visible to those on the deck, including both Newman and Montgomery. Gun flashes and searchlight beams to the north-west had, for the previous 30 minutes, denoted the start of the RAF bombing raid on their targets over Saint-Nazaire, bright ghostly flickers lighting up the skies like distant fireworks, but at this distance without any accompanying noise. In the town itself men and women had wearily taken themselves down to their cellars and designated air-raid shelters on hearing the air-raid warnings begin to wail. It was an increasingly regular occurrence. The night before, some twenty-seven RAF bombers had attacked the docks, with indifferent results, and the loss of a Wellington.

Fifteen minutes later the fleet were passing over the Banc du Chatelier. Far to the left they could vaguely discern the northern shore at the Pointe de Chémoulin, where lay the enemy radar station. With luck, the radar would be pointed skywards to keep track of the air raid, and no attention would be going to the open sea to the south. Their luck held. The subsequent German report on the raid accepted the failure of their radar apparatus to pick up the enemy during its occasional sweeps over the seaward sector, because its primary focus was skywards.

To the right lay the still silent guns on the Pointe de Saint-Gildas on the southern shore. On board Stephens's ML 192 Micky Burn watched two white fringes emerge to the left and right out of the darkness ahead, rather like two low clouds: it was the surf on the two banks of the Loire Estuary. Gordon Holman observed the calm, professional atmosphere on the bridge of MGB 314, Dunstan Curtis steering into the misty blackness, while Ryder used the loudspeaker to convey his instructions, 'shepherding the force along at speed in one compact body'. Bill Green remained busy, diving 'in and out of the little chart room, first taking bearings and then making calculations. Even the mist could not disconcert him and we went steadily on until land was sighted on the port beam.'

But there was a disconcerting silence that appeared strange to those waiting for sight and sound of the diversionary attack on Saint-Nazaire by the RAF. While the noise of the aircraft in the skies above could be distinctly heard, silence largely reigned over the target. It appeared that no bombs were being dropped. No explosive effect could be seen or heard by those travelling up the Loire. Montgomery, for one, was surprised at this relative stillness, expecting to hear the aerial pulverisation of the docks during the run-in of the little fleet. Something had gone badly amiss. On ML 306 Private Bob Bishop of No. 1 Commando (a member of Ronnie Swayne's demolition team) looked skywards with concern. The raid wasn't developing as he had been told in the briefings. Where was the substantial bombing raid he and his mates had been told to expect? 'There was no mass of searchlights with their beams of light criss-crossing in the sky. None of the 88 mm and 40 mm guns were pouring streams of shells upwards.' Would they, he wondered, be aimed into the river instead?

At his bunker complex on the northern shore at Saint-Marc, Kapitän zur See Karl-Conrad Mecke wondered at the unusual conduct of the British planes:

As a rule the English attacked in strong squadrons in waves, but this time they flew only one or two planes at a time into the protected area. This made me suspect that something was wrong. When more and more single planes flew in up to 1 a.m. but only a few bombs were dropped, I think it was about four, I passed a message to all military posts: 'I do not understand the behaviour of the enemy; I suspect parachutists.'

To his own officers at about midnight, after the aircraft had been above them for thirty minutes, Mecke had declared, almost poetically: 'Some devilry is afoot.' He took the precaution of advising his outposts to also look out to sea, and within minutes his own observation post reported that there were several ships without lights in the Loire Estuary. Running into the bunker complex he grabbed hold of the tripod-mounted artillery binoculars in the post and swivelled them to watch the river. He saw at once what he later described as 'sixteen or seventeen ships . . . sailing up the Loire at a fairly rapid pace'. A call through to the duty officer in the harbour HQ confirmed that no German convoy was expected that night.

Unaware of the developing disaster in the air above him, nor of the fact that the flotilla had been spotted by Mecke, and focusing intently on his own task, Curtis found the next buoy (Le Vert) – conveniently lit with oil lamps – at 1.02 a.m. on the right-hand extremity of the Passe des Charpentiers and set a direct course for the next and final waypoint, over the dangerous shallows of the Banc des Morées, to the Les Morées Tower, which lay only one and a half miles from the harbour. Ryder ordered the flotilla to slow to 11 knots, to allow the *Campbeltown* the best chance of getting over the shallows – at higher speeds the destroyer's bows had a tendency to sink deeper into the water. Once this was reached in about twenty minutes' time the flotilla would have only a handful of minutes left to run on to its target. Ryder's plan was that the *Campbeltown* would embed itself in the outer caisson of the Normandie Dock at 1.30 a.m.

Curtis was struck by the 'sweet smell of the countryside as we steamed up the river. One could see both banks and make out hedges and trees on the port hand.' Ralph Batteson recalled how the temperature rose noticeably as they came closer to land and drew further away from the open sea. Curtis had been feeling frightened, but keeping busy during the run-in enabled him to stay calm. His crew, likewise, remained professional and confident, bandying jokes about as they ran in. 'This is a queer do,' Curtis said to his coxswain. 'It will soon be a bloody sight queerer, sir,' was his answer.*

To the rear of MGB 314 *Campbeltown* was making her way nervously over the shallows. Would she have the required clearance? On the destroyer Bob Montgomery's job was to act as the link between Sam Beattie and his commando passengers, a role that placed him on the bridge for much of the run-in. 'We suddenly began to slow down and we heard a lot of churning and we realised we'd hit the top of a sandbank,' he recalled. 'We looked at each other but luckily she cleared. If we'd got stuck we'd have been a sitting duck.' In fact the *Campbeltown* grounded twice, briefly, once at 12.45 a.m. and again ten minutes later, before her screws churned through the mud and propelled the vessel into deeper water. She was across! For Stuart Chant 'those few moments of shuddering and shaking aboard *Campbeltown* were the most dramatic of our whole approach until our actual arrival.'

On ML 446 Sergeant Robert Barron, a member of Captain Bertie Hodgson's assault party and newly transferred from Briault's broken-down ML 341, having raced along at 17 knots to catch up with the convoy just as *Sturgeon* began to make way (in fact, unknown to Barron, ML 446 very nearly collided with *Sturgeon* in the darkness as the latter was submerging), recalled that on entering the estuary the atmosphere was tense. 'It wasn't too dark as we sailed up the river. One could see the outlines of the shores. Everyone was ready for action.' In fact, unbeknownst to the raiders a darkened German patrol vessel was passed on the right flank, but the absence of radio on the ship meant that she was unable to signal any warning to shore. It was almost too good to be true.

A single faltering, suspicious searchlight on the northern bank had swept the estuary but fell to the rear of the flotilla, seeming

---

* This remark is attributed by Lucas Phillips to Tom Boyd, but by Peter Scott to Curtis. As Scott interviewed the survivors and published sooner after the event than Lucas Phillips, I have accepted his account.

to miss all of the British vessels, before being extinguished.* It appeared to be a routine search of the sea, and had not spotted anything untoward. Billie Stephens, leading the formation in MGB 314, watched the beam nervously, worrying that discovery appeared to be inevitable. To 'our indescribable relief and surprise', he later told Peter Scott, 'the light went out as suddenly as it had come on and we continued our approach in the darkness quite unhindered.' Another searchlight was briefly switched on and then off, from the Old Mole directly ahead, and illuminated MGB 314, but nothing came of it, while the flotilla continued into the enemy's lair at a steady speed of 15 knots. It looked likely that surprise would be total.

Almost immediately afterwards, however, the searchlights on the northern bank, from the No. 3 Heavy Coastal Battery, were switched on to illuminate the Passe des Charpentiers. The orders to do so came directly from Mecke, and were the signal for all the searchlights on both banks of the river to be lit up. According to Bill Copland's watch it was now 1.20 a.m., although Ryder recorded it as 1.22 a.m. From that moment the entire force was floodlit, but for what seemed like five minutes no fire was opened, the lights playing over the vessels.

The raiders now had only a handful of minutes left to run, during which time the Germans were attempting to confirm the vessel's identity and the British raiding force was attempting to persuade them that they were German. It took several minutes for the searchlight operators to find the *Campbeltown*, which Mecke knew at once was not a German ship. The large number of smaller vessels gave the game away, however, vindicating Hughes-Hallett's original argument that it would be easier to deceive the Germans with two destroyers than it would be with one destroyer and a host of smaller launches. From MGB 314's

---

* This was the 5-foot searchlight from Blue 1, next to Korvettenkapitän Thiessen's 703 Battalion HQ situated just behind Villès Martin.

bridge blinked the Aldis signal lamp, by Morse code in German, a series of quick signals. To the enquiring harbour defences Pike signalled in Morse the code 'EB' ('Wait'), while he told those on the northern shore at Villès-Martin that the force was 'proceeding up harbour in accordance with previous instructions' (two short flashes, made three times).

Part of the preparation for the raid had been to secure the latest German signalling codes, and the appointment of Signalman Seymour Pike, a fluent German-speaker, to flash the responses to the German defenders. He had spent his time on the journey out practising messages both from the International Signal Book and using a German codebook captured during the raid on Vaagso. In their report on the raid the Germans acknowledged that the 'use of the correct recognition signal by the enemy delayed, even though slightly, our defence measures'. From the bridge of ML 192 Billie Stephens 'saw a Morse lamp flickering from the MGB ahead of us with Commander Ryder on board . . . We waited in breathless suspense for the result.'

There was, as yet, no shooting. It seemed extraordinary that the raiding force had managed to infiltrate into the heart of one of the most heavily defended ports in enemy-occupied Europe, without being fired upon. The entire run-in was a piece of astonishing bluff, and it appeared to be working, spectacularly. Pike then had to rush to the right-hand side of the bridge to repeat the process with the signalling lamp to requests being made by the searchlight stations opposite Saint-Nazaire on the Pointe de Mindin. While he was doing this, however, Mecke ordered a gun to fire warning shots over the *Campbeltown*'s bows from the northern bank, the shells splashing in the water near to the MGB. Pike immediately responded with the signal code for 'a vessel considering itself to be fired-on by friendly forces'. A recognition cartridge was also fired by Curtis's crew in the hope of continuing the uncertainty for as long as possible. This clearly caused some consternation among the German gunners, and it delayed the impending onslaught for perhaps a minute, or slightly less.

Mecke was surprised to see that the signal fired was the current German identification signal: a green rocket that split up into three red stars. Ryder fired another one which fizzled out into the water: it had been designed to drop from an aircraft, not to be fired upwards from the ground. Mecke's confusion was further aroused by a message that then arrived from the harbour HQ duty officer (Kellermann was on leave that night) stating that the vessels were German. Looking through his glasses at the illuminated ships now fast approaching the harbour, Mecke did not believe him. Convinced by now that he was watching the first part of an enemy attack on the port he gave orders to the gun turret to fire 'vigorously' over the bow of the destroyer again.

SEVENTEEN

The Run-In

In the Old Town Monsieur Gordé, who was smoking a cigarette on his balcony in the Rue Thiers overlooking the Loire, was surprised to see a ship making for the harbour wall at speed, illuminated by searchlights. The time was 1.28 a.m. By now the ships had only a handful of minutes and perhaps a mile remaining before the *Campbeltown* would strike the caisson. The opening salvo from Mecke's guns initiated an exchange of fire of such intensity that it appeared to those on the British fleet that the gates of hell had opened. 'It is difficult to describe the full fury of the attack that was let loose on both sides,' Ryder remembered, 'the air became one mass of red and green tracer travelling in all directions, most of it going over.' Ralph Batteson described the noise as being akin to 'being trapped inside a massive dustbin crammed with fireworks at the instant someone tosses a match to ignite them'. The German hesitation about the identity of their visitors was now finally over, and the full fury of the defences in the narrows of the river was launched against the interlopers, at very close range.

The British gun crews had been instructed to open fire only when they had clearly identified their targets, to fire directly into the searchlights to disable them, and to fire at the base of the incoming tracer, which was always coloured blue-green (British tracer was orange-red). In addition, strict instructions had been given about only firing once *Campbeltown* had hoisted her White

Ensign, an action immediately copied by the Fairmiles. This meant that the first enemy fusillade actually received no immediate reply: after about a ten-second pause, however, during which the *Reichskriegsflagge* was rapidly replaced on *Campbeltown*'s mast, the massed guns of the little fleet replied almost in unison, propelling a storm of hot, vicious metal in the direction of their enemies.

In the town, amongst the men and women on duty to put out fires and rescue the wounded from the effects of a bombing raid which had strangely failed to materialise, confusion abounded. Monsieur Grimaud, the deputy mayor, later told Admiral Lepotier that, not knowing what was happening in the roadstead, he first thought that the Germans had lost their heads and were attacking the port themselves.

On the *Campbeltown* the start of the firing was the prompt for Sam Beattie to order full speed ahead, and for the bridge crew to move below to the armoured wheelhouse. On ML 192 Richard Collinson saw the funnel of the destroyer belch smoke as it began to accelerate.

Looking into the river, with the Avant Port rapidly looming to the forward left, a German guard ship was suddenly spotted anchored in the river to the right of the East Jetty, rapidly becoming visible in the tumult of light and fire. This *Sperrbrecher* (a converted merchant ship, the *Botilla Russ*, designed in this instance for anti-ship and anti-aircraft duties, and designated '137') was heavily armed, and placed specifically for the purpose of the close defence of the docks. She was, however, entirely unprepared for the British attack and, as it turned out, unfortunately sited, as she was soon mistaken by the German gun crews on the southern shore as an enemy vessel. As they approached, MGB 314's forward 2-pounder pom-pom, operated by Able Seaman Bill Savage, pumped twenty rounds into her, knocking her main gun (an 88 mm) out of action, and killing some of its gun crew. Slipping between the East Jetty and the anchored *Sperrbrecher* (now to her right) the guns on Curtis's MGB continued to fire, he recalled 'a lot more into her bridge'. Boyd's Fairmile followed closely after, nearly colliding with the darkened enemy vessel because he had been blinded by the light of the searchlights illuminating them from the Old Mole. 'I had to alter course violently to avoid hitting it and gave it a very good burst as we went by,' he told Scott after the battle.

To his left Stuart Irwin's ML 270 poured heavy fire into these searchlights and gun positions to the left of the caisson, reducing the intensity of the enemy fire perceptibly. Following immediately after came the *Campbeltown*, belching fire, which left the unfortunate *Sperrbrecher* a mass of flames. Bill Copland, lying on *Campbeltown*'s deck forward of the armoured bridge, was responsible during the run-in for coordinating fire from the 12-pounder gun and the two sets of 3-inch mortars positioned either side of the vessel commanded by Lieutenant John Proctor. At the outset of the firing he had shouted 'Let her go!' as an instruction to the crews to open fire:

> Almost before I had finished shouting, the first rounds had gone off from the 12-pounder and our mortars. Before the next round was fired by them I was deafened and thrown about by a terrific explosion which appeared to come almost from my feet. The smoke cleared and looking ahead I saw the mortars and crews intact but the 12-pounder crew had vanished and, directly in front of me, yawned a gaping, smoking hole about two-thirds the width of the deck.

Copland had been lucky not to have been killed or wounded by the same explosion.

On the bridge Beattie mistook the searchlight on the end of the East Jetty for the one he was expecting to see on the Old Mole, with the consequence that he had to take sharp avoiding action when the Old Mole loomed suddenly out of the darkness immediately ahead. On the deck of the *Campbeltown* the 23-year-old

Welshman Lieutenant John Roderick of the Essex Regiment and No. 2 Commando had struggled to contain his excitement during the run-in but was now fully occupied. 'One was filled with admiration for the gun crews who suffered severe casualties, I think. Lying behind them we were not entirely inactive as our Bren guns were fitted for this phase with large pans of ammunition which we fired out at as many possible targets as we could make out.'*

Collinson on ML 192 was awestruck by the sight of the *Campbeltown* engaging the enemy, 'her eight Oerlikons pouring out streams of orange tracer-shells towards the docks, which crisscrossed with the green enemy fire. She was surrounded by shell splashes; her own gun-flashes and the glare of shells bursting aboard her lit her upperworks vividly. Tracer shots ricocheted off her, sailing up into the air, in all directions.' Meanwhile, on board MGB 314 a mesmerised Gordon Holman, one of the two journalists accompanying the raid, described the effect of the German fire coming at them from both sides of the Loire as 'forming a strange Gothic archway of fire':

> The match had been set to the conflagration. In a second the whole river was covered with a fantastic criss-cross pattern of fire, marked by the varied coloured tracer shells and bullets. The roar and rattle of gunfire so filled the night that it was impossible to hear orders shouted only a yard or so from the bridges of the motor launches to the gunners on the deck below. Dozens of searchlights lit the scene, but accurate fire from the ships soon reduced the number.

On the same boat as Holman was the 26-year-old German-born Jew Peter Nagel (alias Private Peter Walker), an SOE operative who had only recently been on Lieutenant Colonel John Frost's successful raid to the German radar site at Bruneval in Normandy (Operation *Biting*). Born in Berlin to a Jewish father and Roman

---

* These were circular magazines holding 100 rounds. The normal gravity-fed Bren magazine held 20 rounds only.

Catholic mother, Peter had attended a Protestant school but, fearing the rising tide of anti-Semitism, the family had escaped from Germany, splitting up so as to deceive the German authorities. Peter's mother went to Paris with the children, pretending to go on holiday, while his father went on what he told the Nazis was a business trip to Leicester. They did not return. Peter thereafter made his way to England to join his father, who quickly set up a successful fabric business in Leicester.

Peter enlisted in the Army in March 1940. Speaking fluent German, French and English, he found himself in SOE a short while later. Successfully passing through No. 6 Special Training School at West Court, Finchampstead on 14 August 1941, he was then posted to No. 2 Commando. He is mistakenly described in some accounts as a Sudeten German. Mountbatten (who had personally interviewed Nagel for the Bruneval raid) insisted that he be deployed on Operation *Chariot*. Now, on the receiving end of the Loire defences, he was shocked at the intensity of the firing. He had never seen anything like it:

> The tracer bullets crossed over one another, forming a giant firework display. The enemy anti-aircraft guns installed on the roofs, fired down upon us at point blank range. My gunner [Private Francis Kelly] fired without stopping at the enemy searchlights that were sweeping the waters of the port. The firing was so intense that nobody knew exactly what was going on. Several of our launches were hit and as they were made only of wood and filled to the brim with petrol, they exploded.

Many accounts speak of a Guy Fawkes-type effect that would have been spectacular were it not for the violence and death that accompanied it. Lance Sergeant Don Randall described it as a sort of 'satanic son et lumière', while Hugh Arnold recalled that the battle was unreal:

It was the only time in my experience of the war that the reality approached the fiction that you see on television . . . The enemy had an enormous advantage. We couldn't really see anything. The searchlights blinded us. All we could do was to fire at the searchlights. I saw a ship blow up. I thought it was the *Campbeltown*, and from that moment on I thought that the operation had failed. It was, in fact, one of the MLs.

MGB 314 passed the Old Mole and then veered off to the right in a wide arc, before beginning the turn through 270 degrees to prepare to land at the Old Entrance, leaving the *Campbeltown* to hurtle through the blinding glare of the searchlights onto her objective, spitting fire all the while at each and every target she could engage. After quickly avoiding the Old Mole, Sam Beattie brought the destroyer, a type that was not known for its responsiveness, quickly back on to a track that would take it directly into the Normandie Dock's outer caisson.

In the midst of the noise of the firing a worried Newman suddenly realised that there was no sign of the air raid. What on earth had happened to all the bombers they had been promised, and indeed had heard in the sky above them earlier? He was not to learn until after the war that by 12.35 a.m. all the aircraft had departed for home, after only 65 minutes in the air above the target, most not having found an opportunity to drop their bombs. The thirty-five Wellingtons and twenty-seven Whitleys that eventually got into the air for the raid found that, above the docks, almost comprehensive cloud cover meant that they could not make visual contact with Saint-Nazaire. Flying above 6,000 feet the presence of cloud meant that the bombing raid was abortive. Not willing to abandon the mission entirely and return home, but at the same time unaware of the drama unfolding below them, the aircraft conducted repeated high-level runs over the target area, sometimes diving low to try to break through the cloud so as to identify targets. Unfortunately it was this behaviour, recognised by the

Germans to be unusual in bomber aircraft (staying above a target area, but not dropping bombs), that gave the game away.

Both Fred Willetts and John Hughes-Hallett had arranged to fly in one of the bombers, they alone of all the crews knowing the true importance of the diversionary raid because for reasons of security the crews had not been briefed on the role they were to play in the raid. Willetts's subsequent report suggested:

> Had there been an instruction that if visibility were bad aircraft could bomb on estimated positions the above unfortunate results might, to some extent, have been mitigated, since the target area itself was disclosed by the flash of flak through the clouds.

Willetts concluded that 'an important omission from the plan was the action necessary should aircraft be despatched from this country which, on arrival, found conditions over the target such that aimed bombing could not be done.' The German report on the raid, however, blamed part of the slowness of the German response on the fact that the British succeeded 'in covering the sound of his ship's engines by the propeller noise of low-flying aircraft'. There is some truth in this, as the Fairmile's petrol engines produced a roar that was audible over 3 miles away. After the war Stuart Chant records how Newman was invited to dinner at Chartwell, where Churchill apologised for the lack of air cover because of his concern to avoid collateral damage on French civilian targets. Time would lessen the Prime Minister's sensibilities about causing innocent casualties on the ground. 'I'm sorry about Saint-Nazaire,' he is reported to have said, 'and leaving you alone with no air support; six months later I wouldn't have bothered.'

On the river, Micky Burn on ML 192 watched the *Campbeltown*, just ahead, looking as though she were 'flood lit for a naval review. The troops were lying down at their action stations. I could see the shells all over the place bouncing off every part of the old destroyer. I don't know how she wasn't sunk or crippled.

Everything in the harbour was focused on her.' On the destroyer Roderick, lying with his men, described the racket above their heads of 'one of the Oerlikon Platforms and it was the noise from these and the stuff coming towards them that at one moment made me reach out behind me to find whether Corporal Finch was still in position following a particularly dirty explosion.' Lance Corporal Frank Sumner, who had been targeting searchlights with his Bren gun, had the gun knocked out of his grip by a projectile that left a large, jagged hole in the inner plating. Unhurt but momentarily dazed, he righted his gun and went on firing.

Stuart Chant estimated that three-quarters of all men on deck were injured in some way. He described the moment of his own wounding:

Then there was another explosion and a large report rather like the noise of someone banging a steel door with a sledgehammer. It was caused by a shell which burst alongside me and as I lay there dazed and deafened I wondered what had happened to me. Then suddenly I realised that Sergeant ['Dai'] Davis of No 3 Commando [a member of Lieutenant 'Bung' Denison's protection team] lying just ahead of me had been hit, for his immediate reaction was to try and struggle to his feet, but I kept him still by wrapping my legs round his shoulders. It was then that I realised that my left leg was wet and sticky and my right arm was spurting blood down into my hand. I, too, had been hit, but by some twist of fate there was no pain – just discomfort . . .

I then realised that my hands, which had been shading my tin hat over my eyes, were also covered in blood, but again there was no pain, only a new-found stiffness in my fingers and numerous pinpricks in my face. I didn't realise it then but I was literally peppered with minute pieces of shell all down the front and left side of my body from my face to my legs, but when I wiped the blood off my face there was little or nothing to show what had happened. I began to feel myself all over looking for further damage, but fortunately I still seemed to be intact and mobile.

Newman, standing next to Ryder on MGB 314, completing its arc and preparing to run in to the Old Entrance, observed that the destroyer's 'sides seemed to be alive with bursting shells'. Kenneth Horlock on ML 443 thought that it looked as though it were 'taking part in a pre-war Aldershot Tattoo.' Bill Copland recorded: 'How we got through the next thirteen minutes with anyone left alive, will always pass my understanding.' Tom Boyd's ML 160 was stationed just to the rear right of MGB 314 and slightly ahead of *Campbeltown* (which was to Boyd's rear left) during the run-in. He watched proudly as the destroyer, illuminated by the glare of the searchlights, struck the caisson, commenting that the 'weight of fire caught one's breath'.

On the *Campbeltown* Montgomery recorded that the armoured wheelhouse was hit repeatedly from the outset of the firing. German fire was accurate and intense. The coxswain (Chief Petty Officer Albert Wellsted) at the wheel was quickly killed, the quartermaster taking the wheel before he too was hit and fell away. Seemingly next in line, Montgomery grabbed the wheel himself but, desperately unsure of what to do, was pleased to find more experienced hands, those of Nigel Tibbits, calmly taking the wheel from him. Watching for the moment when MGB 314 ahead of him would turn hard to the right, denoting the point at which he was to turn slightly to the left and make straight for the caisson, Beattie was momentarily blinded by the explosion that destroyed his forward 12-pounder gun, killed all its crew and most of the commando 3-inch mortar men (narrowly missing Copland), leaving the 12-pounder intact but a gaping, smoking hole in the fo'c'sle. Then the moment came and, after nudging the wheel to the left, through the gloom ahead Beattie saw his point of aim, which he described as 'an indistinct black line' in the harbour wall.

Beattie ordered full speed ahead and *Campbeltown* turned onto a line that led straight to the caisson. She struck it moments later at a speed of 19 knots with what Ryder described, from his vantage point ahead on MGB 314, as 'a deep grinding crash'. 'When she hit we saw a burst of flame on her fo'c'sle which seemed to die away after a minute or two, and we could only see her Oerlikons firing hard.' At the time Ryder never gave expression to his fears, but in a radio broadcast in 1946 he admitted that he 'had never really expected that this part of the job would be pulled off, as I thought it was too difficult, but above the din of the battle there was a crash, and there she was.' Extraordinarily the time was 1.34 a.m., only four minutes later than planned. Beattie looked at his watch and in the suddenly still vessel said to Montgomery: 'Well, there we are. Four minutes late!'

'The *Campbeltown* looked glorious as she tore through the smoke and bursting shells and dashed straight into the lock gates with a crash which could just be heard above the terrific gunfire,' Boyd recorded. On the destroyer the shock of impact had thrown Montgomery back against the rear of the bridge, although for the commandos lying on their stomachs on the deck, protected from the worst of the incoming fire by their flimsy metal barriers, the impact was hardly felt at all: Chant recalled a 'slight shudder of the ship and a moment later we came to an abrupt stop'.

In the engine-room Chief Engine-Room Artificer Harry Howard felt nothing at all, only realising that the vessel had stopped when the lights went out. Below decks Corran Purdon and Gerard Brett had heard the hammering and explosions of German shells and bullets striking *Campbeltown*'s hull. 'A shell, glowing red, passed through the Wardroom as we sat there, but continued out without exploding. The intensity of noise increased as *Campbeltown* neared the dry dock. Then came a bump as we hit and passed through the boom, followed by a long shuddering impact as we struck the gate. We had arrived!'

Beattie's feat was all the more amazing given the difficulty of spotting the caisson at all. At the best of times, and in daylight, even today, it simply looks to be part of the harbour wall. To see it, aim for and hit it at night and under intense fire, despite the illumination provided by the searchlights based on the eastern side of the river, was nothing less than extraordinary.

Gordon Holman on MGB 314 also saw *Campbeltown* strike. 'In the face of intense and accurate fire, some at less than five hundred yards range, she steadily gathered speed and crashed fair and square on to the massive dock gate, brushing aside the boom defence as she went. It was an unforgettable sight.' The *Campbeltown* had ridden up onto the caisson on impact – perhaps an angle of 20 degrees – a long section of the bow being ripped back like a tin can, leaving the top of the vessel sitting on top of the caisson (one foot projecting into the dock itself), while 36 feet of hull had buckled back, within a few feet of the point where Nigel Tibbits had judged it would do, and where he had placed his three tons of amatol.

EIGHTEEN

Ordeal in the River

All the while Boyd's guns were engaging and silencing the enemy gun positions on the right-hand side of the *Campbeltown*, and Irwin's ML 270 was dealing with those on the left. Suddenly everything seemed to be happening at once. The noise was phenomenal. On MGB 314 Curtis found himself shouting 'at the top of his lungs the whole time . . .' Boyd looked behind and to the left of him, and saw that the Fairmiles were already being hit by accurate gunfire from both north and south banks, as well as from the dock area.

Some of the little ships were already engulfed in flames. The first to be hit was Billie Stephens's ML 192, the leading Fairmile of the starboard column, which received a devastating shell strike in her engine-room, amongst other damage. She bounced off the Old Mole and was soon ablaze from end to end. On ML 446 Sergeant Robert Barron wondered at the 'fantastic amount of fire and noise, the coloured tracer: it was like a firework display'. Armed with one of the puny Boys anti-tank rifles he carefully fired at the searchlights, and believed that he put one out of action. All the while his vessel was receiving accurate fire from the shore, with a direct hit on the funnel area behind him, wounding him in the foot and leg. On Tom Collier's ML 457 'Tiger' Watson stationed himself beside the Fairmile's funnel with a Bren gun and spare magazines loaded with tracer bullets:

I heard Tom Collier's klaxon giving the order to his bow and stern Oerlikons to open fire, and standing with the Bren gun held at the hip I directed a stream of tracer at the nearest search-light. When by 'hose-piping' the Bren, my tracers were almost on the light, it was hastily switched off. But no sooner had I selected another than the first one would switch on again. It was frustrating. It must have been the unexpectedly intense volume of return fire from our small force which helped to disconcert the German gunners for a few moments, but not for long. We were being hit repeatedly. The ML staggered a little at each impact but kept going.

As Dunstan Curtis was taking his gunboat into the Old Entrance his passengers had a clear view back down the Loire. It was already painfully obvious that many of the wooden Fairmiles were having a difficult time in the face of fierce German fire. Indeed, they could see the first vessel of the port column, Thomas Platt's ML 447 (No. 9), come under a withering assault from the German bunker on the Old Mole. It caught fire at once, and foundered ten feet off the slipway. Many of Captain David Birney's fourteen men, responsible for securing the Old Mole, were killed, although Lieutenant Bill Clibborn and WO2 (TSM) Bert Hewitt managed somehow to get ashore.

Returning downstream after attacking their own targets, Boyd's ML 160 (No. 8) was able to come alongside and rescue those as yet unwounded, including the Frenchman Raymond Couraud ('Lieutenant Jack Lee'), but thereafter most stricken vessels had to be left to their own devices. Boyd recalled Platt's Fairmile when he came alongside to be 'smoking like hell with a red glow coming from the engine room'. Platt had the mournful task of carefully checking the bodies of the dead to ensure that no more could be saved before making good his own escape onto Boyd's vessel. Boyd later commended Petty Officer Leonard Lamb, the coxswain, who helped to carry people off Collier's blazing Fairmile 'and tended ten or eleven wounded. He undoubtedly saved the lives of two of the men.'

Three men were pulled from the water. David Birney also found himself in the water. On ML 307, itself trying to find a way to land, Captain David Paton managed to haul a sodden soldier from the water, now licking with flames, and then heard a voice calling his name. It was Birney, 'a very dear friend. We managed to lock our hands but then the boat's propellers gave a great surge in reverse and our hands were torn apart because of the oily water.' A few minutes later Platt's Fairmile blew up in a bright, savage fireball that lit up the river, and ignited petrol on the surface of the river. Tragically, David Birney was left to drown, his body washed ashore near Escoublac the following day.

On ML 306 Ralph Batteson, as Lieutenant Ian Henderson manoeuvred the vessel towards its designated landing on the Old Mole, was shocked by what he saw:

Coming astern into our line of approach as we neared the jetty was a blazing motor launch. Flames blasted skywards, and I heard the crackle of burning mahogany from her decks. Worse still, I could smell the pungent reek of petrol, which poured from the damaged extra fuel tank, spilling into the water. The launch drifted in a mass of flames, and came to rest at the wall of the jetty, blocking us off from our landing point.

Lieutenant Henderson moved us clear, and aimed for another part of the jetty further on. To our horror, a second motor launch appeared, drifting like a heating fireball on the far side of ML 306. We were in danger of being trapped between the two blazing wrecks. As if this were not enough, the petrol tank of the second launch had exploded, and the flames were actually spreading in the water around us. The force of the heat on our faces and bodies was almost unbearable. Bodies floated in this watery bed of fire, horribly mutilated by the explosions or the flames. I saw men burn alive in the petrol that covered the surface, while others sank in bloody foam as they succumbed to their wounds. With the screams of the dying ringing above the noise of gunfire, and the fierce glare of the flames lighting up the harbour, it was a scene from the worst of nightmares. What made it different was that we ourselves were inside the nightmare, and in imminent danger of being set on fire by the blazing launches on either side.

What horrified Sub-Lieutenant Philip Dark, also on ML 306, was the sight of men jumping off this stricken Fairmile into the water, and having to refuse the entreaties of her skipper to stop and help them: Henderson was determined to get his commandos, commanded by Lieutenant Ronnie Swayne, ashore.

All the while the small vessels in the Loire fought back valiantly against the incoming storm. Once the firing had begun at 1.28 a.m. Ralph Batteson, strapped into his Oerlikon mount on ML 306, fired continuously against targets given to him by Sub-Lieutenant Pat Landy RANVR, many of which were searchlights, gun positions on shore and the *Sperrbrecher*. Likewise, Swayne's commandos were firing at any target within range. But as they drew near the Old Mole, it was apparent that because of the burning craft blocking their route this landing would not be possible. 'We circled around trying to get alongside, but to no avail,' Batteson recalled. 'It was decided finally that we would have to withdraw without putting the commandos ashore.'

One of the blazing vessels encountered by ML 306 was Platt's ML 447 and another was ML 192, the full story of whose dramatic demise was provided after his escape from German captivity by Lieutenant Commander 'Billie' Stephens':

All went well until we were almost abeam of the Old Mole and within two hundred yards of our objective. We had been hit a number of times, but were still quite seaworthy, and whilst we had some wounded, they were none of them serious. Then our luck turned and they got us twice at point-blank range with something very large, probably about 4-inch; the results were sudden and disastrous; both engines and the steering went and the boat was swung hard-a-port by the impact of the shells hitting her. By chance, however, we managed to come more or less alongside the Old Mole allowing a few of the commandos to climb up the wall and get ashore. My signalman also managed to get ashore, the idea being that we should put a line across to him and make fast. Unfortunately he was killed before he could do this and the boat, having hit the wall of the Mole very hard, immediately rebounded some 15 feet and we were left with neither engines nor steering and all the while being subjected to point-blank fire from a 20 mm gun ashore. The damage was simply frightful, there was virtually no engine room left and some incendiaries must have hit our tanks, because we were blazing fiercely in the petrol compartment.

I then decided that as there was no possibility of saving the boat, the best course to adopt was to abandon ship and get ashore in order to join up with our own forces who should by this time, have landed a little further up the river. We got everyone into the water all right, including our wounded, but owing to the number of soldiers we still had on board there wasn't room for everybody on the Carley floats and consequently some of us had to swim ashore. I shall always remember those last moments on board. There was practically no firing at us by this time, it being only too obvious to the enemy that we had already 'had it', and they were concentrating on other targets. I stood right up in the bows and whilst getting out my flask to have a last 'quick one' I looked around me. The scene was indescribable. We were burning furiously as were two other boats astern of us a little further out in the river; it was a very sad sight. Tracer was still flying in all directions and the whole scene was brilliantly illuminated by searchlights. After a very long pull at my flask (little did I realise when I would next taste whisky) I slid over the bows on a line and into the water and my God! it was cold! I started to swim at first quite slowly and casually because it was only sixty or seventy yards to the shore, then harder as I suddenly realised the current was carrying me fast downstream and away from the only possible landing place. I kicked off my flying boots – something I was to regret bitterly later – and swam as I've never swum before. I had to fight to stop myself panicking. Slowly I began to make headway, time seemed interminable, but I suppose I had only been in the water seven or eight minutes when I reached a small slipway and having arrived at it I just lay there half in and half out of the water and quite exhausted. At that moment I didn't really care much what happened to me; however, someone, I think it was my First Lieutenant, pulled me clear and after a minute or two I became more or less normal. We found that only one of our party had not made the shore. Really remarkable considering how strong the current was there.

Just as ML 192 was coming alongside Micky Burn 'felt the whole ship shudder. The tanks were hit, she was ablaze and adrift and her steering had gone, although I didn't know it at the time.' Stephens shouted to him to jump, which he did, swimming to shore and being pulled to safety and saved from drowning by the wounded Lance Corporal Arthur Young of the Gordon Highlanders. Burn was shocked to see the lifeless body of his friend Tom Peyton floating in the water. Only five of the fourteen commandos on the vessel survived. James Laurie, the leading telegraphist, managed to get out of the wheelhouse after freeing the jammed door and destroying some equipment before helping a non-swimmer into the water. It was just like going into a cold bath, he recalled, although of course 'we weren't concerned by the temperature of the water but by the heat of the action taking place. Tracer bullets everywhere, guns booming, shouting all over the place and a real pandemonium.' Miraculously, he considered, he was only one of a handful to escape the blazing wreck unwounded. Lieutenant Tom Collier managed to bring his Fairmile (ML

457) alongside the Old Mole, and deposit his commandos, including Bill Pritchard, Lieutenant Philip Walton, Lieutenant 'Tiger'
Watson, and Sergeants Alf Searson and the German-born Dick
Bradley. As they were landing Watson was 'aware of the awful
screams from another ML which was burning furiously to starboard'. However, it was here that an error was made which was
to have disastrous consequences for the rest of the Fairmiles trying
to dock against the Old Mole. As they were about to land Watson
could see a number of Germans, wearing their distinctive coal-
scuttle helmets, running away from the heavily built pillbox on
the landward end of the Old Mole, with their hands in the air.
On clambering from the Fairmile onto the Old Mole he ran to
inspect the pillbox to ensure that it was empty:

> It must have been quite recently built as there was a strong smell
> of fresh cement. There was also a ladder leaning against it. Now
> my orders were to ensure that the Mole was free of enemy and,
> if nobody else succeeded in landing there, to hold it against all
> comers. This was vital as it was from this spot that the whole
> landing force would re-embark. The whole area seemed deserted.
> Presumably the assault parties had swept on ahead but I had to
> be sure that the Mole was clear of enemy. I climbed the ladder
> to an embrasure. As there was no sound of movement inside, I
> fired a couple of short tommy gun bursts to discourage any
> Germans lurking there. I heard a shout from Bill Pritchard below.
> He sounded exasperated. 'What the hell are you up to, Tiger? For
> God's sake get on!' I was now convinced, as presumably Bill was,
> that the Mole was already in our hands.

Unhappily, this was not so. German soldiers either still occupied
it or managed to get back into it during the confusion of battle.
The pillbox soon began firing again at the highly vulnerable Fairmiles in the river, causing massive devastation. Some of the
immediate victims were the crew of the Fairmile that Watson had

just left. The vessel became the target of enemy soldiers on the Old Mole whom Watson had not seen, who began throwing hand grenades at the vessel, one of which fell into the open bridge, with horrific effect. The explosion took off one of Tom Collier's legs, scooped out a sailor's stomach and killed a third man. One of the sub-lieutenants had already been killed on the fo'c'sle, where the two men manning the gun were also both dead, so the badly wounded Collier gave orders to push off. As they were doing so, however, the ship became the target of heavy firing that set it alight, so Collier, growing very weak, ordered 'Abandon ship'. Able Seaman Herbert Dyer described what followed:

We threw a Carley raft over the side – four got on it. The skipper came on, the young man with his stomach wound, the signalman and myself – we were unhurt. The tide was taking us out. It was similar to the Thames Estuary – it was a wicked tide. We went by a boat that was sunk, with its mast sticking up, and we caught hold of this to hang on there, and tied a rope to it. The skipper wasn't very good – he must have been dying – you could see him change colour. He just let go and went under. The signalman wasn't hurt, but he just said 'cheerio' – he said he couldn't hang on and he went under. In the meantime, the tide was going out, and the rope went too high and was tipping the boy into the water, so we cut it and let it go. We were stuck there until the morning when the Germans picked us up.

As Collier's vessel was burning Burt's ML 262 came alongside and attempted to help, but both craft became casualties of devastating enemy fire. On ML 307, commanded by the Australian, Lieutenant Norman Wallis RANVR, David Paton told the story of their attempt to land: 'We approached the east side of the Mole but as we pulled up beside it we crunched into something submerged.' Stuck fast, it appeared as if the vessel would founder as it was in the direct line of fire from the Old Mole:

Meantime it was all too obvious that the Huns were still on the Mole. We pushed our ladders up against the Mole but anyone who tried to climb up fell off for the ladders were pushed out from above. Now bombs began to be rolled over on to our decks and we were all dancing about kicking them into the water. I turned round to see what was going on behind and saw a Captain of the Inniskilling Fusiliers [Bill Bradley] falling off someone's shoulders. He had been trying to get a Bren Gun up to fire over the angle of the Mole by standing on a soldier's shoulders. He assured me that he had killed a man but the recoil made him fall to the deck.

Meantime the skipper judged that we were not going to manage there and reversed out and tried to get along the other side of the Mole, but the boat ahead of us was now burning fiercely, all lit up like a film river boat. As he hesitated there I saw a German soldier climb up to the Bofors type gun on what was supposed to be my medical post* and load that gun I had warned about with a clip of four large shells. He was all alone but he managed to direct the gun by using two lots of wheels, one for aim and the other for elevation. Then I noticed my Red Cross armband shining white and fluorescent in the searchlights. So I took it off and stuffed it in my blouse. Then my gunner fired his clip, he was only about 25 yards away. The first shot fell into the water only ten yards away, the next was five yards away. I didn't know then what happened to the third but the fourth produced a draught as it shot by me and splashed into the water only ten yards on the seaward side of our boat . . .

And now my medical sergeant came up to me and said 'Do you know, sir, we have wounded below.' I lost my cool and said that we shouldn't be worrying about that but should be on land and in that blockhouse which was firing at us. I looked to

---

* Paton had been instructed to place his medical post in the pillbox on the landward side of the Old Mole. He was assured that it would be empty of enemy by the time he arrived.

see what the skipper was doing but he seemed to be busy enough so I went below to deal with the wounded there. Happily the lights still worked and I was able to check that none needed immediate care. As I had dressed my first casualty I was rising to go to the next when the boat gave a great lurch and I was thrown off balance kicking the poor casualty on the head.

The lurch was Wallis managing to free his vessel from the underwater obstruction. It was clear that a landing was now impossible to achieve given the slaughter in the water around him, so Wallis took his vessel, remarkably still functioning, across the estuary and engaged the batteries on the southern shore, shooting up the *Sperrbrecher* as he passed, and joining up with Boyd's Fairmile.

The next vessel to approach behind Wallis in the port column was Ken Horlock's ML 443, who misjudged his location and overshot the Old Mole. On the bridge with him was Lieutenant Reginald Verity RNVR, the naval beach master. Both men looked at each other and laughed when they realised what had happened: 'it seemed extraordinary that we had got through all that heavy fire and then missed the place,' Horlock recalled. Returning to the Old Mole the Fairmile engaged the German gun positions, of which there were two, producing heavy and relentless fire into the river, although they could not get close to the slipway because it was blocked by a burning Fairmile. 'I opened fire on the two gun positions on the Mole,' said Horlock:

The Hun was going very strong. I saw no signs of life on the burning ML which had prevented me from getting alongside, and there were no MLs alongside the Mole where they ought to have been. My gunfire seemed to be making no impression, and I thought that the German gun positions were probably protected by pillboxes. Lieutenant Eric Shields was in charge of my forward gun and, try as we would, we could not quench the enemy's fire.

It was then that I realised that this part of the operation was a flop.

Ian Henderson's ML 306 and Henry Falconer's ML 446 also failed to get near the Old Mole. Falconer's Oerlikon had received a direct hit, the forward and both twin Lewis guns had jammed, Bertie Hodgson had been killed, the second-in-command seriously wounded and both sergeants were out of action. In the circumstances he decided that it was useless to attempt a landing and proceeded to make his way out of the estuary.

On Falconer's Fairmile Lance Corporal Jack Webb found that keeping himself busy with the wounded took his mind off the horror all around him, a trick he had learned at Vaagso. Lieutenant Neil Oughtred had been badly injured in the neck: it was Webb's colleague Tom Everitt who, going to Oughtred's aid, saved his life. Webb had been sent to administer aid to 'Bertie' Hodgson, but discovered that he had been killed at once by at least twelve machinegun bullets, the result of the first sweep of the enemy's guns across the river.

Of the six Fairmiles of Group 1 only Tom Collier had been able to land his commandos, and the Old Mole – crucial not only as a landing point but also the location for the withdrawal – remained very firmly in enemy hands. It would do so throughout the battle. In retrospect Ryder regretted that the plans had not been flexible enough to allow the Fairmiles to deposit their troops at a safe location if it was discovered that the Old Mole was insecure, rather than attempt repeatedly to land, with the appalling consequences that followed this brave but bloody persistence by the courageous Fairmile commanders.

As MGB 314 turned in its wide arc, straightening up for the Old Entrance, the vessel presented its left-hand side to *Sperrbrecher* 137, moored just off the Old Mole, still firing steadily despite the battering it had already received.* Fearful of the damage it might

---

* The *Botilla Russ* survived the night, suffering two dead and eight wounded, and received 123 cannon strikes.

do if it remained unchecked, Ryder began to make plans for one of the torpedo-armed Fairmiles to attack it. Newman forcefully urged him to ignore it, and land his team ashore first. After what Newman described as a 'hasty argument' he won the day, and Curtis took his Fairmile into a landing, the first to do so, at the south quay of the Old Entrance.

Newman could clearly hear above the din of the heavy guns, the distinct rattle of tommy- and Bren-gun fire so he knew his 'boys were busy on land . . . A handshake with Ryder and we were soon over the side and on French soil!' Curtis then proceeded to tie up alongside Mark Rodier's ML 177. Gordon Holman wrote of the moment Newman jumped ashore, eager for the fray:

> It was a happy, cheerful man who dashed ashore from the motor gunboat accompanied only by his adjutant and two or three Commandos. He waved goodbye to our shouts of 'Good luck!' and I can hear now the confidence in his voice when he said to me during a particularly intensive enemy bombardment just before he landed, 'Don't worry about that, my fellows will get at them in a minute.'

Almost immediately afterwards a tremendous explosion, probably the nearby winding house, brought a good deal of debris raining down on the crew. 'As we crouched to avoid the pattering rain of debris we decided that one more objective had been well and truly accounted for.'

After the leading launch of the starboard column (ML 192) had been disabled off the Old Mole the two following Fairmiles (MLs 262 and 267) overshot the Old Mole entirely, while the fourth, commanded by Bill Tillie (ML 268), who had served happily alongside Ryder in a previous command, received the full brunt of German fire when trying to find a place to land, and blew up in a devastating fireball. Although Tillie and some of his crew managed to escape, only two of the heavily laden commandos did so. All others, including Lieutenants Harry Pennington and Morgan Jenkins, and the Glaswegian Lance Sergeant Bill Gibson, who seemed to have had a premonition of his death, died in the horrifying conflagration.

Meanwhile ML 156 (No. 5), under the command of the well-known British-born American actor, film producer and part-time sailor Lieutenant Leslie Fenton RNVR, was badly hit when abreast of the Old Mole. From his hospital bed he recounted how a shell 'transferred part of the bridge and some shrapnel into my left leg and the leg of Captain [Richard] Hooper, the Commando officer who was on the bridge with me.' The sea ahead and to the side of him seemed to be full of burning and out-of-control Fairmiles. Before he passed out he handed over command to Sub-Lieutenant Noel Machin, a moment before the vessel came under heavy fire from both banks of the river, and from the *Sperrbrecher*. Trying to turn and launch its torpedoes at the *Sperrbrecher* the Fairmile was hit in the engine room and lost power. Machin was himself wounded, but the starboard engine was restarted and at about 2.40 a.m., with the help of a smoke float thrown behind them to distract the German gunners, they started their slow and erratic escape downriver. Only the last in line, Mark Rodier in ML 177, would successfully land his troops.

NINETEEN

The Demolitions

When *Campbeltown* struck the outer caisson of the Normandie Dock at precisely 1.34 a.m., the surviving commandos from the seventy-nine who had embarked gathered their wits with remarkable alacrity and began to make their way forward. Only now could they take stock of the casualties suffered during the run-in. Few men remained unwounded. The man lying next to Sergeant Dai Davis had been killed, and he had himself been wounded, as Stuart Chant has observed, in the feet and arm. His Bren gunner had been wounded in the neck, which meant that as they scrambled down scaling ladders from the fo'c'sle Davis had to carry his spare yoke of magazines.

It was Bill Copland's especial responsibility to ensure a successful exit from the now stricken and smoking vessel. Picking himself up from the deck, immediately above the cache of explosives, and avoiding the hole in front of him caused by the shell that had killed the 12-pounder gun crew, through which a fire could clearly be seen burning, Copland dashed back through the steeply angled ship, stepping over the dead and dying, to bring forward the parties as they had rehearsed. Then it was back to the fo'c'sle to order 'Roderick off – Roy off' followed shortly afterwards by 'Denison off – Hopwood off'. Corran Purdon was impressed by the sight of the second-in-command, standing erect, with his rifle slung over his shoulder, shouting to each party as it presented itself 'Off you go!' just as if it had been a training exercise.

Bamboo ladders had been provided to aid disembarkation, but the men now discovered that many had been smashed. Lieutenant Christopher Gough RN, armed with a single iron-runged ladder, went over the left-hand side first with Nigel Tibbits. On first hitting the lock gate Tibbits had quickly gone below with Sam Beattie to check that the fuses had not been unsettled by the impact. On the deck of the caisson both men held the ladder in place for the men who followed.

With the barrage hurtling about their ears (but surprisingly and fortunately mostly aimed high and flying over the vessel, rather than sweeping the exposed decks), men threw themselves off as best they could. 'The noise was indescribable,' Purdon recalled, 'and tracer was everywhere, crossing the ship and coming towards us in seemingly slow coloured arcs of whites, yellows, blues, reds and greens, which suddenly whipped past on nearing us.' Lance Sergeant Don Randall glanced half-left to the massive pump house only a hundred yards away, to see one of the anti-aircraft guns firing at the ship at almost point-blank range.

When *Campbeltown* had shuddered to a sudden stop, John Roderick 'went quickly forward to reconnoitre the way off the ship; it was a bit of a shambles with many wounded chaps lying about the deck. Flames met me in opening the Forward Companion way door and I had to shut it quickly. On trying again shortly afterwards they had died down.' The quiet, soft-spoken Corporal Donaldson, 'with a charming smile' as Roderick recalled him, had been wounded during the run-in, and his bamboo ladder broken by shell splinters.

Corporal 'Buster' Woodiwiss of No. 2 Commando, part of Roderick's assault team, was the first man ashore, with his comrades close behind. Because the *Campbeltown* had ridden up onto the caisson Woodiwiss found that his assault ladder was too short, so he ended up simply jumping off. Many others were forced to do the same. Roderick found himself shimmying down a length of cable. Their immediate target was the three sets of guns firing onto the ship from the right-hand side of the dock. Without pausing for breath Woodiwiss raced towards his target, a sand-bagged gun emplacement. Kicking aside a German hand grenade on the way, he killed the sentries with his Thompson sub-machine-gun before getting on to the gun position and doing the same, singlehandedly, to the gunners. He then destroyed the gun with some pre-prepared plastic explosive before returning to join the rest of Roderick's team who had run past, Lance Sergeant Arnold ('Arnie') Howarth sustaining shrapnel wounds in his back on the way.

After clearing the second gun position – a concrete bunker with a 37 mm gun on its roof – and killing the fleeing crew, they then swept forward into the vast area of warehouses and oil storage tanks, sharing fire and movement with Lieutenant John Stutch-bury's team, killing a number of Germans in buildings with their Thompsons and grenades. They had a large amount of ground to cover, with a substantially reduced number of men to do it. The wounded, such as Arnie Howarth and Private Harold Simpson, were sent back to the casualty collection point at the bridge at Point G.

Campbeltown emptied quickly, the men eager for the fray, as well as to escape the smoking metal coffin in which they had travelled all those agonising minutes through the furious barrage of enemy shot and shell. Captain Donald Roy's assault team went over the left-hand side of the fo'c'sle as best they could, before making their way to the pump house, Chant's demolition target, which had the two anti-aircraft guns on the roof. Whilst on the *Campbeltown* Roy had asked for a volunteer to help him destroy the two guns, and Lance Sergeant Don Randall had immediately stepped forward. Private Johnny Gwynne, a Thompson sub-machinegunner, would help the two men clear the roof of enemy. If the stairs were inaccessible, they would take a bamboo ladder.

Fortunately the guns turned out to be unmanned. Thomas Boyd's Fairmile ML 160 had already engaged these two guns from a distance of about 200 yards, Boyd giving them '30 rounds of high explosive and buckshot from the 3-pounder'. He directed the fire through a megaphone, and McIver, the gunner, kept on saying: 'Och! that's hit the bashtards again.' Fortunately, the enemy could not depress their guns sufficiently so could not respond. With the gun's breeches destroyed by plastic explosive Roy then led his men to the bridge at the Old Entrance, where they were to provide a secure bridgehead through which all the men from *Campbeltown* would need in due course to retire on their way to the disembarkation point at the Old Mole. Lieutenant Mark Woodcock and his demolition team were supposed to have been there preparing the bridge for demolition, but Roy found the area deserted, empty of friends and enemy. Settling down into their firing positions, they waited for the next stage, the withdrawal of the demolition teams and their protection teams, to begin.

Stuart Chant and his demolition team (Sergeants Bill Chamberlain, Ron Butler, Bill King and Arthur Dockerill) followed Roy off the *Campbeltown*. Making his way forward to the fo'c'sle Chant stumbled over the bodies of the dead and dying, crew and commando alike. He spoke briefly to the badly wounded Lieutenant John Proctor on the way, then fell part-way into the gaping hole in the deck next to the 12-pounder gun, but was saved from falling further by his pack and his men hauled him out.

Somehow they clambered down the vertical scaling ladder and took off at a run towards their target, the huge, two-storey pump house, here to be met by 'the bespectacled and square little figure of Lieutenant ['Hoppy'] Hopwood, Essex Regiment and No 2 Commando', their protection team leader, who had left the destroyer before them. Now they faced an unexpected problem: the door to the pump house was locked. Fortunately Bob Montgomery arrived at the moment at which the frightened and wounded Chant was wondering what to do, and applied a small explosive charge to the lock. It did the trick.

Four men quickly entered the building (Sergeant Chamberlain

had been wounded, so he stayed at the door, armed with a Colt automatic) and made their way carefully down a series of galleried landings to the pump-house floor. The torches on their webbing belts showed them that the massive layout was identical to what they had practised on at Southampton: the four main impeller pumps at the base of the subterranean complex connected by drive shafts to the large electric motors on the ground floor far above. Chant recalled later that they:

> had been training for this moment for weeks past and our movements ashore followed like drill. We had studied models and aerial photos to such a point that each of us had the whole layout memorised. I know I used to dream of the place long before I ever actually saw it. Sure enough, when we got there everything was in its proper place.

The men laid 40-pound charges on the impellers as they had practised, linking them all by cordtex to twin igniters. The whole process, Chant judged, took twenty minutes, during which they heard the explosion, far above them, caused by Captain Donald Roy and Lance Sergeant Don Randall destroying the German guns on the roof.

After setting the charges the men rushed in the darkness as fast but as carefully as they could up the metal stairs. They had ninety seconds to get out of the building, which they managed with only moments to spare before 'there was a deafening explosion and the large blocks of concrete protecting the building from air-raid damage flew up into the air and crashed down on the quayside where we had just been standing.' When he had seen the men exit the building Bob Montgomery shouted to Chant and his men to get further away, which he recalled 'they somewhat reluctantly did – out of range of the heavy blocks of stone which came crashing down where they had been lying.' Copland, by then near the bridge at Point G, was startled to hear a roar of sound that 'cracked into our eardrums, followed immediately by a colossal burst of continuous yellow fire to our left rear. With relief I realised that it was the big Dock Pump House demolition going up.' After the massive chunks of debris had ceased to fall they ran back to inspect the building to see whether the 15-foot-high pumps also needed blowing, but were glad to see that they had also been destroyed, and were lying at crazy angles.

Running behind Chant and his men on leaving the *Campbeltown* Lieutenant Chris Smalley and the four men of his demolition team made straight for their target, the left-hand winding house. It was locked, and after failing to open it with a slug from a Colt 45 they climbed in through the windows and had planted their charges within ten minutes. The first attempt at ignition failed, the second worked spectacularly, and the explosion rained debris on to the Fairmiles in the Old Entrance a few yards away.

By the time Chant and his men had finished with the pump house they could see, through the illumination of the searchlights, Smalley and his men, their task completed, running down to the water's edge at the Old Entrance to climb aboard a Fairmile for the return home. Although they didn't know it at the time, it was Edward Burt's ML 262, which had just taken on board Lieutenant Dick Morgan and his team. A horrified Chant watched, mesmerised, as he then saw the vessel emerge from the sanctuary of the Old Entrance and come under sustained and savage fire from the German guns, probably from the Mindin Point battery on the south bank of the river. Parts of the vessel were very soon ablaze, and it was clear that serious casualties were being caused on board. He had first shouted to the vessel to stop also for them, but his voice did not seem to carry over the din. Watching the vessel limp away into the estuary he thought: 'Rather him than me, I hope they make it.'

Chant did not learn till after the war that Smalley and most of his men had been killed within minutes of setting foot on the boat. The torpedo-armed ML 298 of Lieutenant Bob Nock, whose task was to wait offshore and engage the enemy until it was time to withdraw the commandos, likewise was struck heavily by enemy guns, the ship burning out of control and the survivors taking to the water.

Moving away from the Old Mole after leaving Tom Collier's Fairmile, Second Lieutenant 'Tiger' Watson went directly towards his objective, the Southern Entrance Gate at Point D, which the demolition team under Lieutenant Philip Walton was to destroy. Tiger was immediately struck by a strange, spicy smell in the air that suddenly told him that he was in France, a reality soon confirmed by the arrival of a group of excited Frenchmen on the street in front of him, brought out of their air-raid shelters to see what all the commotion was about. Concerned that they should not get in the way, he urged them, in what he described as his appalling French, to get inside before they were hurt. A burst of sub-machinegun fire at their feet finally persuaded the reluctant crowd, perhaps imagining that this was the moment of their liberation from tyranny, to disperse.

Seeing a group of Germans running down an alleyway, Watson, who knew nothing of the havoc caused to the Fairmiles on the river, could not understand why the area had not already been cleared of the enemy by the assault parties. Attempting to chase these Germans and yelling '*Hände hoch*' after them he was lucky to get away with his life. The enemy turned on him with sub-machinegun fire and grenades, sending bullets clanging into a metal litter bin on a lamp-post above the roadway where he had been forced to throw himself.

Watson returned whence he had come, and made for his primary task, determined not to be sidetracked again. In the confusion he had lost track of Philip Walton, although he managed to meet up with Walton's demolition team. Walton's men said that they had seen him fall when crossing the Place de la Vieille Ville (Old Town Square). While Watson was calling out his name a burst of machine-gun fire from a nearby rooftop struck Sergeant Dick Bradley in the chest, went through his lung and came out through his back below the shoulder blade. As he bent over to inject him with a syrette of morphine Watson himself was struck in the left buttock by a ricocheting bullet.

Their location, the Place de la Vieille Ville, was clearly very dangerous. It was now also apparent that the assault parties under Captains David Birney and Bertie Hodgson had not arrived, and the area was teeming with an alert and hostile enemy. Determined to carry out his objective – the destruction of the bridge at Point D, in order to prevent the enemy using it to reinforce the Old Town – Watson decided to try to approach the bridge indirectly alongside the Bassin rather than through the Place de la Vieille Ville, which seemed to be thick with enemy. As they approached along this route, however, they came under fire from a German vessel in the Bassin itself.

As we went along, this malevolent vessel insisted on keeping us company and when no building was interposed between, gave us the benefit of its gun crew's marksmanship. But as they could not hear us and we had no intention of affording them more than a momentary glimpse of their target, no harm was done. However that ship was going to prove a nuisance to others before the night was out.

Retracing his steps to ask Colonel Newman for reinforcements, he found that there were none. 'Bad luck, Tiger,' Newman told him. 'You've done your best. Yes, I think you should have another try, but I can only let you have two tommy-gunners. We're a bit short of men.' Watson returned for a second attempt to get through to the bridge, again avoiding the Place de la Vieille Ville but returning that way to collect two packs of explosives they had left. Throwing caution to the wind, and aware of the need for speed, Tiger ran down the road. Luck was on his side. A bunched group of Germans did not disperse when they saw him and his men approach, and were felled in a hail of sub-machinegun fire. Before they could go any further, however, a runner arrived from Charles Newman, ordering him to move immediately to the disembarkation rendezvous. The raid was over. Furious that he had not managed to achieve anything concrete, Watson marshalled his men and returned through the warehouse and railway sidings to the Old Mole.

Separating from Tiger Watson shortly after leaving the Old Mole, Bill Pritchard reached the bridge at Point D with his team, and found no sign of the demolition or protection teams (Bill Bradley, Walton and Watson). Pausing to lay charges against two moored tugs (the *Champion* and *Pornic*), Pritchard and Corporal Ian Maclagan then went off in further search of the demolition teams.

As he moved left through the streets to the Avant Port, Pritchard likewise could not find the Commando teams who at this point should have been swarming all over their targets in the Old Town. At this point, setting off back through the Old Town and turning a corner quickly in the darkness, he ran straight into a German soldier before stumbling backwards. Corporal Ian Maclagan shot the German dead. Pritchard was breathing heavily and appeared to be badly wounded, but he ordered Maclagan to report back to headquarters. Returning to get help, Maclagan passed by the bridge, where a pillbox on the opposite side was spitting fire into the Old Town. He stumbled over the body of Lieutenant Philip Walton.

Pritchard had in fact been mortally wounded in the encounter – in all likelihood by a bayonet – and bled to death on the cobblestones before help could arrive. An especially poignant photograph of him lying dead on the dockside, taken the next morning by a German photographer, sits in the German Military Archives in Koblenz. Charles Newman was later to acknowledge the central role the immensely popular Bill Pritchard played in planning and executing the demolition component of the raid:

Right from the beginning the idea of using demolitions and the possible use of troops to smash an enemy dockyard had been his, his own hard work had trained the demolition troops, and his arrangements for placing charges etc, had entirely made possible the success in the Dry Dock destruction. To have died in the battle before he could be told of the success of it all, was a cruel fate for one who had worked so hard and untiringly for it.

While this was going on in the Old Town the demolition teams from the *Campbeltown* had spread out alongside the Normandie Dock to secure their various targets. Corran Purdon and his little party of corporals (Johnny Johnson, Ron Chung, Bob Hoyle and 'Cab' Callaway) came together on the caisson. Bob Montgomery remembered Corporal Callaway's trousers catching fire as he climbed down and he had to take them off, carrying out the whole operation in his underpants.

The men then ran as fast as their heavy packs would allow to their objective, the northern winding house at Point A. Corporal Johnson was hit and wounded. Lieutenant 'Bung' Denison led from the front, helping to clear an enemy post on the way. Bertie Burtinshaw and Gerard Brett, who both had tasks to destroy the inner caisson, followed. The racket was tremendous, Purdon later considered: the moving lights from searchlights, fires and the intensity of small-arms and cannon fire, together with the re-peated shock, noise and flashes from explosions made the whole affair surreal.

When they arrived at their target they encountered a problem they had not considered: like Chant's pumping house, the heavy metal door was padlocked. Purdon tried and failed to shoot it off. Corporal Ron Chung broke through with a sledge hammer. Once inside, their training paid off: the charges were quickly laid and connected to the igniters. When they were ready, Ron Chung ran across the fire-swept ground to Gerard Brett's party on the caisson, telling him that they would blow the winding house as soon as Brett had concluded his own task and withdrawn back through them.

On the caisson, however, Brett and Burtinshaw were struggling to deal with their own task. The Germans had laid timber and tarmac along the top to use it as a road, and it proved impossible to break in to place their explosive charges inside the lock gate. Some of the external 18-pound charges designed to be lowered down against the outer wall of the caisson were successfully put in place, but the commandos' activities were soon spotted by the Germans across the Pont de la Douane, who unleashed a heavy and effective fire against them. Before long Brett was injured in the arm and leg and Burtinshaw was killed, having first been wounded several times. Sergeant Frank Carr of the Royal Engineers took responsibility for the task:

Time was passing and we should have been ready to 'blow'. The fact that we could not complete the whole task caused us some concern and I realised that we would have to blow the underwater charges only. We again came under fire, and the withdrawal rocket was also fired so I decided to set off the charges.

I checked that the caisson was clear and removed the pins from the igniters. The resultant explosion seen from quite close by myself and Lance Corporal Fred Lemon was heavier than originally planned because we combined both sets of charges rather than waste the ones we couldn't lay inside the caisson. We could see the water boiling as a result of the explosion.

To check, I walked the caisson to estimate the damage. I could hear running water at both ends and realised that the caisson was badly damaged, probably enough to move it off its seating and make it useless.

They then withdrew through Purdon at the winding house, the wounded Brett being helped along by Corporals Bob Wright and

'Fergie' Ferguson. Accordingly, Purdon fired his igniters, and the whole building seemed 'to rise several feet vertically before it exploded and disintegrated like a collapsed house of cards'.

Wasting no time, the men, now considerably lightened, ran back alongside the railway line to the rendezvous point, through Donald Roy's bridgehead, running singly over the fire-swept bridge at Point G. Accompanying the remnants of his demolition teams back to Donald Roy's position, Bob Montgomery was elated that most of the demolitions had gone according to plan. With spare explosives to hand he now enjoyed himself: 'I found a railway truck and lit an explosive and hurled it in. The truck disintegrated in flames. It was lovely.' Crossing the bridge on the seaward side and using the girders underneath to avoid the enemy fire sweeping the surface, the men reported in to Newman as they had been instructed to do.

It was at about this time that, on the right-hand side of the Normandie Dock, Roderick's and Stutchbury's parties saw what they thought were the withdrawal signals in the night sky (they were not: all of Newman's signalling flares had been lost in the destruction of Eric Beart's ML 267, so what they saw must have been German tracer), and began retracing their steps across the bows of *Campbeltown*, which as Buster Woodiwiss recalled 'was uncannily silent in contrast to the bangs going on around'. 'I could not see nor hear any sign of life on her. Our movements were obviously being watched as we had to move in between bouts of fire.'

When they reached the now-quiet destroyer Woodiwiss climbed the lashed ladder up to the bows and then pulled it up behind him to prevent pursuit.

A burst of fire indicated a counterattack, pretty quick work. A large group of Germans were forming to cross the open area we had just left. Lying abandoned on deck behind the shrapnel shields were Brens with 100-round magazines, which had been fired as we sailed up the Loire. I set up three of these behind the shields and began firing each in turn to prevent their advance and forced them to withdraw. I dropped all the spare weapons I could find into the Loire, collected all the Tommy magazines I could carry, rejoined my section and shared out the ammo.

It was while running for cover, carrying the Bren guns, that Roderick was shot through his left thigh. 'It came as a complete surprise,' he recalled. 'I was only aware of being knocked head over heels and the Bren leaving my hands. I moved quickly behind a stanchion and eventually made my way towards Colonel Newman's assembly point where the rest of my party had foregathered.'

TWENTY

Dash for Freedom

As soon as Bill Copland was sure that the wounded had been taken off the *Campbeltown* he made his way first alongside the Normandie Dock to the inner caisson and the Pont de la Douane (Point M), before returning along the Bassin de Saint-Nazaire through the bridge over the Old Entrance (Point G) and thence to the Old Mole, there to arrange the evacuation of the commandos onto the waiting Fairmiles. This journey was a hazardous one, enemy fire sweeping all the open areas from vessels in the Bassin and on the top of buildings on the other side.

No radio communications could be established during this time with Newman, as had been hoped. New lightweight (24 pounds) No. 38 man-portable radios, especially designed for assault troops, with a throat microphone for the operator but a range of only two miles, had been carried on the raid, even though they had been trialled unsuccessfully on Exercise *Vivid*. Whilst the sets worked after a fashion in and around Falmouth, neither Sergeant Ron Steele on Newman's staff nor any of the other signallers found that they could communicate with each other during the fighting.

At the flak towers near Purdon's northern winding house (Point A) Copland came across a lonely Micky Burn, who was waiting to see whether the demolition team under Morgan Jenkins was going to arrive to destroy the Pont de la Douane. Unable to enlighten him, Copland set off to make his own way back. He turned left to follow the dock road to Point G, all the while darting from cover to cover to avoid the heavy fire strafing the docks from various points along the Bassin de Saint-Nazaire. After his hair-raising journey he eventually made contact with Donald Roy and crossed the bridge under fire, some of his party being hit and wounded in the process.

With comforting visions of taking charge of embarking the survivors into the fourteen empty Fairmiles lined up and awaiting them at the Old Mole, Copland first reported to Charles Newman at Commando HQ, which was situated just to the left of the bridge at the Old Entrance. Copland could see that Sergeant Major George Haines was directing Bren and 2-inch mortar fire against the two enemy machineguns on a roof on the other side of the Bassin.

A few minutes after stepping ashore from MGB 314 Newman and his team had reached the point designated for his HQ location, but there was no sign of any of the other troops, including WO1 Alan Moss, the regimental sergeant major. He was not to learn until much later that Moss and many others had died on the river after Eric Beart's ML 267 had to be abandoned to the flames. On arriving at the building he had chosen as his HQ Newman literally bumped into a German on the doorstep: a hurried interrogation by Captain Antony Terry revealed that the building was the German dockyard HQ, and there were more Germans inside.

Just then heavy fire began to be aimed at them from one of the several vessels moored in the Bassin, perhaps at only 70 yards' distance, forcing Newman and the others to retire behind the building. Fires on the ground and at least one searchlight near the roof of the U-boat pens opposite unhelpfully illuminated the entire dock area. Thereafter a heavy plunging fire was brought to bear on Newman's position, alleviated only by the firing by Haines of the puny 2-inch mortar and his Bren guns. The enemy positions were too well protected, however, and Haines's Bren-gunner was wounded in the face.

With the demolition teams having withdrawn across the bridge at the Old Entrance (Point G) the two parties now withdrew through the empty dock warehouses some 300 yards to the rendez-vous next to the Old Mole, after warning Roy on the bridge to follow them, there to meet with all the withdrawing commandos. Sergeant Major Haines went forward with a screen of Thompson sub-machinegunners; reaching and hiding among a group of railway wagons, they saw a party of Germans coming towards them through the shadows dancing off the harbourside. Newman told the men to hold their fire until the last minute: the entire enemy group was then wiped out at close range.

Two things struck Newman as he looked around. First, that the area was not clear of the enemy: a fair-sized but sporadic clash was raging. Unhappily, one of the guns on the Old Mole was still firing. It became clear later that a sizeable German contingent was close to the dockside and had already picked up many half-drowned and wounded men from the water. Second, that there was no beach master on the harbour wall, and no Fairmiles lined up in the water. From what he could see, the river was a scene of sinking and burning craft, one that reminded Bill Copland of images from Dante's *Inferno*:

> Close into the Mole, the shells of nearly burnt-out MLs still glowed red on the river, whilst in the night behind them, and seemingly suspended in mid-air, blazed a sea of burning petrol through which came shells and tracer fire of all kinds, some of the shells exploding with a rather futile little 'crack' in the air just ahead of us. To our left, as we looked at this rather foreboding picture, still blazed a fiercer fire – the Pump House still going strong – from all quarters still shone the searchlights, fortunately not upon us.

A short while later, having made his way safely across Roy's bullet-swept bridge, Corran Purdon arrived at the rendezvous. There he found:

Colonel Newman, cheerful and kindly as ever, standing near some railway wagons with the imperturbable Major Bill Copland at his side. I reported that our demolition task had been successfully completed, and that my party was present and correct. 'Well done, old boy,' said Colonel Charles. 'Just like some of our exercises, we've been let down by transport again!'

Looking out over the harbour – bathed as it was in the white light of German searchlights and criss-crossed by coloured tracer – Purdon noted without much surprise that 'heavy pillars of smoke and orange bursts of explosions denoted that there were indeed no ships to take us home to England'. Don Randall recalled the assembled men looking on 'in awe at the scene of the sinking vessels, aware of the crews and comrades struggling in the burning river'.

Newman's quiet, even humorous disposition in the midst of the slaughter on the dockside was an inspiration to those who saw him in action. Micky Burn was encouraged to see him at his HQ, officers coming in to report from across the battlefield, under heavy fire from many sides, standing there showing a 'complete disregard of any danger. He seemed to be enjoying himself.'

The time was now about 2.45 a.m., calculated Stuart Chant, who arrived at the rendezvous shortly after Purdon. He estimated that about seventy men (Newman guessed closer to a hundred), of whom more than half were wounded to some degree or another, gathered in the area of the railway trucks on the landward side of the Old Mole. The enemy were close – Chant could hear their shouts – but they seemed reluctant to mount a direct attack on the Commandos' position.

Newman determined at once that they had no choice but to fight their way through the Old Town, across the bridge (Point D) into the New Town, and to seek their fortune and freedom in the open country beyond. There was no thought of surrender. Aware that *Campbeltown* could blow at any minute, Newman's first thought was the absolute necessity to get everyone away from the dockside as quickly as possible: the *Campbeltown* was due to explode by 3 a.m., and that time was fast approaching.

None of this had been planned, but the atmosphere was calm, even positive. Spain and Gibraltar were their next objective. Ammunition was low, but there were no complaints. Copland had already formed a defensive perimeter, some one hundred by thirty yards, while Sergeant Lionel Wickson of Tiger Watson's protection team fired his Bren gun at the position on the Old Mole that Tiger had at first believed cleared. Frustratingly, it was continuing to bring fire to bear on the river.

All the while the Germans were closing in, in small groups, on Newman's assembly point, the only physical protection provided by the carriages. Indeed, they were so close at one moment that a German hand grenade exploded at the feet of Newman, Day and Copland as they stood next to a carriage discussing the plan. Amazingly, they were unharmed.

Newman then softly called the officers together. They were going to break out through the bridge at Point D (luckily, perhaps, not destroyed after all), and try to escape into the countryside. They were to fight until they were out of ammunition, and, if they could, men were to make for neutral Spain using their own resourcefulness and ingenuity. There were no maps, either of France or Spain. They would move towards the bridge in groups of about twenty, to attempt to cross the bridge. Men from the assault and protection teams with their Thompson sub-machine-guns and grenades would lead, with the lightly armed demolition teams (armed only with Colt pistols) and the walking wounded in the middle, and a small rearguard led by Lance Sergeant Don Randall.

Without pause or any further orders, the troops moved out in fighting order on both sides of the roads, running in and out of cover towards the bridge at Point D that crossed the Southern Entrance and gave access to the town. Donald Roy and Tiger

Watson with what remained of their assault and protection teams led the way, attempting to beat a path with fire through any opposition that might present itself. It was a dangerous passage, the commandos suffering many more casualties during this period. The bridge was later to be known to those who crossed it under intense fire that early spring morning as 'The Bridge of Memories'.

Many wounds were not life-threatening, however. Earlier, on the bridge at Point G, Don Randall had been hit by a 20 mm ricochet in his left forearm: it hammered into his arm, making a hole down to the bone, but did not break it. He saw a large bullet fall out, then wrapped a First Field Dressing on it and carried on. Soon after they set off a grenade landed at Bob Montgomery's feet and he received a piece of shrapnel in his buttock. Stuart Chant recalled bursting out laughing when Corran Purdon caught his feet in some barbed wire and tripped up. A German bullet struck the cobbles inches from Purdon's head, throwing up sparks and chips of stone, but within minutes Chant found himself sprawled on the ground, a bullet, probably a ricochet, embedded in his knee. Carried for a short while by two of his men, he eventually persuaded them to leave him, and they departed into the darkness in the direction of the Southern Entrance bridge.

As the remaining commandos crossed the open, bullet-swept ground, running flat out, pausing in dark patches of cover to re-form for the next bound, Corran Purdon was immensely moved by the sight of Captain Donald Roy, 'moustached, kilted, upright, disdaining cover and holding to the centre of the street', as well as Roderick, Tiger Watson, Sergeant Major George Haines and Sergeant Bill Challington, fighting aggressively from street to street, covering each other with sub-machinegun fire and hand grenades. He likened their rush to the bridge to a charge by rugby forwards, the men calling words of encouragement to each other and building unstoppable momentum.

Copland was impressed with the energy and clinical profes-sionalism of Sergeant Major George Haines who, armed with a Bren gun, cleared a path to the bridge for their group. Taking a circuitous route that led them alongside the Bassin where Tiger Watson had been a little while before, they eventually reached the bridge. It was being swept by enemy fire. Newman, however, worked on the assumption that the Germans would act like any other soldiers untrained in the art of night fighting, and would aim high. He was right. Halting by the side of a large low building before the bridge, Haines saw a large group of German sailors, distinguished as such by their uniforms (he estimated about fifty), some 250 yards away to the left. Sending two Bren-gunners to disperse them, Newman then gathered all the other Bren-gunners, under Haines's command, and rushed the bridge under intense enemy fire.

The time was now about 3 a.m. If the fuses were working correctly, this was the moment that the *Campbeltown* was due to blow. Newman shouted 'Away we go lads', and led the way to the bridge. The historian Brigadier C.E. Lucas Phillips memorably described the scene in *The Greatest Raid of All*:

> To all those who took part it was the most inspiring moment of the night, like a charge of olden times across fire-swept ground right into the heart of the enemy. In the stirring pages of British history, there have been many glorious charges, many heroic assaults on battlemented walls and ramparts deemed impregnable, but, on its smaller scale and in its more modest intent, the break-out of the Commandos at Saint-Nazaire ranks high among them as a manifestation of soldierly purpose and of the will and deter-mination to defy odds.

'There was clanging against the girders on the bridge,' Bob Montgomery remembered, 'but we got through.' The fighting was furious and at close quarters. Corporal Ed Douglas saw four of his fellows fall. Bill Copland fired his Thompson sub-machinegun into the aperture of a pillbox on the far side of the bridge that only moments before had been firing at them. A German grenade exploded at Purdon's feet as he got to the far side of the bridge, lifting him off the ground and wounding him in the left leg and shoulder, and wounding Captain Stanley Day at the same time. His left battledress trouser leg was wet with blood, but though it felt numb, it still worked and he quickly forgot about it. He relieved some of his frustration on the hapless crew of a German motor-cycle combination who unwisely came round the corner ahead of him soon afterwards. Lance Corporal Jimmy Brown of 5 Commando and Argyll & Sutherland Highlanders, part of Copland's party from the *Campbeltown*, was knocked out by the blast of a mortar bomb on the bridge. When he came to, he saw the rest of the party disappearing up one of the side streets. He managed to crawl underneath the girders and hide, where he was found the next morning.

But it was during the approach to the bridge that Tiger Watson received the bullet that finally ended his war. He had spotted a German rifleman ahead of them, occasionally popping out from cover to take shots at the approaching commandos. As they drew near to the spot where the German was positioned Roy threw a grenade, Tiger then racing to reach the street corner to deal with the German when he showed himself again. When the man's rifle barrel appeared some 20 yards ahead as predicted Watson pulled the trigger of his sub-machinegun. Nothing happened. The magazine was empty. 'It was too late to stop,' Watson recalled, and he had:

> no clear idea of how I was going to tackle him when I got there, but tackle him I must. As I ran I could see the rifle muzzle swing round until I was looking straight at the black 'O' of the barrel. I felt nothing but a numb resignation. I only had time to think 'Well, this is it.' The bullet broke my left arm just above the elbow.

Stopped in his tracks, Watson dropped his tommy gun and sat down abruptly on the road. His assailant was killed by men following behind. Johnny Roderick injected some morphine into the back of Watson's right hand, and Hoppy Hopwood, despite Tiger's vehement objections, gently relieved him of his Colt and spare tommy-gun magazines. Left propped against a wall like Stuart Chant before, the unarmed Watson now awaited the uncertain mercies of the Germans. His comrades disappeared towards the bridge in the distance, men calling out farewell as they passed.

Not everyone was able to cross the bridge, however. The rearguard, led by Lance Sergeant Don Randall, supported by Corporal Bertie Johnson (originally from Captain Chris Smalley's demolition team, he had survived the sinking of ML 262), Private Peter Honey (from Hoppy Hopwood's protection team) and three others, followed the main party, watching for enemy infiltration between the buildings as the column zigzagged in the direction of the Old Entrance, then sharply left by the side of the inner Bassin with warehouses on the left. Progress was slow, however, as Johnson's knee was badly injured. Randall heard a great burst of fire nearly 70 yards ahead which he assumed to be the main body of the group crossing the open, heading for the bridge into town, and an even greater interchange of fire as they charged the bridge. 'The flashes from so many automatic weapons in that concentrated area with many tracers striking the steel structure of the bridge and ricocheting in all directions, seemed akin to an explosion in a firework factory. Just as suddenly as it all started, it stopped.'

Johnson couldn't go on. As he slumped to the ground, in great pain, wondering momentarily whether he could steal a boat from the Bassin to his right, a large group of German soldiers led by a Feldwebel suddenly appeared out of the darkness, shouting '*Hände hoch*' and levelling their weapons at him. Disarmed, the commandos were marched under guard across the bridge only a matter of minutes after their comrades had escaped across it. They were taken into the U-boat pens and locked in the guardroom.

After leaving Watson, Roderick (who by this time had been wounded in the head by grenade fragments), Hoppy Hopwood, Sergeant Alf Searson (badly wounded in the left shoulder) and a few others judged that attempting to cross the bridge was suicidal, and sought hiding places in the warehouses on the river side of the lock. There they remained until dawn.

Those who managed successfully to cross the bridge were met by rapidly intensifiying German opposition. An armoured car of some kind controlled the next crossroads some 150 yards further on from the bridge. The men now broke into small groups in an attempt to break through the town into the countryside beyond.

The confused and disparate activities of the next few hours have become known as the Saint-Nazaire Obstacle Race, as men clambered over backyard walls and into and out of houses in their attempt to escape. Purdon was among a group with Newman and Copland. 'We came on a lorry parked by the roadside and Bill Copland tried to get it started. All he succeeded in doing was to switch on the headlights, illuminating, among others, the Charles Atlas figure of Bung Denison, our protection party commander, to cries of "Put those bloody lights out!"' An armoured car passed them at one stage; the men pressed themselves, unseen, into the shadowed walls. Bill Copland recalled being fired on from front and rear, sheltering in alleyways, and dashing through a churchyard and throwing themselves over a six-foot wall. He remembered Private Thomas Hannan 'causing some amusement by falling into a hen-coop, [we] crossed a back garden, opened some good housewife's back door and found ourselves in a French kitchen.'

I went through the house to find the front door locked and the key missing so back again and out, grabbing a drink from the kitchen tap on the way. Next door was locked too so we smashed in the kitchen windows with rifle butts, got in and ran through the house and down the front steps into the street beyond. We were greeted by machine gun fire from both ends of the street.

We went back to our desirable furnished residence again and let the firing continue; as they were all Germans firing at each other it appeared to be a fairly sound policy.

By now, however, ammunition was low and many of the wounded were struggling to keep up. Newman's group of sixteen (only four of them unwounded) came upon a tall house showing a light from its upper windows. They considered knocking on the door to seek refuge, but found instead that the door to the house opposite was open. They piled in, moving down to the cellar, which had been prepared with mattresses as an air-raid shelter.

The dawn was beckoning: sunrise that morning was shortly before 7 a.m. Newman hoped that this location might give them a reprieve, time to reconsider their situation and make use of the next period of darkness. It was not to be, however. The cellar they had chosen was the air-raid shelter for the house opposite – the one with the illuminated window – which happened to be Kellermann's HQ, the Kommandantur. The usual occupants of the air-raid cellar were at that very moment out on the streets of the town hunting down British commandos.

Perhaps it was the irony of this situation – Newman and his men letting themselves involuntarily into their own prison – that prevented the Germans simply throwing grenades into the cellar when they were discovered, as Bob Montgomery and Bill Copland first feared they would do. Newman had decided, because of the state of the wounded, not to contest the cellar if they were found, and a tense first few minutes after the appearance of heavily armed Germans were followed by the men being unceremoniously bundled across the road into the HQ building, there to be briefly interrogated by their captors.

The civilian population of the Old Town had no choice but to be caught up in the fighting. According to Lepotier's careful accounting, three civilians were killed during the night of the raid at the hands of Germans who mistook them for combatants.

Passive or otherwise, the Germans were to punish them collectively for the raid. Madame Loréal lived in the old Hotel Blanconnier in Old Saint-Nazaire, on the corner of the Place de la Vieille Eglise and the Rue Vieille Ville. She and her family had gone down to their cellar rather grumpily at the onset of the air raid, but now found themselves in the middle of the battlefield. In their cellar they heard the noisy clatter of the German boots, before hearing other, more discreet, muffled footsteps, which they later realised were the rubber-soled boots of the commandos:

> Suddenly a German sailor, in a white cap, navy blue jacket, white fabric trousers, with one arm wrapped in a kitchen cloth stained with blood and a rifle held in front of him, shouted . . .
> 'Tommies! Tommies!'
> 'Nix Tommies . . . ici français,' we replied.

They were left alone, for the time being. Nearby, at No. 32 Grande Rue, near the Café du Morbihan, the nineteen-year-old Jean Bouillant lived with his mother and aunt. He decided to go down to the cellar only when the aircraft above strangely persisted in droning on without dropping any bombs. He was suspicious and, unable to sleep for the noise, decided to seek the sanctuary of the cellar. It also provided a useful refuge for a German patrol during the evening: the German officer gave Jean a cigarette. Half an hour after they left three more soldiers arrived at the cellar, but to everyone's astonishment they were British. One of the men, two of whom were in kilts, was wounded, and bleeding. The Britons offered Bouillant a cigarette. 'In the space of half an hour,' he considered, 'I therefore smoked a German cigarette and an English cigarette!' His mother dressed the soldier's wound, before taking them to an old, empty house at the bottom of the court-yard, to escape the searching Germans.

Gérard Pelou, a member of the local civil defence organisation (the 'Défense Passive'), was conscripted to be a stretcher-bearer in the aftermath of air raids. When the warning sounded he was to report to a makeshift first aid post in the cellar of the Service Sanitaire Maritime, together with Dr Bizard, the chief warden of the Naval Prison. This night was strange, he thought, as the noise of the bombers was not accompanied by falling bombs. At about 1.30 a.m., Pelou walked out onto the street, just in time to see the searchlights from La Glacière and the Bureau du Port suddenly sweep towards the harbour and catch a warship in the beam. Thinking that it was one of the German torpedo boats returning to port, he immediately thought that it would be hit by the British bombing raid. The next moment the firing began and Pelou realised in an instant what was happening. 'The English are landing!' he told his friends excitedly. Running to warn his father in a building close to the Place de la Vieille Eglise, in the Loire Fluviale, he crossed the narrow streets across the Old Town, shouting into the cellars 'The English are landing! Do not move!' The first reaction was disbelief, followed quickly by excitement, as the locals believed that liberation was imminent.

The sixteen-year-old Alain Bizard, son of Dr Bizard, also acted as a stretcher-bearer, with his friend Gilles Chapelan. Operating from the first aid post in the cellar of the Service Sanitaire Maritime the two boys were instructed at about 2.45 a.m. to collect a badly burned British sailor from the dockside. Bringing the man back to their first aid post, they gave him the only drink they had: warm whisky. The sailor tried to tell the young men to stay away from the destroyer, an instruction that made no sense to them at the time.

TWENTY-ONE

Escaping from the Loire

While many of the Fairmiles were fighting desperately for their lives along the entire length of the harbour, Curtis had safely docked MGB 314 on the south side of the Old Entrance, alongside Mark Rodier's ML 177 – the last vessel in the starboard column – which deposited its commandos (Sergeant Major George Haines together with thirteen others). Frank Arkle watched them go silently ashore in their rubber boots and disappear into the shadows, little knowing that only a fraction of the Fairmile-borne commandos would get ashore that night. After firing a number of shots across the Old Entrance into the area of the submarine pens Ryder came alongside and, using his loudhailer to make himself heard above the din, instructed Curtis to bring MGB 314 alongside the north quay, and Rodier to take his Fairmile alongside the *Campbeltown*, pick up as many crewmen as he could, and begin to make their way home. Frank Arkle recalled:

> Some of the anti-submarine nets were still hanging off its sides as we were trying to come alongside and we had to be very careful of this in order not to get them tangled around our own propellers. However we managed to get our bow alongside and took off a lot of the crew including the Captain and several of his officers, including the medical officer [the Canadian Surgeon Lieutenant William 'Jock' Winthrope RCNVR], a lot of the wounded and some commandos.

Those embarked by Rodier included Sam Beattie and Nigel Tibbits. At 2.20 a.m., forty-six minutes after the *Campbeltown* had struck, ML 177 signalled to say that she was leaving the destroyer for the open sea. She now had to run a gauntlet of fire as she attempted to escape with her heavily laden craft out of the Loire. She did not make it. After some thirty minutes, straddled by shells, her engines knocked out and on fire, she started to drift, a target for even heavier enemy attacks. The survivors were forced to take to the water, some onto a damaged Carley float and others reliant on their life jackets and planks of wood. The loss of life was considerable, and included Mark Rodier, Nigel Tibbits and Jock Winthrope. Sam Beattie, Frank Arkle and a handful of other survivors were plucked from the water by the Germans the following morning.

Soon after ML 177 had left the Old Entrance to go over to the *Campbeltown*, both ML 262 (Lieutenant Edward Burt RNVR) and Lieutenant Eric Beart RNVR (ML 267) also managed to dock their vessels on the northern side of the Old Entrance, after first overshooting their objective. The demolition team under the command of Lieutenant Mark Woodcock and the protection team under Second Lieutenant Dick Morgan made their way successfully to shore, but Lieutenant Eric Beart's Fairmile, carrying Regimental Sergeant Major Alan Moss's HQ reserve team, did not. Battered by heavy gunfire, the stricken Fairmile drifted out into the river. Most of those on board died in the bitter inferno that followed, or in desperate circumstances in the flame-flecked water.

When MGB 314 came alongside the northernmost part of the Old Entrance Robert Ryder climbed onto the harbour wall, making his way through the darkness towards the now disabled *Campbeltown*. It was a dangerous journey with indiscriminate machinegun and cannon fire sweeping the dockside and buildings exploding at random, spraying dangerous debris aross the dockside. He made his way to the side of the destroyer, successfully negotiating an alert commando sentry on the way (calling out 'Ryder' in response to the commando's challenge). He found the vessel appeared deserted. Waiting for ten minutes he heard the scuttling charges explode, before returning along the dockside to the motor gunboat. Wynn had by this time brought his MTB 74 into the Old Entrance and tied up alongside MGB 314. Now no longer required for the Normandie Dock, Ryder ordered Wynn to discharge his heavy time-delayed torpedoes against the Old Entrance gate. The time was about 2 a.m.

This done, Dunstan Curtis took MGB 314 a hundred yards off the Old Entrance to observe events on the river. The view was shocking. It was apparent that few, if any, Fairmiles had managed to go alongside the Old Mole, and the pillbox was still spitting fire, searchlights illuminating the river like day. Seven or eight vessels were burning furiously. Using her own 2-pounder Vickers gun, operated by Able Seaman Bill Savage, to attempt to silence the pillbox and searchlight on the Old Mole, MGB 314 very quickly became a target in her own right. Curtis observed that Savage's pom-pom seemed to have a more destructive effect on the German positions than the Oerlikons. Hit many times, and piled high with sailors and soldiers evacuated from the Old Entrance, many from *Campbeltown*, some of them wounded (including John Proctor), it was only a matter of time before she too was destroyed. Reluctantly, Ryder ordered Curtis to retire out of the Loire.

The time was now 2.50 a.m., an hour and sixteen minutes after *Campbeltown* had struck the outer caisson. On board the motor gunboat Gordon Holman recorded the accuracy of Bill Savage's shooting:

Our gunner, on the exposed forward three-pounder [*sic*], took careful aim as we went in and hit the double-decker German pill-box fair and square on the top. Part of it disappeared but it was so strong that the men lower down in it were able to go on firing. It was a great shot and fully justified the 'Skipper' [Curtis] leaning over the bridge to shout, 'Well shot! Do it again!' But it was not to be. The gunner was fatally wounded immediately afterwards and died with those words of congratulation ringing in his ears.

As she made way from the Old Mole Henry Falconer's surviving Fairmile (ML 446) followed her out. With the Germans now fully alert for any attempt by vessels to escape, the journey out of the Loire was to be far more dangerous than the entry. Intense fire was directed from both banks of the river, the vessel surrounded by near-misses until near the Le Chatelier Shoal, about four miles from land. For Gordon Holman it was 'a nightmare experience. There were guns and searchlights all the way. The heavy batteries at the mouth were thirsting for our blood, having missed us altogether on the way in.'

A large flash behind them at 4.25 a.m. suggested to Ryder that the *Campbeltown* had gone up. They had to swerve violently to avoid an armed trawler, perhaps the guard ship they had avoided on entry hours earlier, but its heavy fire was nevertheless wide, and they managed to pass with ease. Ten minutes later they overhauled Stuart Irwin's ML 270, and the group of three vessels made their way together to Position Y, which they reached at 4.30 a.m. They saw no sign of the five enemy torpedo boats. As dawn arose they spotted a further Fairmile in the distance (it was ML 160) before the silhouettes of HMS *Atherstone* and *Tynedale* appeared over the horizon. On the motor gunboat Holman recorded that as they were bailing out five feet of water from their damaged forward compartments, the sight of the British destroyers was never more welcome. To Irwin's immense relief they were able to begin transferring their wounded to the *Atherstone* at about 7.30 a.m.

Few boats escaped unscathed from the river of fire that night. On departing the Old Entrance Wynn's MTB 74, having taken aboard *Campbeltown* survivors from MGB 314, was powering downriver when directly ahead they spotted two survivors on a

Carley float. Wynn had to make a snap decision: stop, or carry on. If they did the latter the two men on the Carley float would have been washed off and drowned. His instincts took over, and he stopped. As they picked up the two men, however, disaster struck, as two enemy shells slammed into the vessel. Wynn was blown from the bridge and looked as though he was dead. His chief motor mechanic, Bill Lovegrove, before jumping over the side, decided to make one final check to see whether his captain was alive. Wynn had lost an eye in the explosion and was unconscious, but Lovegrove realised that he was still breathing. He pulled Wynn up on deck and jumped over the side with him, tying him to a Carley float, and in doing so saved his life. The very intense cold killed many of those who had survived the sinking: when they were rescued by a German vessel at 2 p.m. the following day, only three from the MTB were still alive.

Boyd, on ML 160, could not believe the intensity of the fire. 'We were never out of the searchlights,' he recalled, 'and every time the tracer got too close I took violent avoiding action. Somehow we managed to keep clear of the heavier stuff.' Off the harbour wall disaster struck:

> I was held in searchlights, and I could feel the ship shudder as she was constantly hit. Then came a blinding crash behind me and clouds of smoke issued from the engine-room; both engines cut and all lights went out. 'Well, this is it,' I thought. 'What a bloody end.'

Unbelievably, however, both engines cut in again almost immediately and the vessel struggled forward. Hit repeatedly thereafter as it limped downriver, Boyd's luck held, despite losing an engine for a period. He was determined to get back to England, even if this involved stealing 'a French fishing-boat to get back in. Whatever the odds, I was going to get my crew and myself back somehow.' Boyd noted later that Motor Mechanic Walker 'carried on with repairs in the engine room although wounded and bleeding freely. With the help of Motor Mechanic trainee, Frederick Morris, he started the port motor, which had been hit, and it was without question this which enabled us to get the ship back.'

At sea, HMS *Atherstone* and HMS *Tynedale* were engaged at a seven-mile range by the German torpedo boats at about 6.30 a.m., but to Jenks's amazement the Germans broke off after the first few salvoes, concerned perhaps to ensure that they prevented any further Fairmiles from escaping from the river, and unsure of how many British destroyers were lurking further out at sea.

The first Fairmile the *Atherstone* encountered was ML 156, commanded by Sub-Lieutenant Noel Machin while Leslie Fenton lay wounded below decks. Before the two British destroyers had appeared on the horizon Lance Corporal Stan Stevenson and Lance Corporal George Owen took off their boots and hung them around their necks, as they feared that with their vessel sinking they might soon have to rely on their life jackets. Fortunately this did not prove to be necessary. Once emptied of crew and commando passengers, the Fairmile was abandoned to its fate. Shortly afterwards both MGB 314 and Irwin's ML 270 reached the destroyers. On MGB 314 Ryder transferred his wounded to the *Atherstone* and at 8 a.m. the two destroyers, together with ML 270, 446 and MGB 314, began the journey home.

The Luftwaffe had already shown itself. At 7.45 a.m. a Heinkel 115 float-plane had appeared, shadowing the vessels for some twenty minutes, before disappearing. It satisfied itself with bombing the sinking hulk of Fenton's ML 156. At about 8.20 a.m. a twin-engine, multi-role Junkers 88 arrived overhead, and was immediately engaged by an RAF Beaufighter which managed to shoot the German down, but in so doing crashed itself, with the loss of its crew. Just after 9 a.m. the five vessels met up with the newly arrived *Cleveland* and *Brocklesby*, and Ryder placed himself under the command of Commander Guy Sayer, commanding officer of HMS *Cleveland* and the senior officer present. HMS

Brocklesby shot down a further Ju 88 a little while later. The fear was that these aircraft would presage a large-scale attack on the fleet from the air. During the withdrawal long-range heavy fighters of No. 19 Group of the RAF's Coastal Command, flying from St Eval and Predannock, carried out twenty sorties in Beaufighters (which had a range of 1,750 miles), Blenheims and Hudsons, totalling 105 flying hours, keeping the enemy at bay as the little ships struggled homeward. Two aircraft did not return.

By now it was clear that the three vessels (MLs 270, 446 and MGB 314) would not survive the journey home, and because they were slowing the destroyers down and increasing their vulnerability to attack from the air, the gallant wooden vessels which had seen and survived so much were sunk by gunfire. The four destroyers were then left to steam homewards at 25 knots, shaking off the threat of shadowing aircraft. While *Cleveland* and *Brocklesby* turned back to search for three Fairmiles also making their way home unescorted (ML 307, 160 and 443), *Atherstone* and *Tynedale* reached Plymouth at 2.30 a.m. the next morning.

On Norman Wallis's escaping ML 307 Captain David Paton tended to the eight wounded on board, none of whom had serious injuries. Looking through a hole in the side of the ship he could see that they were zigzagging downriver in clouds of smoke, Wallis attempting to move from one shadow on the river to another, to provide a difficult aiming point for the guns. After meeting up with *Atherstone* and *Tynedale* they were judged sufficiently seaworthy to make their way home unescorted. Meanwhile Boyd (ML 160) saw HMS *Cleveland* and HMS *Brocklesby* steaming south, and at a distance had a few worrying moments as he thought they might be German and had to throw his charts and confidential documents overboard to prevent their capture before the two destroyers could be identified.

Later in the day the little fleet (the two destroyers and Boyd had now been joined by Horlock's ML 443) was attacked by German aircraft. At about 3.25 p.m. a Heinkel lined up in an

attack run, but as it did so was met by the combined weapons of
the Fairmiles, and every man on board who was able to fire back.
Boyd saw its demise: 'The first rounds hit him in the glasshouse
and he crashed at once. It was a fine sight to see the iron crosses
smash into the sea and the plane break up. We all cheered and I
gave the boys two rations of rum.' Then, two hours later, an enemy
seaplane dropped a 1,000-pound bomb on Boyd's vessel from a
height of only 300 feet, but it missed and the aircraft flew off.
Ryder was later to claim that up to a hundred Luftwaffe aircraft
were preparing to leave airfields around Rennes but the German
spotter aircraft were unable to locate the main body of the escaping British vessels and a massive counterstrike from the air did
not materialise.

When the enemy aircraft finally left them alone the three vessels
came together and, despite the heavy swell, Paton jumped from
one to the other to tend to the wounded and one sailor who, for
want of a blood transfusion, was dying. Picking up the Lizard at
9 a.m. the following morning (Monday 30 April) they entered
Falmouth Harbour on little more than the smell of petrol:

> Soon a couple of ambulances drove down to receive us. All our
> chaps made loud booing noises, which naturally the airmen didn't
> understand till we told them that the RAF had been a total
> washout in our experience, noticeable only by their almost total
> absence. The only medical person on land was a crisply starched
> and very officious VAD girl, who told me that the doctors would
> not be out of bed yet. It was about 9 a.m. Now we had been
> ordered not to shave so as to save water and I had about three
> days growth on. She took me to one side and said 'Doctor. You
> haven't shaved!'

The journey of ML 306 out of the Loire did not end so happily.
Ralph Batteson was shocked at the 'murderous, scything hail of
fire that poured in on us from both sides of the river', thinking

that it was only a matter of time before they met with catastrophe. When it came it was from an unexpected quarter. Surviving the relentless barrage downriver as a consequence of Ian Henderson's fine seamanship, the badly battered vessel eventually outran the guns, silence finally descending on the gallant ship for the first time in several hours. Henderson stood as many men as possible down to rest, while Batteson wondered at the fact that so few men seemed to have been injured in the vicious exchanges of the previous hours. The men were quietly satisfied with their performance:

'That little lot has given a good tweak to Hitler's moustache', one of the lads commented.

'More like a bloody good pull', I replied, with great satisfaction.

Then, at 5.30 a.m. when they were some 45 miles out to sea, from the darkness ahead loomed what he described as 'four ghostly shapes'. They were, in fact, the five enemy torpedo boats, returning at speed into the estuary. Alerted by Kelbling's sighting early the previous day, they had deployed to sea to counter-attack what they believed to be a British anti-mining flotilla, but received their urgent recall to Saint-Nazaire at 3.52 a.m. local time (i.e. 4.52 a.m. BDST). Henderson tried to hide his vessel in the darkness, urging the fourteen crew and fourteen commandos on board to absolute silence, but as the German ships passed, one of them, the *Jaguar*, turned in a great arc to intercept the little British vessel, which it had spotted as a vague shape on its right-hand side.

The next moment *Jaguar*'s searchlight was bathing the Fairmile. Warning shots were fired before an order came over the loudhailer, in broken English, to surrender. The response was instantaneous, the tiny David spitting fire from every available weapon against the German Goliath. There was to be no surrender without a fight.

Batteson fired his Oerlikon at the enemy vessel, and heard glass smash on the enemy's bridge.

Retreating a little distance, the German called again for the Fairmile to surrender, but this was received again by a contemptuous volley of fire. The German response was numbing, Batteson recalled: it was clear that this would be a very one-sided battle. Nevertheless, both sailors and commandos continued to bring every weapon they could to bear on their hated enemy. Sergeant Thomas Durrant, part of Ronnie Swayne's demolition team, had been engaging the enemy with a Bren gun. Badly wounded, he nevertheless saw that the sailor manning one of the vessel's twin Lewis guns had fallen and so, dropping his now empty Bren, he ran to take the man's place, firing back without hesitation.

The next call to surrender was again met with machinegun fire. The response, and the result of this resistance, was now inevitable. The *Jaguar* struck the Fairmile a glancing blow, and a number of men were thrown overboard in the collision and lost in the sea, including Lieutenant John Vanderwerve. With the enemy vessel virtually alongside and towering above her, a storm of small-arms fire plunged into her. As *Jaguar* circled for another attack her captain, Friedrich Paul, called yet again for surrender. Swayne, by now the senior officer alive, agreed, seeking to avoid further and wholly unnecessary bloodshed. By now twenty of the twenty-eight on board were casualties. 'Thank God,' thought Batteson, who had been blown away from his Oerlikon, but who was miraculously still alive, 'it was over.'

The damage was appalling. Henderson was dead, and most of the crew were wounded, some very seriously. Bodies and wreckage littered the boat, the deck slippery with blood. The courageous Durrant lay dead at the base of his Lewis guns, his body riddled with bullets. Captain Paul brought the *Jaguar* alongside, and German sailors descended on rope ladders to help the wounded and transfer the survivors on board. Throughout, German treatment of the wounded was exemplary. As Batteson was later to comment ruefully, this represented the end of his involvement in Operation *Chariot*, and the start of a long period as a prisoner of war.

Paul recorded that the damage to his ship included three wounded, 25 machinegun hits, 16 cannon hits of approximately 20–30 mm calibre, and his port forecastle, bridge, funnels and antennae were shot through. His report of the action noted that *Jaguar* fired three rounds of 105 mm high explosive, 212 rounds of 20 mm mixture (incendiary, anti-armour and high-explosive shells), 40 rounds from their MG34 machinegun and ninety 9 mm rounds from Schmeisser machine pistols.

Returning to Saint-Nazaire, Philip Dark noted that the *Jaguar* anchored among the debris of the harbour at about 9.30 a.m. The men, British and German alike, looked on in amazement at the smoking ruins of the dockside, the still smouldering wrecks of Fairmiles in the river, and the grey bulk of the *Campbeltown* embedded in the Normandie Dock. The dark waters of the river were filled with debris, and the angled deck of the scuttled British destroyer seemed to be covered with Germans picking their way over her forlorn grey carcass. The British were depressed that the destroyer had not exploded as planned. What could have gone wrong?

As the wounded were slowly lowered into boats from the *Jaguar*, Korvettenkapitän Moritz Schmidt, the commander of the torpedo flotilla and captain of the *Seeadler*, came on board, and began questioning Dark, the senior surviving naval officer, in broken English. 'Suddenly,' Dark recalled, 'in the middle of our conversation, there was an almighty explosion. The ship shuddered from stem to stern. [Schmidt] leapt from his chair and rushed outside. Sitting in the cabin peacefully by myself, I seemed to be surrounded on all sides by complete pandemonium.' The *Campbeltown* had

---

* Moritz was to be sunk in *Seeadler* in the English Channel off Dover later in the year, by a British MTB. He became a POW.

completed the task required of her, blown up in a spectacular conflagration.

Ralph Batteson was alongside the *Jaguar* in a little picket boat at the time, sheltered from the blast by the bulk of the German vessel, helping the transfer of the wounded:

Suddenly the entire harbour shook, as though hit by an earthquake. The explosion that followed was so vast, it swallowed up every other sound and sensation within itself. I have never experienced its like before or since. For an instant, I felt that the whole of Saint-Nazaire was being seized and shaken apart.

Our little picket boat, low in the water and protected by the looming bulk of the *Jaguar*, rocked crazily to the force of the blast. The world appeared to blow itself to fragments and come hurtling down on us with the fury of a hailstorm. The air was thick with clouds of dust, thickly studded with steel chunks torn from the ships, and every other kind of wood and metal. Shuddering vibrations pulsed through the sea beneath us, and gradually subsided. The hail of lethal missiles slackened, became a spattering fall. Then nothing, only the awareness of a terrible, deafening silence.

The time was 11.35 a.m. BDST. *Campbeltown* exploded some 8½ hours later than expected (i.e. at 3 a.m with the 2½-hour fuses) and three hours after Tibbits had expected his fail-safe detonators to explode. But as the noise, dust and debris died, no one was quibbling.

TWENTY-TWO

Aftermath

Lying out of action and in pain in the shadow of the warehouses on the wet, cobbled road, propped up against a cold dockside wall, worrying about his closeness to the three tons of amatol lying in the *Campbeltown* no more than 500 yards away, Stuart Chant could see in the distance the giant, dark entrance to the U-boat pens across the Bassin. At about 4 a.m. he was joined against the wall by a young commando whose name he did not know. All around him were the sounds of German troops calling to each other. A hundred options ran through Chant's head, from stealing a boat to rescue by friendly Frenchmen, but these were dreams as long as he could not move, and soon to be shattered in any case by the arrival out of the darkness of three black-uniformed Germans armed with Schmeisser machine pistols. They were very jumpy and reacted violently to the sight of the two British commandos on the cobbles, screaming nervously at the two men.

Chant quietly warned the soldier not to move: Chant himself, of course, was unable to. The soldier, in fear of his life, however, obeyed the shouted commands and came slowly to his feet, only to be promptly shot dead, in cold blood and at point-blank range. For some unknown reason, the men did not shoot Chant. They realised perhaps that he posed no threat, but perhaps they were also repelled by their own initial lack of humanity, the reaction of terror and anger rather than of self-defence. After a few moments of further shouting they began dragging Chant several hundred yards to a crossroad junction and into a dark building that morning would reveal to be the Café Moderne, full of German soldiers and some other wounded commandos. There he was propped against the wall, and left.

Tiger Watson had a similar experience. Lying back against the wall where he had been left, the effects of the morphia still coursing pleasantly through his veins, he watched three nervous Germans edging their way towards him in the inky blackness and felt a detached amusement as they nearly jumped out of their skins when he addressed them, quite calmly and in English: 'There is nothing to be afraid of, I can't hurt you.' Watson was lifted to his feet and searched. The discovery of his Commando knife caused an anxious moment, but the situation was saved by the arrival of another party of Germans bringing along the painfully hobbling Gerard Brett, who had been wounded in the foot. Speaking in German, he calmly pointed out that there was no difference between the knives the Commandos carried and the Germans' bayonets. Grudging agreement was reached before the two men found themselves deposited in the café along with Chant, Private Thomas McCormack and Sergeant Richard Bradley.

Many of the sailors, unprepared for fighting or escaping, were rounded up by the Germans soon after they reached land. Billie Stephens, George Davidson and James Laurie, for instance, recognised the hopelessness of escape almost the moment they came ashore from their sinking ML 192. Germans seemed to be everywhere around the docks and the Old Town. They were spotted by enemy soldiers before they had gone twenty yards, and despite trying to hide behind some rolls of wire netting on the quay were soon captured. There were about a dozen of them, Stephens recalled, 'and a very bedraggled bunch we must have been, all dripping wet and with very little of our clothing left.'

After much shouting and with Huns on all sides we were moved off in a bunch and made to double half a mile or so out of the dock area. We were then halted in a Church yard and lined up with our backs to the Church, with three of the enemy facing us in a very menacing way with their machine guns at the ready. I shall never know what was supposed to happen next, but I do know that I was very frightened.

By daylight the Café Moderne had filled up with German sailors and French civilians on stretcher-bearer duties, who offered the men oranges and brandy. At one point a German sailor looked at Watson's distinctive rubber-soled boots. '*Fallschirmjager* [Paratrooper]?' he asked. Watson tried to look non-committal. 'Well, you could not have come up the river,' the sailor added, before turning away. The idea that an enemy force could sail directly up the Loire, through some of the heaviest defences on the European seaboard, unchallenged, was an unpalatable thought for the Germans: it proved that even the most vaunted defences could be breached.

At daylight the five men were taken outside for the benefit of the German cameras, which were already clicking and whirring across the docks, capturing the scenes of devastation – and of British captives and bodies – for the benefit of the voracious German propaganda machine. These shots show Dick Bradley lying on his back, the exit hole to his bullet wound now safely bandaged after several hours of bleeding; Stuart Chant, still wearing his steel helmet for fear of an imminently exploding *Campbeltown*; the severely wounded and only semi-conscious Thomas McCormack, unaware of what was going on around him; Tiger Watson and, closest to the camera, Gerard Brett.

From across the dockside, and in both the Old and New Town,

* Stephens was in due course to become a celebrated escaper, escaping three times before successfully reaching Switzerland and then returning home across Vichy France and into Spain.

individual commandos were being prised from their hiding places. The nineteen-year-old Pierre Brosseau, who lived with his grand-parents on the Boulevard Président Wilson, remarked on the panic that seemed to consume the Germans, who went 'into all the houses like madmen, to see that there weren't any English hidden in the wardrobes, in the cupboards, or I don't know where'. Madame Loréal finally managed to get to bed at daybreak after a tiring night, climbing up the stairs from the cellar, clad in pyjamas and slippers, with a coat to keep out the cold. She had only just got into bed when there was the sound of heavy boots on the stairs, and lots of shouting:

> The doors are thrust open. A German comes into my bedroom, throws back the bedcovers and sheets to the foot of the bed, and sticks a revolver and torch under my nose. Then he let loose a volley of blows at my small corner cupboard, hoping to find an Englishman behind it . . . they searched in all the houses.

Hidden with some of his crew, two of whom were wounded, in the base of the lighthouse on the Old Mole, Richard Collinson was captured at dawn and taken by his captors to the U-boat pens, noting furtively that the password for access was 'East Prussia':

> We were taken to the enormous dimly lit echoing U-boat shelters, and along the gallery running across the ends of the huge berthing pens. Each bay of the shelter had two sleek 360 foot long Type VIIc U-boats, berthed alongside their own jetties. It was pure Hollywood: the U-boats had been 'flooded down' to prevent the commandos placing demolition charges on the pressure hulls. The crews were at defence stations, in steel helmets and carrying small-arms. As we came in the boats were being 'blown' up again, now that the commando-danger was considered to be past. The shelters shook and reverberated with the roar of high-pressure air blowing the water out of the ballast-tanks, amidst shouted commands.

One of the men Collinson would have met was Kapitänleutnant Herbert Sohler, who had rushed into Saint-Nazaire from his hotel in La Baule after first alerting Dönitz to the news. Sohler was back at his HQ by 2 a.m. The first soldiers of the 679th Infantry Regiment did not arrive from their base at Guérande, a few miles inland from La Baule, until 3.45 a.m., and their commander, Colonel Hans-Hugo von Schuckmann, until 4 a.m. This delay greatly irritated Sohler because of the clear threat to the precious U-boats. On his arrival Schuckmann had told Sohler that he did not intend to enter Saint-Nazaire until dawn. Sohler, normally a calm man, was apoplectic and according to his subsequent account, and ignoring Schuckmann's superior rank, retorted: 'If you do not send in your battalion immediately and something happens to the submarines, you will end up with a court martial!' The threat was only partly effective, but one company of the 679th was dispatched immediately to begin house searches. By 5.05 a.m. German forces had regained control around the Normandie Dock, and they announced the end of the clearing operations at 5.50 a.m. It was fast and efficient work.

Lying in a shell hole into which he had crawled during the night, Peter Nagel was depressed at the apparent outcome of the raid. He knew that the *Campbeltown* should have blown up hours before. In his worst imaginings he could already imagine himself in a concentration camp, particularly if the Germans learned his identity. Soon after sunrise a German patrol started firing into his hiding place and he was forced to surrender. With several others he was pushed against a wall and searched thoroughly. His captors talked among themselves about shooting their prisoners, but were deterred by the arrival of an older German NCO, who sent them under guard to a nearby boat.

This appeared to be a common thought among some of the nervous Germans that night, encountering British commandos for the first time. Unable to get over the bridge during the fighting, Micky Burn hid in the boiler room of one of the merchant ships in the docks. He was a fluent German speaker. When, long after dawn, he had been rounded up, he overheard his captors talking about whether they should shoot him. He spoke up in German at once, claiming to be a very important prisoner and handing over his precious prismatic compass in an attempt to persuade them to keep him alive. 'None of us expected to be taken prisoner,' he later reflected. 'We all expected to get away with it, blow up the docks and return safely to England without a casualty.'

By 8 a.m. the Germans considered that the bulk of the Old Town had been cleared of the commandos and sailors, and brought in trucks to transport the prisoners out of Saint-Nazaire along the coast to the seaside resort of La Baule, there to process their captives and treat the wounded. Lance Sergeant Don Randall was relieved when the moment came and the trucks left the dock area, at about 9 a.m. He was keen to put as much distance between him and what he still confidently expected to be the coming explosion.

It was a short but painful journey for the wounded, Tiger Watson feeling every jolt and bump as they made their way slowly out of the town. Bill Copland was delighted to see large numbers of the French population surreptitiously giving them V for Victory signs as they passed, although Collinson thought that they looked sullen and resentful, not because of the British attack, he concluded, but offended by the German occupation. Within only thirty minutes they had stopped outside the luxury Hôtel l'Hermitage in La Baule, which the Germans had commandeered in 1940, and were now using part of as a makeshift hospital.

At this point the wounded were taken into the hotel, while the others were segregated and then loaded onto trucks for the uncomfortable seven-hour journey to a prisoner holding centre in Rennes. It was the first opportunity the men had to gauge the success of the operation, and to see who had survived. Watson was delighted to see Johnny Roderick and Hoppy Hopwood again, although they were strictly forbidden to talk to each other. The men waited patiently for treatment, the German wounded being seen to first. The wounds in Frank Arkle's hand, hip and foot were not treated until later the following day. To his relief, however, the Germans had anaesthetics. Somehow, in his fevered imaginings, he thought that the enemy would seek to punish him for the raid by operating without them.

The big issue on many minds was the fate of the *Campbeltown*. Why had she not exploded when planned? The answer came quickly. Not long after their arrival at La Baule, a dull boom in the distance, accompanied soon after by a new level of anger and hostility from their German guards, confirmed that the destroyer had gone up.

It is clear that the 2½-hour-delay fuses had failed (or had not been inserted: with Tibbits dead, no final clarity can be determined on the matter), and that the eight-hour-delay fuses took three hours longer to explode – eleven hours from their first insertion – than planned. Why that should be the case remains a mystery, although Tibbits's decision to add the eight-hour fuses as fail-safes, if this is what happened, ensured that the *Campbeltown* was destroyed as planned. Without this precaution the primary purpose of the raid, the destruction of the outer caisson of the Normandie Dock, would not have been achieved and the sacrifices of so many would have been in vain.

When the destroyer exploded the outer caisson was wrenched from the dock, completely torn apart. The *Campbeltown* itself split into two major chunks of metallic debris, the remains falling into the Normandie Dock with the inrush of the river, leaving it entirely unrecognisable as a ship. Extraordinarily, the two merchant vessels in the dry dock survived the cataclysm, bashing up against the inner caisson but remaining afloat. As the deep boom of the detonation died away and an eerie silence descended over the entire environs of Saint-Nazaire, a huge pall of black smoke rose high above the docks. The blast smashed windows across both Old and New Towns and blew tiles off roofs.

A deep sense of shock accompanied the physical blast – it had not entered the heads of the complacent Germans that any form of danger might be posed by this Trojan Horse in their midst. By contrast a feeling of quiet satisfaction settled on their British captives, vindicated at last.

Sam Beattie, back on shore after being picked up from the sea by *Jaguar*, was, at the moment of detonation, being interrogated by a German officer in a room on the dockside. A photograph shows him sitting at a desk, shirtless but covered by a blanket, a uniformed clerk in the foreground writing as Beattie's statement is taken. The German questioned the British decision to send such a puny vessel to attack so large a target, suggesting that it wouldn't take very long to repair the damage the *Campbeltown* had caused. As the noise of the blast died away Beattie remarked quietly in response to his shocked interrogator: 'That, I hope, is proof that we did not underestimate the strength of the gate.'

Like Herbert Sohler, Klaus Ehrhardt, 7th U-boat Flotilla's Chief Engineer, had rushed into Saint-Nazaire from his billet at La Baule when roused earlier that morning. After making his way through the security cordons thrown up around the town and reaching the U-boat bunkers he was briefed on the situation, which by that stage comprised the rounding up of British sailors and commandos who were attempting to hide among the local population. 'Already a number of British soldiers had been captured,' he recorded, 'and a lively exchange of cigarettes was going on.'

As dawn arrived the dramatic sight of the *Campbeltown* embedded in the lock gates excited widespread interest, and as the security situation improved to the point at which trucks began taking the British wounded to La Baule, curious military sightseers began making their way to the dockside. Ehrhardt was one of these tourists. He spent what he described as a 'considerable period of time on the ship', and left her only when his driver suggested that they go to lunch. It was a lucky decision: he was only a few hundred yards away, sheltered from the direct impact of the blast, when the vessel exploded. 'It had occurred to no one until that moment,' he reflected, 'that a time bomb had been placed in the hold of the destroyer.'

Estimates vary of how many people were killed when *Campbeltown* exploded, and at this remove in time it is impossible to be precise about the actual numbers of casualties. In 1946 Ryder calculated that 380 Germans had been killed, and four years later Rear Admiral Lepotier came to the similar figure of 360, some of them on the vessel at the time of its demise, and others on the dockside. Other reports significantly reduce this figure, the Germans suggesting about one hundred dead. Although they do not give the whole picture, of course, German photographs show only a handful of men on the outside of the stricken vessel, with others – souvenir hunters as well as naval officials – undoubtedly below decks.

Lepotier interviewed many local people after the war about the events of these days. By his account, access to the dockyards was prevented until the morning of 29 March, when local dock workers were able to re-enter the devastated port and were co-opted to help the shocked Germans with clearing up the human debris that littered the area, and it was the vast quantity of human remains scattered across the dockside that enabled the casualty estimations to be made. 'The quays near the outer lock gate were literally piled with corpses,' he recorded. 'Others were floating in the lock . . . Fatigue parties were fishing the bodies out of the water and piling them up.' A mechanic employed at the main electrical workshop in the dockyards reported being astonished by the carnage when he was allowed access to his workplace on 30 March. The local *pompiers* were tasked by the Germans with recovering bodies from the river, both British and German. One of them, Serge Potet, recalled that this 'macabre work lasted many days'.

What is not in doubt is the profound sense of astonishment the explosion caused the Germans, a deep and uncomfortable feeling of vulnerability, even of embarrassment that the British had managed to thrust so deeply into the heart of their defences. German reactions to the French citizens of the town in the days that followed are at least in part attributable to this sense of humiliation.

In their makeshift hospital at L'Hermitage over the following days Stuart Chant picked up whispered rumours from some of the French women co-opted as nursing staff, who passed on the story, upon which they were insistent, that large numbers of Germans had been lured onto the carcass of the *Campbeltown* by the actions of two British servicemen, who persuaded them that the vessel was safe. Impossible to verify after the event, the story remains one of the legends of a legendary raid.

To their credit the occupying authorities carried out a funeral at Escoublac near La Baule on the afternoon of Wednesday 1 April, with full military honours for the men, both British and German, whose bodies had been recovered in the clear-up operation. Twenty-eight British bodies were prepared for burial. They allowed scores of French men, women and children to attend and to lay flowers on the newly turned soil of the mass grave.

But the ramifications of the raid for the citizens of the Old Town were profound. According to excited Free French news reports the Germans reacted aggressively against the local people, believing them to have encouraged the raiders, and in some cases abetted them. The commentary attached to some news reports was lurid, when not utterly unfounded, not least the suggestion that the population of Saint-Nazaire 'rose as one man and for three and a half days fought beside the Commandos while terrific explosions were still blasting the submarine base'. It was reported likewise that the Germans showed signs of panic, expecting a full-scale British invasion, and ordered two thousand of their sailors to evacuate inland immediately, and that about five hundred French civilians were killed. Admiral Lepotier's much more considered investigations suggest that sixteen civilians were killed and twenty-six wounded in the four days between Saturday 28 March and Tuesday 31 March. But the detonation of the nearly two tons of explosives in Wynn's two delayed torpedoes against the Old Entrance, the first at 4 p.m. local time on Monday 30 March and the second an hour later, served to whip up German hostility to a new pitch.

Reports from local sources at the time indicated that at the sound of the two explosions the several hundred Todt Organisation and local French workers at the dockside stampeded to leave through the Pont de la Douane (Point M), rushing a German military cordon in their determination to escape what many supposed to be further actions by British commandos who had somehow remained at large. German troops rushed back onto the streets and a cordon was thrown across the Rue Carnot. Shortly thereafter shots were fired by nervous German soldiers and sailors, fearing another attack, and it was during this time that a number of French civilians were shot.

Initial but subsequently unsubstantiated reports suggested that the Germans had opened fire on the mass of workmen attempting to flee the dockside after the second of Wynn's torpedoes, killing up to 400, of whom 280 were French. These numbers have never been independently verified, and are not borne out by other reports from French sources at the time. They are undoubtedly greatly exaggerated. But the incident was serious enough to convince the German regional HQ in Angers that the French had contributed to the raid, and that a threat of a general uprising existed. Madame Loréal worried about the sudden anger of the Germans that evening. 'The Germans are nervous, furious, and accuse the French of having helped and hidden the English,' she recorded.

At midnight the mayor, Monsieur Pierre Toscer, and his four deputies (Grimaud, Georgelin, Garrec and Gauffriau) were arrested in their beds by German military police and taken to the Collège-Lycée Saint-Louis on the Boulevard Albert Premier on the river front west of the port, where they were berated for the fact that

French civilians had supposedly fired on German soldiers. The Germans threatened to shoot one in every ten men in the town if the guilty parties were not produced. Instances of civilians supporting the raiders had been claimed by the Germans, and although this undoubtedly happened, the number of men who joined in the fight was equally certainly very low (no greater than fifty according to local estimates at the time). The French were as caught by surprise as the Germans, and any pro-British action was spontaneous, but without serious effect.

In any case, civilians in Saint-Nazaire had no access to weapons or ammunition, outside of the odd illegally held shotgun or low-calibre rim-fire which in the days of peace had been used to pick off hares in the countryside to supplement the family pot. French civilians in the town did, nevertheless, give the raiders their moral support, and showed it in myriad ways, from sheltering escaping commandos and caring for the wounded to flashing the now famous 'V' sign at those who had been taken prisoner.

Pierre Toscer succeeded in persuading the Germans that there had been no uprising, and that their fears were exaggerated, but he could not change one radical decision taken by the occupying power, namely to raze the Old Town to the ground to improve security for the dock area. All inhabitants – upwards of two thousand souls – lost their homes to German demolition. Rounded up without ceremony on Tuesday 31 March, they were transported en masse and under armed guard by bus to a disused prison camp 17 miles east-north-east at Savenay. Allowed back three days later, they were given time only to recover essential possessions before being rousted from their homes, which were subsequently demolished, and forced to move elsewhere across the region.

The German clearance of British sailors and commandos from across Saint-Nazaire was thorough, but not comprehensive. On 16 June 1942 Wing Commander Casa Maury at Richmond Terrace sent a short memorandum to Brigadier Haydon: 'Advice has been received that Corporal Ed Douglas and Private Victor Harding have reached Spain safely.' A delighted Haydon scribbled in the margin: 'This is first class news.' It was indeed. In fact, three other men escaped from Saint-Nazaire that day, and made successful 'home runs' through Spain and Gibraltar: Corporal George Wheeler, Lance Corporal Sims and the wounded Lance Sergeant Arnie Howarth. All five were from No. 2 Commando.

There is a suggestion that Howarth was taken prisoner after the raid and transported to Rennes with the others, where he managed to escape, although as there is no evidence of an escape of this kind from the transit camp in Rennes it is more than likely that, as a lone evader, he hid in Saint-Nazaire until darkness before making his way east to Nantes. Here he was befriended by the daughter of Monsieur Barrate, the head of the Collège Public Aristide Briand on the Rue Louis Blanc, and was hidden in the college itself, where four hundred Germans were also billeted. Treated by a local doctor for his wounds, he was given civilian clothes and after a period of recuperation was taken by Mademoiselle Barrate on the train to Bordeaux. With the help of local farmers he crossed the Demarcation Line into the Zone Libre and got as far as Toulouse before he was arrested by the Vichy French and sent to Fort de la Rivère prison at La Turbie in the hills above Nice. While he was on the train under guard to La Turbie he was befriended by a young Jewish boy, Alexander Rotenberg, himself an evader, and the story of their extraordinary encounter is contained in Rotenberg's autobiography, *Emissaries*.* Howarth escaped from La Turbie in a mass breakout of British prisoners in September and was sheltered by the Pat O'Leary escape line led by the legendary Albert Guérisse. He was then evacuated from Canet beach near Perpignan on MI9's 20-ton Moroccan felucca *Seawolf* (which had sailed from Gibraltar with a Polish crew) on the night of 11 October in Operation *Rosalind*, one of thirty-two

---

*   It is this account that suggests that Howarth escaped from Rennes. Alexander Rotenberg, *Emissaries* (Secaucus, New Jersey: Citadel Press, 1987).

escaping Allied servicemen who were delivered safely to Gibraltar in that operation.

Wheeler and Sims fought their way across the Bridge of Memories into the New Town at about 4 a.m., but out of ammunition they sought sanctuary until the hullabaloo had died away. Finding a long, dry drain beneath a house, which they later found was close to the German Kommandantur, they remained hidden during the day, hearing scattered gunfire and the blast of the destructing *Campbeltown*, then creeping out at midnight in bright moonlight to make their way out of town, heading north-east. They had already made the decision to travel only at night, to stay away from major roads and towns, and to seek refuge only in isolated farmhouses where they could quickly make their escape if required.

During the first day they took shelter in a haystack where they were discovered by a friendly farmer, who fortified them with food and wine and equipped them with civilian clothes and money. Their journey was slow and careful. Moving east towards the Demarcation Line with Vichy France they found themselves well looked after by the farmers with whom they sought refuge, each night sleeping in barns or haystacks. Local villagers warned them about the presence of German patrols and provided information as to what towns to avoid because of the presence of German garrisons. On occasion they were taken into the home itself. Both men were regularly asked when the British would invade. Guided by advice gleaned from local villagers they continued eastwards, often following railway lines, when on 10 April, after passing Montreuil-Bellay, they bumped into a gendarme walking alongside the railway. Suspicious, he began interrogating them, and eventually Wheeler confessed, in his schoolboy French, that they were British soldiers escaping from Saint-Nazaire. To their immense relief the policeman was a patriot and warned them of the presence of Germans in the nearby town of Loudun.

As they continued on their way, they found that every single house they approached for help gave freely and generously. They stayed the night of 11 April at a farm near the village of Pouant, and the very pro-British farmer 'almost wept when we left', Wheeler recalled. At 4 a.m. on the morning of 13 April they left, in the company of a woman from Tours who was crossing into unoccupied France, wading across the chest-high river La Creuse at midday. The danger was not yet over, of course, as the Vichy authorities had a policy of incarcerating Allied escapers and evaders, and occasionally of repatriating individuals to the Germans. But luck remained on their side. At La Bousse the owner of a château provided accommodation and money, and put them on the bus to Châteauroux. A local cafe there announced by means of a sign in the window that English was spoken, the proprietor having lived in both Brighton and London between the wars. In the company of a Belgian teenager called Gilbert Mahun, who was also making his way to Spain, they caught the train to Toulouse at midday on 16 April, where they fell into the expert hands of the sixty-year-old Mademoiselle Marie-Louise Dissard ('Françoise'), who worked for Albert Guérisse, and who placed them in the hands of the Ponzan-Vidal *réseau* in early May to take them across the Pyrenees to Spain. By 7 May 1942 Wheeler and Sims were safely in the hands of the British embassy in Madrid.

Ed Douglas and Victor Harding had a similar adventure. After fighting their way into the New Town they holed up in a cellar on the Rue de Saille, but were not discovered next day, despite a German soldier looking into the cellar and pronouncing it empty. At 9.45 p.m. that night they left their sanctuary and, having discarded their kit and gaiters, went slouching through the town, passing German sentries with a nonchalant '*Bonne nuit*'. To put any pursuers off the scent they travelled north for three days without approaching any local farmhouses for help until they were finally forced to do so by hunger, having exhausted the iron rations they had carried since Saint-Nazaire. Turned away from the first farm they approached, they sought sanctuary in a wood, where the next day they were very nearly caught by a German patrol. As the two of them lay in a thicket a German tracker dog came up to Douglas and sniffed his head, but made no sound and wandered off, its minder, just feet away, none the wiser.

On the morning of 30 March they found help in the form of a Frenchwoman who fed them, gave them civilian clothes (corduroy trousers, sabots and old coats), six hundred francs and two bicycles. In the days that followed they began to make their way eastwards, moving from farm to farm and avoiding the German roadblocks leading into and out of the larger villages. By 9 April they had made their way to Langeais, a few miles west of Tours on the Loire, where they crossed with the help of the local priest, in a ferry shared with a number of German soldiers. The priest, a veteran of the First World War, wrote a note calling on all good French people to help the men get to safety. The first address he gave the men was at Vallères, where the men were sheltered on a farm for a fortnight from 12 April by a family determined to get them into the Zone Libre. They worked on the farm, the villagers providing them with books and food. At the end of April they were taken on a pony trap, a Frenchwoman riding ahead by bicycle to check the route. They crossed the Demarcation Line in the company of a Frenchman and his daughter whose farm straddled the boundary. After shaking hands the two men walked to Esvres before catching the train to Loches and thereafter to Marseille. At the end of May both men were taken across the Pyrenees by the Ponzan-Vidal *réseau*, reaching Madrid in mid-June. Soon, they were home.

---

* Space does not allow for any telling of the subsequent adventures of those taken prisoner at Saint-Nazaire. Six ended up in Colditz (Billie Stephens, Micky Burn, Corran Purdon, Dick Morgan, Micky Wynn and Sergeant Ronald Steele) and five subsequently escaped their captivity (Billie Stephens, Micky Wynn, Sergeant Richard Bradley, Private Jimmy Brown and Sergeant Alf Searson).

Epilogue

Buried deep in the pages of Saskatchewan's *Leader Post* newspaper on Tuesday 31 March 1942 was a short editorial commenting on the outcome of what was headlined as a 'Commando Achievement' scored a few days before on the German-held French Atlantic coast. 'British' Commandos, whom the newspaper reported to involve 'Canadian boys', had landed at the French Atlantic port of Saint-Nazaire the previous weekend and attacked the harbour installations – the only ones on the Atlantic coast, it noted, large enough to host a visit by the 'huge Nazi warship Von Tirpitz'.

The *Post* observed that the information it had about the raid, in which a 'small but highly-trained British commando force crept into the mouth of the Loire river under cover of darkness', came from a British and Reuters newspaperman, Gordon Holman, who had accompanied the force, but that Holman's version had been preceded days before by a breathless German communiqué carried on Radio Berlin on the evening of Saturday 28 March, announcing the colossal failure of a British raid on the port. According to the German story 'British losses in casualties and prisoners had been high [. . .] a ship laden with explosives had been blown up before it reached a vulnerable point in the Saint-Nazaire docks'.

English naval forces attempted during the night of March 27 to land troops in the Loire Estuary in order to attack the submarine base at Saint-Nazaire and destroy the harbour gates. Under fire of German naval batteries an old American destroyer laden with explosives, which was to have rammed the lock gates, blew up into the air before attaining its objective. The bulk of the enemy's speed and assault boats were also destroyed or heavily damaged by naval artillery. Such enemy forces as succeeded in landing were wiped out by troops from all sections of the German forces when they attempted to attack the dock and penetrate into the town. According to information so far to hand a destroyer, nine speed boats and four torpedo boats of the enemy were destroyed. Apart from heavy losses the enemy left over 100 prisoners in our hands. On the German side not a single war vessel was lost. No damage of any kind was done to the submarine base. When daylight came German torpedo boats encountered a superior formation of British destroyers, which broke off the engagement after having received several hits.

The speed with which the German propaganda ministry had dispatched the news of the raid meant that for several hours the world's press had only the German version of events to rely on. In the evening edition of *The Pittsburgh Press* on Saturday 28 March the newspaper led with the headline 'British Land at German Sub Base. In France, Battle Reported Raging'. It reported French sources in Vichy confirming that 'British forces including Canadian parachute troops struck at the port installations at the German-held submarine base at St Nazaire today and one report said the paratroops still were fighting in the buildings at the entrance to the Loire river'. The raid, it observed, was the fifth against Occupied Europe by what it described as the 'black phantom' Commandos.

Hidden among the small print on page 5 of the Monday 30 March edition of the *Sydney Morning Herald* came the news of the raid. The British government on Saturday had announced that a small raid had taken place, but that further information would not be forthcoming until all the forces involved had returned home. Now, more detail was emerging.

The first British communiqué, issued by Combined Operations Headquarters, was prompt, but understandably sketchy. It was published on the morning of the raid – Saturday 28 March 1942 – and picked up for publication in the daily newspapers across Britain on Monday 30 March, followed by those of the world on Tuesday 31 March and Wednesday 1 April. Later that day a second communiqué was issued:

A signal has been received from the Saint-Nazaire Raiding Force which is returning safely from the raid, saying that HMS *Campbeltown* rammed the main dock gate at 1.34 this morning, only 4 minutes late on programme time. This ex-American destroyer had had her bows specially stiffened and filled with 5 tons [*sic*] of high explosive. A delayed action fuse had been fitted to give our Forces sufficient time to complete other demolition work and withdraw before the main explosion took place. The signal states that at 4 a.m., after the Force had withdrawn, a heavy explosion was heard and seen.

The majority of the *Campbeltown*'s crew were evacuated by motor launch.

Special Service troops were landed and carried out pre-arranged demolitions in the dockyard in the face of very heavy opposition.

There is every hope that this raid accomplished, though not without some casualties, their main task, mainly the destruction of the gate of the large dock at Saint-Nazaire, the only one on the Atlantic Coast capable of taking the 45,500 ton *Tirpitz*. Beaufighters and Hudsons of Coastal Command covered the return of our Forces, one Beaufighter damaging [a Heinkel]. Some diversionary bombing was carried out by bombers of Bomber Command during the raid, in spite of unfavourable weather conditions.

The *Sydney Morning Herald* attempted some prescient analysis, comparing the raid with a similar attack on the port of Zeebrugge in 1918:

This was the first of the raids on the European seaboard that possessed more than a local tactical significance. Its aim was to deal a blow at German strategy in the Atlantic, because Saint-Nazaire was primarily a submarine base. The immobilisation of the harbour would also limit Germany's use of the French Atlantic coast, because Saint-Nazaire docks are the only ones large enough to accommodate the largest modern battleships . . .

From a broader point of view, the raid showed that even the most strongly held enemy positions on the French coast are no longer immune from British assaults. If Saint-Nazaire can be assailed by land, sea and air, there is virtually no point along the entire coast of occupied France that can be termed safe . . .

The possibility of such raids must have the effect of immobilising large German forces: and it may very well be that the power to hold the enemy offensives in Russia and the Middle East will depend to an ever-growing degree on diversionary activities in Western Europe.

The *Pittsburgh Press*, however, made an even more telling observation: that the raid 'came at a time when there was renewed clamour for the opening of a second front in the west to take the edge off whatever offensive the Germans are planning to launch against Russia this spring'.

Less informed speculation, such as that represented in *The Evening Independent* in Florida on Monday 30 March, suggested that, according to a 'well-informed source', the raid would have crippled the German submarine base for a year, curtailing U-boat activities in the north Atlantic for some time: submarines in the basin had been 'probably left high and dry, experts declared'. Next day's *Melbourne Age*, featuring a report by its London correspondent, observed that the value of the raid had to be calculated not just by military factors: 'It threw the enemy's defence into confusion, and stepped up the morale of those people opposed to the Nazi regime. It also encouraged the British, who, by the avidity with which they have seized on the raid for discussion, showed that they are hungry for action.'

The second German communiqué sought to minimise the British attack, reporting that those 'forces which the enemy succeeded in landing were encircled and annihilated by the quick action of troops of all services. A comparatively large number of prisoners remain in our hands. Numerous enemy ships were sunk and the rest took to flight.' However, on 31 March a German radio broadcast from Breslau let the cat out of the bag, inadvertently acknowledging that HMS *Campbeltown* had succeeded in her mission:

> Every German can only feel respect in fact sympathy for the poor devils who tried to get the utmost out of an operation which had been imposed on them by a command completely deprived of reason . . .
>
> The crew of the *Campbeltown* which forced the Northern lock gate [i.e. the Normandie Dock] under the hail of fire of German artillery and the crews of the British torpedo boats and speedboats which in vain tried to reach and torpedo the southern lock gave of their best in pursuing what could only be described as a mad undertaking. They persevered until they were killed or captured.

Mark Twain observed that truth can often be stranger than fiction. The scattered and confused newspaper reports from across the globe in the final days of March 1942 could only guess at the dimensions of one of the most dramatic feats of the Second World War, in which 621 men, commandos and sailors, threw themselves at the French Atlantic port of Saint-Nazaire in a daring attempt to change what they believed to be the entire direction of German maritime strategy. The survival of their cause, country and civilisation lay at stake. Disaster once again threatened Britain. This was not a time for half-measures, but for decisive, determined and dramatic action.

Writing shortly after he returned safely from the Saint-Nazaire raid, one of the few to do so, the journalist Gordon Holman observed that when the time came to write the full story of Commando exploits after the war it would 'be a volume of immortal memories'. Striking back at the German behemoth striding arrogantly across the carcass of a once-free Europe, even if it was but a tiny pinprick compared with the scale of German military might at the time, was a stirring sight. Holman stated proudly that the raid:

> put this generation of Englishmen, at one bound, on a par with all the fearless fighting men of any bygone generation that helped to make our history. I wish that all my fellow countrymen, indeed all free and freedom-loving people, could have witnessed that scene from some great invisible bandstand. Their hearts would have been stirred and uplifted, their faith strengthened and they would have said a prayer of proud thanksgiving.

In some small measure this book is an attempt to help build that volume of immortal memories of which Holman wrote so movingly only hours after returning from the scene of bloody battle.

Mountbatten's diary on Saturday 28 March 1942 revealed that the day was an anxious one, as he awaited news of the raid. Had he known the ferocity of the German defences encountered by the raiders he would have had reason to worry. Dieckman's battery at Le Pointeau that night fired 1,300 rounds, and the big 6.6-inch guns at Pointe de l'Ève fired no fewer than four hundred.

The first intimation of the outcome of the raid came with the arrival in Plymouth early the following morning of the destroyer group carrying Ryder, who was able to provide a brief but prompt update to Combined Operations HQ by telephone. He suggested that, although expensive in casualties – many of whom must now be prisoners of war – the operation had been successful. Within a few days Forbes had debriefed Ryder in Plymouth and sent his findings to Richmond Terrace. Worried at first that the raid was tantamount to suicide, he now considered it to have surpassed the achievements of the fabled attack on Zeebrugge in 1918. 'Not only was this a highly successful frontal assault on a heavily defended port,' he observed, 'but it was also mounted through a difficult and even treacherous estuary, utilising all the effects of surprise and bluff to the full.' Forbes and Mountbatten were not the only ones to be relieved. Congratulations started to flood in.

Given the fierce intensity of fire that he had seen with his own eyes in the Loire during the run-in, the battle in the dockside and during the withdrawal, Ryder feared that the butcher's bill would be high. It was. Of the 621 men who departed Falmouth on the afternoon of 26 March 1942, some 382 became casualties, a rate of 62 per cent, 27 per cent of whom were killed (169). Five escaped to Spain, 213 (34 per cent), many wounded, were taken prisoner and the remainder (234, or 38 per cent), made it back to Britain. Of the 264 commandos who set sail 72 per cent were killed, wounded or taken prisoner (190); 25 per cent (66) of whom were killed and 124 taken prisoner, many of whom were wounded. However, bald presentations of the statistics for the dead, wounded and missing represented battlefield arithmetic, for those at the time, of a misguided kind. It had always been considered that Operation *Chariot* was a high-risk venture. The idea of success-fully ramming a destroyer packed with explosives into the heart of a strongly defended enemy harbour, there to self-detonate and destroy the massive external caissons of the largest dry dock in Europe, and to disgorge commandos to carry out additional dockside demolitions, was preposterous, unless of course one believed that the very audacity of such an operation might itself contribute to its success.

Forbes concluded that taking 'into consideration the extreme vulnerability of the coastal craft, neither the losses in men or material can be considered as excessive for the results achieved'. Ryder, likewise, observed that the casualties were 'what one would expect from any land operation against such formidable military defences'. Both men were right. Relative to combat elsewhere during the war the figures for Operation *Chariot* were not dramatically different, although they were more severe than the losses sustained during the Dieppe Raid later that year – a raid that has gone down in history as much for its many operational and tactical errors as for its human cost. At Dieppe on 19 August 1942, widely regarded as a bloodbath, 4,963 Canadians deployed as part of a combat force of nearly 6,000 troops. Of this number 68 per cent of the Canadians (3,367) became casualties; 18 per cent were killed and 39 per cent became prisoners of war. The percentage of those killed at Dieppe therefore equated to similar operations in this theatre of war at this time but was significantly less expensive in terms of dead than Saint-Nazaire.

A reasonable comparison is with battle casualties in infantry combat in North West Europe in 1944–5. The historian John Ellis has calculated that across eleven separate US infantry divisions fighting during this period of high intensity, between 16 and 18 per cent of soldiers were killed, and between 57 and 65 per cent were wounded. In a selection of British infantry battalions over the same period and in the same geography, the figures are between 16 and 28 per cent killed, and between 66 and 72 per cent wounded.

On 22 June 1942 the Admiralty's Naval Intelligence directorate assessed German casualties at Saint-Nazaire to be 320, 'and therefore comparable to our own . . .' The Germans acknowledged 42 dead and 127 wounded, together with 'over 100 missing', presumably those killed when the *Campbeltown* blew up. The best estimate of French casualties suggests that during the raid and the week that followed 16 were killed and 26 were injured. In addition, up to 2,000 civilians were forced permanently from their homes in the subsequent weeks.

Of the eighteen coastal craft employed, ten were sunk by enemy action, four were scuttled or destroyed and four returned safely but damaged. The raid has been roundly criticised for taking the vulnerable wooden Fairmiles into the teeth of the action. Was it really necessary to carry out the raid without the proper resources? Ryder gives this argument very short shrift, observing that Britain was badly prepared for war across its entire spectrum of military capabilities, not merely in the arena of amphibious operations. 'To have suggested that this important objective was not to be attacked on this account,' he considered, 'would surely have been a defeatist attitude and should find no place in our thoughts.'

Hughes-Hallett's initial plan to use two destroyers fell at the hurdle of available resources. It is also important to recognise that one of the reasons for the deployment of so many Fairmile launches was Newman's concern that in one or two destroyers his commandos would be 'bunched', and vulnerable to devastating counter-action. In his report Ryder presented a third option, in abbreviated form, which would have avoided the risk to so many vulnerable Fairmiles, especially during the withdrawal, namely 'to use *Campbeltown* and [the Eureka assault landing craft] carried by two fast Infantry Assault Ships. Using possibly four MGBs to give supporting fire. Speed of withdrawal 22 knots. Total time 34 hours instead of 60.' Ryder's idea remains untested, however. Arguably the Eurekas would have been as vulnerable in the close reaches of the Loire as the Fairmiles.

One issue not raised at the time, officially at least, was the lack of contingency plans for the Fairmiles if they found their designated landing places untenable because of enemy fire. Time and again the extraordinarily brave Fairmile commanders drove in against the Old Mole despite seeing boat after boat destructing in front of them under a vicious and relentless enemy fire. The planning of an alternative landing place, or the freedom to choose one, would almost certainly have made a significant difference to the casualties, both of men and Fairmiles, on that bloody night. It would have required flexibility, both from crews and commandos, to adapt at the last minute to a change of plan, but the commandos had demonstrated time and again their power to think on their feet, as Newman's withdrawal across the Bridge of Memories demonstrated. All this, of course, is hindsight.

Did the Germans know about the raid? The strength of the German counter-fire during the run-in shocked and surprised Newman, and led him to wonder whether the Germans were waiting for them. In his after-battle report he mused on the possibilities that their plans had been rumbled, either by spies in England, aerial reconnaissance during the journey out, or from information provided by U-593, assuming that it had managed to send a message to Saint-Nazaire after successfully evading the attentions of HMS *Tynedale*. 'Whichever of these conditions prevailed,' he wrote, 'it was amazing that the number of enemy troops in the area was so great.'

> Within minutes of landing, heavy fighting was going on in the dock area with considerable numbers of enemy troops about. Very soon afterwards in the street fighting the enemy were everywhere. It appeared that every crossroad and street junction had a machine gun post and patrols were moving in most of the streets. Armoured cars and mobile troops in motor cycles and sidecars were in operation. Were they waiting for us or was it just very quick work in bringing the troops in from their barracks?

The truth is, however, that the raid came as a complete surprise to the enemy. Despite the shock of the attack, they reacted fast to the threat to the port. In the first place, the failure of the bombing diversion meant that whilst many Germans were hidden in air-raid shelters, a large number of others were manning weapons along both banks of the river; it took only a matter of seconds to switch them from the anti-aircraft to the anti-ship mode. The German post-operation report, while critical of many of their failings that night, nevertheless recognised that the local troops and sailors, many of them only partially trained in what they described as 'land fighting', reacted with commendable alacrity and professionalism when the threat was recognised for what it was, noting that the 'passing of intelligence and the alert worked quickly and smoothly'.

Only twenty minutes after the *Campbeltown* struck the outer caisson of the Normandie Dock, men of Thiessen's *Marineflakbataillon* 703 from Villès-Martin had crossed Bridge D into the Old Town, followed shortly afterwards by men of Koch's *Marineflakbataillon* 705 – a remarkable achievement. By the time that Newman's men were attempting to rush the Bridge of Memories, men of the 679th Infantry Regiment had arrived in the New Town from La Baule with armoured cars and machineguns, reinforcing the guards and base crew of the 7 *Unterseebootsflottille*, the anti-aircraft gunners of the 703rd and 705th *Marineartilleriebataillone* and local troops of two *Arbeitseinheiten* (labour companies). Likewise, the morale and bearing of the men was regarded as excellent. The reality for Newman is that the British were fighting a first-class enemy who, when roused, and despite having no intimation of the attack, fought back tenaciously.

Was the raid successful? Forbes was adamant that in so far as its object was to put the Normandie Dock 'out of action for a considerable time' it was undoubtedly so. In this he is unquestionably correct, at an operational level: the enemy could no longer rely on the use of any of the French Atlantic ports to repair a capital ship of the size of the *Tirpitz*, should they wish to (and it is clear that they did not). At a tactical level a number of subsidiary benefits were tabulated, such as the 'certain damage, and probable sinking, of a U-boat by HMS *Tynedale*', the 'probable diversion of troops and armament to Biscay ports' and the 'moral effect on the enemy of an attack on one of his principal bases'.

But at a strategic level it is also true that different people had varying views of the purpose and value of the raid. The Admiralty had, at least superficially, bought Mountbatten's argument that the rationale for the raid was to change the balance of maritime power in Europe by ensuring that the *Tirpitz* could no longer find refuge on the French Atlantic coast. But it is also clear that this argument, in Mountbatten's mind, was always the means to an end, and the 'end' was not the emasculation of the *Tirpitz*, but the successful prosecution of raiding as a discrete strategy of offensive containment at a time when it was not possible for Britain to engage in decisive land battles in Europe. That this was also a view held by Churchill can be seen by General Sir Alan Brooke's comment to General George Marshall on 9 April: 'We were executing a number of raids on the enemy-occupied coastline from Norway to the Bay of Biscay,' he wrote, 'in order to force on the enemy a feeling of insecurity and uncertainty.' Sir Leslie Hollis (Senior Military Assistant Secretary in the Office of the War Cabinet) observed that Saint-Nazaire 'spurred on the already aggressive Prime Minister in the face of Brooke's attempts to restrain him'.

The moral impact of the raid must also not be forgotten. It undoubtedly gave Britons hope, at one of the lowest points in Britain's modern history. The fact that, straitened as she was, Britain could still launch damaging attacks on German-held Europe was a message of priceless value to Britain and her allies, a point understood only too well by Nazi propagandists, who attempted to discredit the raid from the very start.

In this respect British 'public relations' were much slower and more considered than German media efforts, as befitted the information provided by a democracy, but for the short term at least the only information available across Europe came from Nazi sources. The Nazi reporting was an exercise in the careful insertion of lies amongst a smattering of half-truths. According to two reporters, Heinricht Schmidt and Kurt Ettars, supposed eyewitnesses of the raid, the events of the early morning unfolded dramatically in Germany's favour:

> An old American destroyer is sent against lock gates. The organisation appears to be good. The weather is quite favourable for a surprise attack. There is some moonlight, obscured from time to time by light sea mist. The alarm is given, the guns start firing, and the staccato noise of machineguns fills the air. A mighty explosion is heard, then others. The destroyer has advanced further . . . makes off towards the sea at full speed. He is not allowed to get far. A small boat of the harbour-protection flotilla immediately opens fire; the English reply, and a violent artillery duel ensues between the unequal adversaries. Suddenly a motor torpedo-boat is rent by a vivid flash. We hear an explosion, and the vessel disappears. The crew jumps overboard and is picked up by the German boat. One of the prisoners is the destroyer's commander. By dawn the whole excitement is over. Those of the enemy not killed have been taken prisoner – well over 100. One destroyer, nine motor torpedo-boats, and four torpedo-boats have been sent to the bottom of the Loire.

The initial German line was to suggest that HMS *Campbeltown* had blown up short of its intended target, although this claim was undone later in the day when pictures were published by the German authorities showing quite clearly that the vessel was wedged tightly in the lock gates. The story now changed to assert that whilst the *Campbeltown* had indeed struck the lock gates, it had nevertheless failed to detonate, the pictures (together with many others taken that day) supposedly demonstrating the veracity of the German position. It needed subsequent PRU photographs to demonstrate the truth of the British claim, although this, of course, took time. Meanwhile the Nazi regime exulted in its supposed triumph. Evidence that the British attack had in fact succeeded also came from an unexpected source, a German civilian radio broadcast, some weeks later. In this a German naval officer observed:

> We would not wish to deny the gallantry of the British. Every German is moved by a feeling of respect for the men who carried out this action. The crew of the *Campbeltown* under fierce fire forced their ship through the northern [i.e. Normandie] lock gates, and carried out a crazy enterprise as well as it could be done. They fought until death or capture.

The Germans in secret, of course, were shocked by the daring of the British plan and the skill of its execution, acknowledging that 'the enemy did achieve his principal aim: "The destruction of the lock gates and installations of the large Saint-Nazaire docks."' Indeed, the British raid concentrated on destroying facilities for battleships, the aim of which 'they accomplished with outstanding skill and thoroughness'.

Hitler was furious, and a gale of recrimination swept through the senior echelons of the Wehrmacht. Together with the mosquito bites along the Norwegian coast in 1941, the cross-Channel raiding in early 1942 and the raid on Dieppe (Operation *Jubilee*) in August, Operation *Chariot* led Hitler to determine that the Commando menace could only be countered by the most extreme and brutal measures. On 18 October 1942, in his infamous *Kommandobefehl* (Commando order), he instructed his forces from that time forth to exterminate all captured commandos without mercy. Although the POWs in German captivity were safe from this secret and unlawful edict, a number of men who had been on Operation *Chariot* and who had successfully returned to Britain were subsequently captured and executed in later Commando raids on the European continent. One of these was Lieutenant Joe Houghton. A pre-war Territorial soldier with the Honourable Artillery Company, the 31-year-old Houghton of No. 2 Commando was taken prisoner in September 1942 after being captured during the raid on the Glomfjord hydroelectric plant in Norway (Operation *Musketoon*). He was murdered at Sachsenhausen concentration camp, outside Berlin, on 23 October 1942.

What were the causes therefore of *Chariot*'s undoubted success? Forbes stressed, pre-eminently, the role of surprise, at several levels:

> The unseen passage – to the Loire – was due partly to favourable weather conditions, which helped to prevent the force being detected from the air, and partly to careful routing to keep the force out of the tracks of Zenits (daily meteorological reconnaissance flights) and reconnaissance flights by the enemy. It was also due to the almost certain sinking of a U-boat at 0815 on 27th March by HMS *Tynedale*. [This assumption, of course, turned out to be false.] Surprise in the final approach was . . . due to the methods employed by Commander Ryder to deceive the enemy. It was also fortunate that there were no patrols covering the approach over the mud flats. That surprise was not complete was principally due to the noise of the M.L.s' engines (which, on a still night, are clearly audible three miles away) and to the inability of our bomber aircraft to locate their targets in the difficult weather conditions.

But the most important point was one that Forbes did not feel necessary to mention, namely the operational chutzpah exhibited by Combined Operations in planning and carrying out this sort of raid. It was brazen and bold, a David versus Goliath type of strike that had a chance of succeeding by virtue of its very audacity. It was a gutsy plan, requiring luck, bluff and surprise in abundance to come off. It also called for high-quality intelligence, excellent planning, the committed professionalism of all the servicemen involved, some of whom were highly trained volunteers, together with decisive and determined leadership. All of these features Combined Operations, for this raid, displayed in abundance. The success of Operation *Chariot* was therefore a product of brilliant planning and superb intelligence, executed with cool heads and outstanding bravery.

Whether Britain would have entertained an Operation *Chariot* if its survival was not as seriously threatened as it had been in 1942, and when its ability to fight back was as dramatically constrained as it was, is a moot point. Britain's desperation to strike back actually increased the chance that a 'rapier thrust from the sea' (as Churchill described it) would be successful. Its triumphant denouement can be seen in part in the array of awards for bravery from a notoriously parsimonious state: five Victoria Crosses (Savage, Durrant, Ryder, Beattie and Newman), four Distinguished Service Orders, seventeen Distinguished Service Crosses, eleven Military Crosses, four Conspicuous Gallantry Medals, five Distinguished Conduct Medals, twenty-four Distinguished Service Medals and fifteen Military Medals. Fifty-one men were Mentioned in Dispatches. Four men were awarded the Croix de Guerre.

The Admiralty's own damage assessment on 11 April 1942 concluded that even if the South Entrance remained intact, the outer caisson to the Normandie Dock had been destroyed, as had been the lock gate to the Old Entrance (by Wynn's torpedoes), although the Germans were quickly building a dam across this gap to prevent the Bassin becoming subject to the tide. Intelligence sources had reported that some of the civil population had joined in the fighting. The most important outcome, however, was the state of insecurity the raid engendered among the German defenders of the Atlantic coast. 'The Saint-Nazaire raid has had a more far-reaching effect than any previous one,' the report stated, 'and has created a state of nerves and disorganisation.'

This was no mere wishful thinking. Concerned about the potential for a similar raid in the north, presumably aimed either at the U-boat pens or the dock facilities that had sustained the *Scharnhorst*, *Gneisenau* and *Prinz Eugen* the previous year, a state of siege was declared in Brest. Further afield, the British naval attaché in neutral Sweden reported that his Vichy opposite number had commented on the great impact of raids such as Operation *Chariot* on French opinion. Wheeler and Sims had observed the same reaction during their journey through France. One German who seemed especially affected by the prospect of further British raids was Admiral Dönitz, who within days of the assault on Saint-Nazaire was moved away from the danger zone to an anonymous apartment block in the Avenue du Maréchal Maunoury in Paris, but continued to believe that he had been the mission's target.

What of Operation *Myrmidon*, the raid designed to accompany and complement *Chariot*? To Richmond Terrace's discomfiture it proved to be a monumental cock-up, a deeply embarrassing contrast to the brilliance of Ryder and Newman's *Chariot*. The force, embarked on HMS *Queen Emma* and HMS *Prinses Beatrix* disguised as Spanish merchant ships, escorted on the surface by the destroyers HMS *Calpe* and *Badsworth* and three MTBs and in the air by a Sunderland flying boat, left Falmouth on 2 April but returned, without undertaking any action, five days later. The raid proved to be a flop, the result of poor planning and intelligence. The originally ambitious plan to destroy the coastal batteries defending Bayonne and Saint-Jean-de-Luz, seize and demolish the Adour Estuary port facilities and do likewise to the explosives factory at Blancpignon, reported to be a significant manufacturer for the Germans of TNT, was reduced in scale by a third on 25 March, Churchill limiting the raid to the destruction of ships in the port. On 5 April the ships, carrying a thousand commandos, approached the mouth of the Adour Estuary in order to carry out the landing, but in the midst of bad weather encountered an unexpected sandbar and, lacking local navigational expertise that would enable them to proceed, were forced to return to Britain.

On reflection, and even at the time, it was clear that the noise made about the raids in terms of the exultant post-action publicity seemed overblown, relative to their tiny size and seeming strategic irrelevance, and in the context of the seismic military events taking place elsewhere. And yet, all the commentators at the time recognised the light that such raids shone in the otherwise Stygian gloom of the moment. The seemingly impossible had been achieved. Morale at home had been improved (confirmed by Ministry of Information analysis for April, which detected 'a steady improvement in spirits', partly as a result of the Combined Operations raids), fighting troops were inspired, offensive momentum was maintained in the face of potential criticism that Britain was not doing enough to fight back against the enemy (accusations that came, primarily, from the United States and the Soviet Union), and the enemy was forced to divert resources that would otherwise be used elsewhere.

Important also was the fact that these *strategic* raids had a solid *operational* objective: in the case of Bruneval it was the recovery of a new German radar; for Operation *Chariot* the destruction of the Normandie Dock, and later in the year Operation *Frankton* (the famous Cockleshell raid) would damage the Axis blockade-running capabilities between Europe and Japan. In addition, successful small raids would continue to be launched against strategic targets in Norway, with mixed results.

Together, it is unarguable that these raids had a serious strategic purpose, and to a significant degree achieved that purpose. The triumph of the Charioteers lay not in keeping the *Tirpitz* out of Atlantic waters – from December 1941 Raeder and Hitler had determined that she would serve better as a deterrent and a 'force-in-being' to tie up a significant part of the Royal Navy in Scapa Flow, than to deploy for war in the Atlantic where, like the *Bismarck*, they might lose her. Instead, the Charioteers succeeded spectacularly simply by virtue of *raiding*: the very act of taking the war to the enemy in Europe, at a time when Britain otherwise had few other offensive options, constituted Combined Operations' greatest achievement, voicing through decisive action Britain's collective determination to continue fighting, David against the Germanic Goliath, in spite of the seemingly enormous odds against them.

In no small way also, through the courage and sacrifice of the Charioteers, Britain was able to serve notice to the subjugated nations of Europe that in time she would be back, and that they would no longer be slaves. This was their ultimate triumph.

The day after HMS *Tynedale* had deposited Lance Corporal Jack Webb and his fellows at Plymouth they spent in a state of dazed disbelief at the loss of so many of their colleagues. That night was the first of a lifetime of nightmares:

> I was not the only one who, in bed that first night back, wept away the tension until sleep finally obliterated thoughts of our comrades lost in small boats or ashore in a hell ten times worse than the one we had been through.

When Dr David Paton returned with the commando survivors to their base in Ayr two weeks after the raid the whole world knew about the gallant raiders, and the blow they had struck against the mighty Teuton. But it didn't stop the tears. Paton proudly marched what he described as his 'sorry little' group of three officers and twenty-five men from the railway station half a mile back to their HQ at No. 2 Wellington Square through crowded though silent streets, numbers down from the 'rumbustious 400' the townsfolk had 'learned to live with for months'. The sight told its story: the 'people of Ayr stood in the streets and the women wept as we marched'.

Glossary

AOC	Air Officer Commanding
ASDIC	Anti-submarine detection equipment (Sonar)
BCRA	De Gaulle's intelligence organisation, the 'Bureau Central des Renseignements et d'Action' (Central Bureau of Intelligence and Operations)
BDST	British Double Summer Time
BEF	British Expeditionary Force to France, 1939–40
BST	British Summer Time
Cdo	Commando
C-in-C	Commander-in-Chief
CIU	Central [Photographic] Intelligence Unit, Medmenham
CO	Commanding Officer
COHQ	Combined Operations Headquarters
DCM	Distinguished Conduct Medal
DSC	Distinguished Service Cross (an officers-only award)
DSM	Distinguished Service Medal (an other-ranks-only award)
DSO	Distinguished Service Order
GOC	General Officer Commanding (i.e., a divisional commander)
ISSB	Inter Services Security Bureau
ISTD	Inter-Service Topographical Department
ISTDC	Inter-Services Training and Development Centre
LOTI	Liverpool Observatory and Tidal Institute

LSI	Landing Ship Infantry
MACO	Military Adviser to Combined Operations (Brigadier Haydon)
MGB	Motor Gunboat (MGB 314, a Fairmile 'C'-class boat)
MI9/MI19	The branch of Military Intelligence in the War Office concerned with escape and evasion and with enemy interrogation
ML	Motor Launch (Fairmile 'B'-class boat)
MO	Medical Officer
MPI	Mean Point of Impact
MTB	Motor Torpedo Boat
NAAFI	Navy, Army and Air Force Institutes (the British Armed Forces' 'shop')
NCO	Non-Commissioned Officer
OBWest	German Army Command, West (*Oberbefehlshaber West*)
OC	Officer Commanding
OIC	Officer-in-Command
OKW	Supreme Command of the Armed Forces (*Oberkommando der Wehrmacht*, Hitler's supreme military HQ)
passeur	A French helper in an escape network
PJC	HMS *Prinses Josephine Charlotte*, a converted cross-Channel ferry, deployed as a Landing Ship Infantry (LSI)
POW	Prisoner of War
PRU	No. 1 Photographic Reconnaissance Unit, RAF Heston
RA	Royal Artillery
RAMC	Royal Army Medical Corps
RANVR	Royal Australian Navy Volunteer Reserve
RCNVR	Royal Canadian Navy Volunteer Reserve
RE	Royal Engineers
réseau	Resistance or escape and evader network
résistant	A member of a resistance group, or an individual resister

RN	Royal Navy
RNVR	Royal Naval Volunteer Reserve
SIS	Secret Intelligence Service (MI6)
SKL	German Naval Warfare Command, Berlin (*Seekriegsleitung*)
SNO	Senior Naval Officer (R.E.D. Ryder)
SNOIC	Senior Naval Officer in Command (*Kriegsmarine*)
SOE	Special Operations Executive
STC	Special Training Centre, Lochailort
TSM	Troop Sergeant Major, a Warrant Officer Class 2
WFSt	The operations department of the OKW (*Wehrmachtführungsstab*)
WO1	Warrant Officer Class 1 (a Regimental Sergeant Major)
WO2	Warrant Officer Class 2 (a Company or Troop Sergeant Major)
WRNS	Women's Royal Naval Service
Zone Libre	French free zone (i.e. Vichy-controlled)

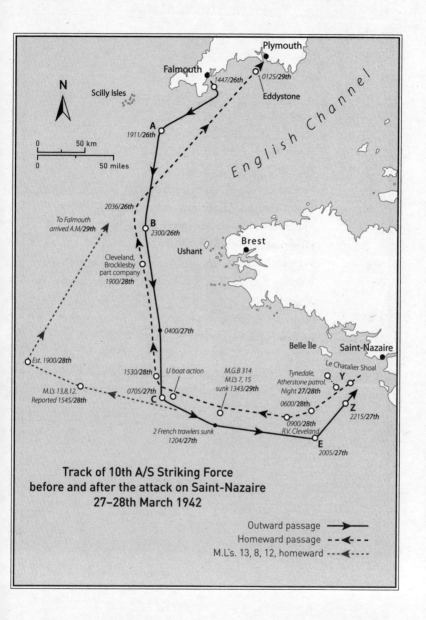

N

Plymouth

Falmouth

1447/26th

0125/29th

Eddystone

Scilly Isles

English Channel

A
1911/26th

0   50 km

0   50 miles

2036/26th

To Falmouth
arrived A.M/29th

B
2300/26th

Cleveland,
Brocklesby
part company
1900/28th

Brest

Ushant

0400/27th

Belle Île

Saint-Nazaire

Le Chatalier Shoal

Est. 1900/28th

1530/28th

U boat action

M.G.B 314
M.L's 7, 15
sunk *1343/29th*

Tynedale,
Atherstone patrol.
Night *27/28th*

Y

M.L's 13,8,12.
Reported *1545/28th*

C
0705/27th

0600/28th

Z
2215/27th

2 French trawlers sunk
1204/27th

0900/28th
R.V. Cleveland

E
2005/27th

**Track of 10th A/S Striking Force
before and after the attack on Saint-Nazaire
27–28th March 1942**

Outward passage ⟶

Homeward passage ⟵- -

M.L's. 13, 8, 12, homeward ⟵· · ·

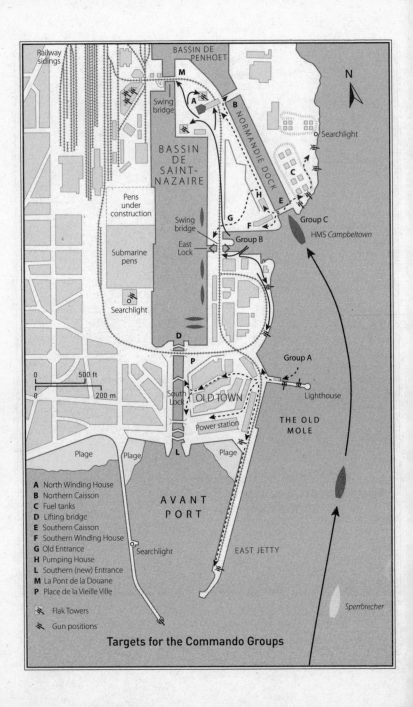

Targets for the Commando Groups

Railway sidings

BASSIN DE PENHOET

M

Swing bridge

A

B

N

NORMANDIE DOCK

Searchlight

BASSIN DE SAINT-NAZAIRE

C

Pens under construction

H

E

Submarine pens

G

F

Swing bridge

Group B

Group C

East Lock

HMS *Campbeltown*

Searchlight

D

P

Group A

South Lock

OLD TOWN

Lighthouse

THE OLD MOLE

L

Power station

0   500 ft

0   200 m

Plage

Plage

Plage

AVANT PORT

A North Winding House
B Northern Caisson
C Fuel tanks
D Lifting bridge
E Southern Caisson
F Southern Winding House
G Old Entrance
H Pumping House
L Southern (new) Entrance
M La Pont de la Douane
P Place de la Vieille Ville

Searchlight

EAST JETTY

⚡ Flak Towers

⚡ Gun positions

Sperrbrecher

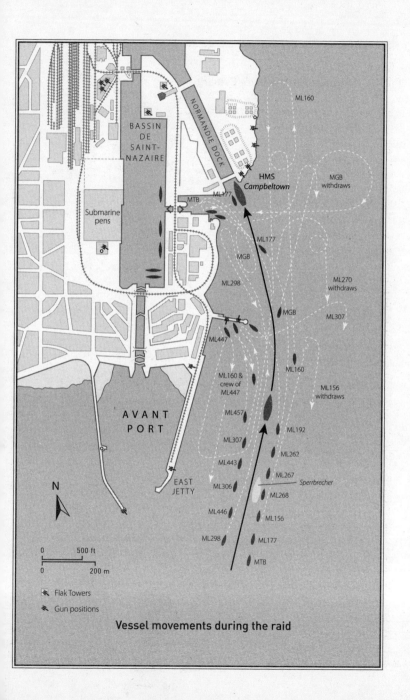

Vessel movements during the raid

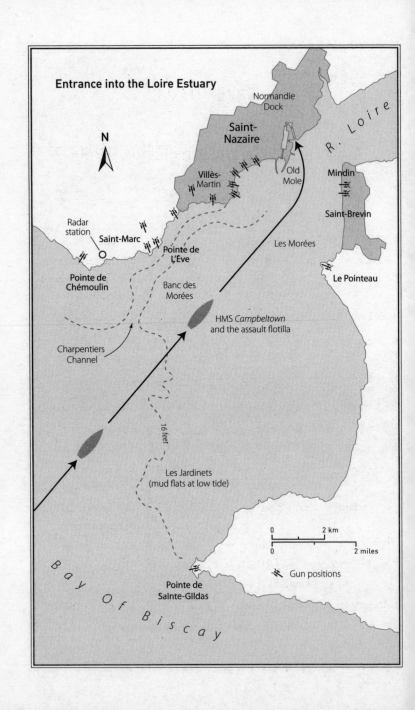

Entrance into the Loire Estuary

N

Normandie Dock

Saint-Nazaire

Villès-Martin

Old Mole

Mindin

Saint-Brevin

Radar station

Saint-Marc

Pointe de L'Eve

Les Morées

Pointe de Chémoulin

Banc des Morées

HMS *Campbeltown* and the assault flotilla

Le Pointeau

R. Loire

Charpentiers Channel

16 feet

Les Jardinets (mud flats at low tide)

0   2 km

0   2 miles

Gun positions

Pointe de Sainte-Gildas

Bay Of Biscay

APPENDIX 1

Combined Operations Raids, 1940–2

1940

Collar	Boulogne	24.6.40	11 Independent Company, 3 and 4 Commando
Ambassador	Guernsey	14.7.40	11 Independent Company, 3 Commando

1941

Claymore	Lofoten Islands	04.03.41	3 and 4 Commando
Chess	Ambleteuse	27.07.41	12 Commando
Acid Drop	Hardelot/Merlimont	30.08.41	5 Commando
Chopper	Saint-Vaast/ Saint-Aubin	27.09.41	5 Troop, 1 Commando
Astrakhan	near Calais	12.11.41	101 Troop, Special Service Bde
Sunstar	Ouistreham	23.11.41	9 Commando
Anklet	Lofoten Islands, Norway	26.12.41	12 Commando
Archery	Vaagso, Norway	26.12.41	2 and 3 Commando

1942

Chariot	Saint-Nazaire	27.03.42	Special Service Brigade, 2 Commando
J.V.	Boulogne	11.04.42	101 Troop, Special Service Brigade
Abercrombie	Hardelot	21.04.42	4 Commando
Bristle	Boulogne	03.06.42	6 Commando
Barricade	Pointe de Saire	14.08.42	Small-scale raiding force
Jubilee	Dieppe	19.08.42	Canadians, 3, 4 and 40 (Royal Marine) Commandos
Gauntlet	Spitzbergen	25.08.42	
Dryad	Île Casquets	02.09.42	Small-scale raiding force
Brandford	Île Burliou	07.09.42	Small-scale raiding force
Aquatint	Port-en-Bessin	12.09.42	Small-scale raiding force
Musketoon	Glomfjord, Norway	20.09.42	12 Commando
Basalt	Isle of Sark	03.10.42	Small-scale raiding force
Fahrenheit	Pointe de Plouézec	11.11.42	Small-scale raiding force
Frankton	Bordeaux	07.12.42	Royal Marine Boom Patrol Detachment (the 'Cockleshell Heroes')

APPENDIX 2

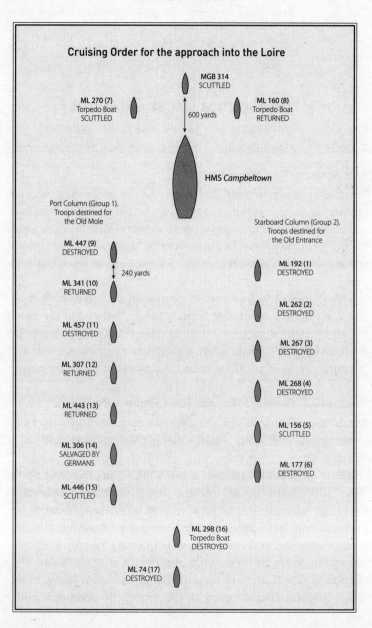

Cruising Order for the approach into the Loire

MGB 314
SCUTTLED

ML 270 (7)
Torpedo Boat
SCUTTLED

ML 160 (8)
Torpedo Boat
RETURNED

600 yards

HMS *Campbeltown*

Port Column (Group 1).
Troops destined for
the Old Mole

Starboard Column (Group 2).
Troops destined for
the Old Entrance

ML 447 (9)
DESTROYED

ML 192 (1)
DESTROYED

240 yards

ML 341 (10)
RETURNED

ML 262 (2)
DESTROYED

ML 457 (11)
DESTROYED

ML 267 (3)
DESTROYED

ML 307 (12)
RETURNED

ML 268 (4)
DESTROYED

ML 443 (13)
RETURNED

ML 156 (5)
SCUTTLED

ML 306 (14)
SALVAGED BY
GERMANS

ML 177 (6)
DESTROYED

ML 446 (15)
SCUTTLED

ML 298 (16)
Torpedo Boat
DESTROYED

ML 74 (17)
DESTROYED

APPENDIX 3

The Victoria Cross Citations

Able Seaman W.A. (Bill) Savage

For great gallantry, skill and devotion to duty as gun layer of the pom-pom in a motor gun boat in the Saint-Nazaire raid. Completely exposed, and under heavy fire he engaged positions ashore with cool and steady accuracy. On the way out of the harbour he kept up the same vigorous and accurate fire against the attacking ships, until he was killed at his gun.

This Victoria Cross is awarded in recognition not only of the gallantry and devotion to duty of Able Seaman Savage, but also of the valour shown by many others, unnamed, in Motor Launches, Motor Gun Boats and Motor Torpedo Boats, who gallantly carried out their duty in entirely exposed positions against enemy fire at very close range.

Sergeant T.F. (Tommy) Durrant, No. 1 Commando

For great gallantry, skill and devotion to duty when in charge of a Lewis gun in HM Motor Launch 306 in the St Nazaire raid on 28 March 1942.

Motor Launch 306 came under heavy fire while proceeding up the River Loire towards the port. Sergeant Durrant, in his position abaft the bridge, where he had no cover or protection, engaged enemy gun positions and searchlights ashore. During this engagement he was severely wounded in the arm but refused to leave his gun. The Motor Launch subsequently went down the river and was attacked by a German destroyer at 50 to 60 yards range, and often closer. In this action Sergeant Durrant continued to fire at the destroyer's bridge with the greatest of coolness and with complete disregard of the enemy's fire. The Motor Launch was illuminated by the enemy search-light, and Sergeant Durrant drew on himself the individual attention of the enemy guns, and was again wounded in many places. Despite these further wounds he stayed in his exposed position, still firing his gun, although after a time only able to support himself by holding on to the gun mounting.

After a running fight, the Commander of the German destroyer called on the Motor Launch to surrender. Sergeant Durrant's answer was a further burst of fire at the destroyer's bridge. Although now very weak, he went on firing, using drums of ammunition as fast as they could be replaced. A renewed attack by the enemy vessel eventually silenced the fire of the Motor Launch, but Sergeant Durrant refused to give up until the destroyer came alongside, grappled the Motor Launch and took prisoner those who remained alive.

Sergeant Durrant's gallant fight was commended by the German officers on boarding the Motor Launch. This very gallant non-commis-sioned officer later died of the many wounds received in action.*

Lieutenant Commander S.H. (Sam) Beattie RN

For great gallantry and determination in the attack on St. Nazaire in command of H.M.S. *Campbeltown*. Under intense fire directed at the bridge from point blank range of about 100 yards, and in the face of the blinding glare of many searchlights, he steamed her into the lock-gates and beached and scuttled her in the correct position. This Victoria Cross is awarded to Lieutenant-Commander Beattie in recognition not only of his own valour but also of that of the unnamed officers and men of a very gallant ship's company, many of whom have not returned.

---

*   This award was first suggested to Lieutenant Colonel Charles Newman in the prison camp at Rennes by Kapitänleutnant Friedrich Paul, who wanted to make him aware of Durrant's exceptional bravery. The VC was awarded to a commando, therefore, fighting and dying on a Royal Navy vessel, on the recommendation of a German officer.

Lieutenant Colonel A.C. (Charles) Newman, No. 2 Commando

On the night of 27th/28th March, 1942, Lieutenant-Colonel Newman was in command of the military force detailed to land on enemy occupied territory and destroy the dock installations of the German controlled naval base at Saint-Nazaire.

This important base was known to be heavily defended and bomber support had to be abandoned owing to bad weather. The operation was therefore bound to be exceedingly hazardous, but Lieutenant-Colonel Newman, although empowered to call off the assault at any stage, was determined to carry to a successful conclusion the important task which had been assigned to him.

Coolly and calmly he stood on the bridge of the leading craft, as the small force steamed up the estuary of the River Loire, although the ships had been caught in the enemy searchlights and a murderous cross-fire opened from both banks, causing heavy casualties.

Although Lieutenant-Colonel Newman need not have landed himself, he was one of the first ashore and, during the next five hours of bitter fighting, he personally entered several houses and shot up the occupants and supervised the operations in the town, utterly regardless of his own safety, and he never wavered in his resolution to carry through the operation upon which so much depended.

An enemy gun position on the roof of a U-boat pen had been causing heavy casualties to the landing craft and Lieutenant-Colonel Newman directed the fire of a mortar against this position to such effect that the gun was silenced. Still fully exposed, he then brought machine gun fire to bear on an armed trawler in the harbour, compelling it to withdraw and thus preventing many casualties in the main demolition area.

Under the brilliant leadership of this officer the troops fought magnificently and held vastly superior enemy forces at bay, until the demolition parties had successfully completed their work of destruction. By this time, however, most of the landing craft had been sunk or set on fire and evacuation by sea was no longer possible. Although the main objective had been achieved, Lieutenant-Colonel Newman nevertheless was now determined to try and fight his way out into open country and so give all survivors a chance to escape.

The only way out of the harbour area lay across a narrow iron bridge covered by enemy machine guns and although severely shaken by a German hand grenade, which had burst at his feet, Lieutenant-Colonel Newman personally led the charge which stormed the position and under his inspiring leadership the small force fought its way through the streets to a point near the open country, when, all ammunition expended, he and his men were finally overpowered by the enemy.

The outstanding gallantry and devotion to duty of this fearless officer, his brilliant leadership and initiative, were largely responsible for the success of this perilous operation which resulted in heavy damage to the important naval base at Saint-Nazaire.

Commander R.E.D. (Robert) Ryder RN

For great gallantry in the attack on Saint-Nazaire. He commanded a force of small unprotected ships in an attack on a heavily defended port and led H.M.S. *Campbeltown* in under intense fire from short range weapons at point blank range. Though the main object of the expedition had been accomplished in the beaching of *Campbeltown*, he remained on the spot conducting operations, evacuating men from *Campbeltown* and dealing with strong points and close range weapons while exposed to heavy fire for one hour and sixteen minutes, and did not withdraw till it was certain that his ship could be of no use in rescuing any of the Commando Troops who were still ashore. That his Motor Gun Boat, now full of dead and wounded, should have survived and should have been able to withdraw through an intense barrage of close range fire was almost a miracle.

Sources

Second World War Experience Centre, Leeds
George Davidson DSM; Frank Arkle RNVR; Lieutenant John Roderick MC

Jewish Military Museum, London
Peter Nagel

Mountbatten Papers, Hartley Library, University of Southampton
MB1/B	Combined Operations 1940–1942
MB1/28	Haydon Papers
MB1/B32-47	Memoir of Vice Admiral John Hughes-Hallett

Churchill College Archives Centre, Cambridge University
GBR/0014/RDER	Robert Ryder VC

Bundesarchiv, Koblenz
IIIM 1000/31	Seekriegsleitung War Diary (1–31 March 1942)
Box 484/PG 32550	1 Seekriegsleitung Ib Handakte: The English Landing at Saint-Nazaire, 28 March 1942
Box 1981/PG 17394c	1 Seekriegsleitung – Telegraph and Radio Collection Vol. 61
M/325/37525-26	Navy Group West, Vol. 23 (1–31 March 1942)

M/300/37525-26	Commanding Admiral, France, Vol. 43 (16–31 March 1942)
M/280/37174	Naval Commander Loire, Vol. 2
M/947/70261-5	5th Torpedo Boat Flotilla, Vol. 9 (1–31 March 1942)

Imperial War Museum, London

Department of Sound
11361: George Russell Wheeler; 13406: George Gonin; 10963: Herbert Reginald Dyer; 9247 and 29615: Michael ('Micky') Clive Burn; 10231/3: Sir Ronald Swayne MC; 10251: Glyn Salisbury; 29823: Bill 'Tiger' Watson; 29822: Bert Shipton; 26204: John Roderick; 9976: Ernest Chappell; 29826: Frank Carr; 26203: David Paton; 18534: Hugh Arnold; 13406: John Wingate; 2528: 'Free French Officer' (Raymond Couraud); 17158: John Stanley Roberts; 29825: Thomas Sherman; 29821: William Etches; 29820: Eric de la Torre; 29605: Ernie Chinnery; 29616: Richard Bradley; 11289: Thomas O'Leary; 2531: Robert Ryder; 2530: (British Officer); 2529 and 10501: Stuart Chant; 9721: Robert Wynn; 10241: Robert Butler; 17157: Louis Brown; 12029: Arnold Tillie; 11075 and 29617: Robert Montgomery; 11477: George Haines; 12584: William Etches; 6985: Tony Pinder et al.; 10887: Robert Barron; 12159: Thomas Sherman; 26814 and 1365: Alfred Leggatt; 5191: James Laurie; 12554: Donald Randall; 22671: Harold Roberts; 17896: Corran Purdon; 22668: Ralph Batteson.

Department of Documents
12029: Lieutenant Commander George Congreve Bt DSO; 13707: Corporal Buster Woodiwiss; 3028: PJC Dark; 2397: Brigadier JC Haydon; 11510: Admiral Sir Guy Sayer; 1927: Commander WL Stephens DSC; 78/43/1: Captain The Reverend Joe Nicholl MC; 66/213/1: Brigadier Cecil Ernest Lucas Phillips.

Department of Film
9940: BBC Radio 4 recording of St-Nazaire raid; Ernie Chinnery Tapes 16–20; Micky Burn Tapes 52–5; Richard Bradley Tapes 55–8; Robert Montgomery Tapes 59–62; Corran Purdon Tapes 63–6; John Roderick Tapes 72–3; Eric de la Torre Tapes 74–7; David Paton Tapes 78–9; Bill

Etches Tapes 80–3; Bert Shipton Tapes 84–5; Bill 'Tiger' Watson Tapes 86–8; Bob Hoyle Tapes 89–90; Tom Sherman Tapes; Frank Carr; Ralph Batteson; Richard Scott.

Liddell Hart Archives

GB 0099 KCLMA	Papers of Brigadier Gerald Montanaro, late RE
GB 0099 KCLMA	Papers of Major General Sir Robert Edward Laycock

National Archives, Kew, London

ADM 1/12238	Lieutenant Mark F Rodier, RNVR
ADM 1/11888	COMBINED OPERATIONS: Operation Chariot
ADM 1/11970	COMBINED OPERATIONS: Operation Chariot
ADM 1/11970	ADMIRALTY: Operation Chariot
ADM 1/20019	Despatch of report by Commander-in-Chief Plymouth
ADM 1/18251	Request for approval to write an account of St-Nazaire raid
ADM 1/20718	Naval participation in ceremonies of commemoration
ADM 1/13983	Presumption of death of missing personnel
ADM 1/20019	Despatch of report by C-in-C Plymouth
ADM 199/1199	Stuart Chant
AIR 8/870	Operation 'Chariot'
AIR 14/694	Operation 'Chariot'
AIR 15/611	Operation 'Chariot'
CAB 79/18/30	COS(42) 63rd meeting
CAB 79/18/35	COS(42) 68th meeting
CAB 79/19/24 6	COS(42) 94th meeting
CAB 79/20/1	COS(42) 101st meeting
CAB 79/56/13 6	COS(42)(O)13
DEFE 2/125	Operation Chariot Part 1
DEFE 2/126	Operation Chariot Part 2
DEFE 2/127	Operation Chariot Part 3
DEFE 2/128	Part 4: photographs and drawings.
DEFE 2/130	Operation Chariot Vol. 1

DEFE 2/131	Operation Chariot Vol. 2
DEFE 2/132	Operation Chariot Vol. 3
DEFE 2/137	Operation Chess
DEFE 2/142	Operation Claymore
DEFE 2/697	History of Combined Operations
DEFE 2/698	History of Combined Operations
DEFE 2/699	History of Combined Operations
DEFE 2/843	Commando casualties 1940–45
DEFE 2/851	Honours and Awards
DEFE 2/879	Drugs for Fatigue
DEFE 2/881	Reports on Exercises
DEFE 2/956	Honours and Awards
DEFE 2/960	Special Service Brigade 1942–44
WO 218/33	War Diary, No. 2 Commando
MFQ 1/302	Maps & Diagrams
MFQ 1/304/3	Maps & Diagrams
MFQ 1/306/2-7	Maps & Diagrams
PREM 3/376	Publicity
WO 193/384	13 June 1940
WO 208/3264	MI9
WO 231/2	Operation Claymore
WO 231/4	Operation Sunstar
WO 231/5	Operation Archery
WO 231/6	Operation Bristle

Admiralty Battle Report 1736 (34) *The Attack on St Nazaire* (1948)

Saint-Nazaire

Souvenance *L'Operation Chariot* No. 1
Souvenance *L'Operation Chariot* No. 2

U-Boot Archiv, Cuxhaven

Report by Kapitänleutnant Herbert Sohler, *A Contribution to the history of the 7th U-Boat Flotilla: The English Landing in Saint-Nazaire*
Hermann Schlicht, *The 7th U-Boot Flotilla in the War Years, 1942*

Select Bibliography

Allan, Stuart *Commando Country* (Edinburgh: National Museums Scotland, 2007)

Barnett, Corelli *Engage the Enemy More Closely* (New York: W.W. Norton, 1991)

Batteson, Ralph *Saint-Nazaire to Shepperton: A Sailor's Odyssey* (Derby: Highedge Historical Society, 1996)

Binney, Marcus *Secret War Heroes: Men of the Special Operations Executive* (London: Hodder & Stoughton, 2005)

Blumenson, Martin *The Vildé Affair: Beginnings of the French Resistance* (London: Robert Hale, 1977)

Brooks, Richards *Clandestine Sea Operations to Brittany, 1940–1944* (London: Routledge, 2004)

Burn, Michael *Turned Towards the Sun* (Norwich: Michael Russell, 2003)

Chant-Sempill, Stuart *Saint-Nazaire Commando* (London: John Murray, 1985)

Clarke, Dudley *Seven Assignments* (London: Jonathan Cape, 1948)

Cobb, Matthew *The Resistance* (London: Simon & Schuster, 2009)

Cobb, Richard *French and Germans. Germans and French* (New England: Brandeis, 1983)

Cooksey, Jon *Operation Chariot* (London: Leo Cooper, 2005)

Darling, Donald *Secret Sunday* (London: William Kimber, 1975)

—— *Sunday at Large* (London: William Kimber, 1977)

Dark, P.J.C. *In Captivity: Images from WW2* (Honolulu Academy of Arts, 15–23 October 1994)

Dorrian, James *Storming St. Nazaire: the Gripping Story of the Dock-Busting Raid, March, 1942* (Annapolis: Naval Institute Press, 1998)

—— *Saint-Nazaire: Operation Chariot – 1942: Battleground French Coast* (Barnsley: Pen & Sword, 2006)

Downing, Taylor *Spies in the Sky: The Secret Battle for Aerial Intelligence during World War II* (London: Little Brown, 2011)

Dunning, James *It Had To Be Tough: The Origins and Training of the Commandos in World War Two* (Barnsley: Pen & Sword, 2012)

Durnford-Slater, John *Commando* (London: William Kimber, 1953)

Fergusson, Bernard *The Watery Maze* (London: Collins, 1961)

Foot, M.R.D. *Resistance* (London: Eyre Methuen, 1976)

—— and Langley, James *MI9 Escape and Evasion 1939–1945* (London: Bodley Head, 1979)

Ford, Ken *Saint-Nazaire,1942* (Oxford: Osprey, 2010)

Fourcade, Marie-Madeleine *Noah's Ark: The Story of the Alliance Intelligence Network in Occupied France* (London: Allen and Unwin Ltd, 1973)

Guériff, Fernand *Saint-Nazaire sous l'occupation allemande Le Commando – La poche Edition revue et augmentée* (La Baule: Editions des Paludiers, 1974)

Harriman, William Averell and Abel, Elie *Special Envoy to Churchill and Stalin 1941–6* (New York: Random House, 1975)

Hinsley, F.H. *British Intelligence in the Second World War* vol. 1 (London: HMSO, 1979)

Holman, Gordon *Commando Attack* (London: Hodder and Stoughton, 1942)

Holt, Thaddeus *The Deceivers* (London: Weidenfeld & Nicholson, 2004)

Hopton, Richard *A Reluctant Hero. The Life of Captain Robert Ryder VC* (Barnsley, Pen and Sword, 2011)

Hutton, C. Clayton *Official Secret* (London: Max Parrish, 1960)

Jackson, Julian *France, The Dark Years* (Oxford: Oxford University Press, 2001)

Jeffery, Keith *MI6 The History of the Secret Intelligence Service 1909–1949* (London: Bloomsbury, 2010)

John, Evan *Lofoten Letter* (London: Heinemann, 1941)

Kedward, H.R. *Resistance in Vichy France* (Oxford: Oxford University Press, 1978)

—— *Occupied France* (Oxford: Blackwell, 1985)

Kellas, Arthur *Down To Earth* (Edinburgh: The Pentland Press, 1990)

Kennedy, John *The Business of War* (London: Hutchinson, 1957)

Keyes, Elizabeth *Geoffrey Keyes, V.C., M.C., Croix de Guerre, Royal Scots Greys, lieut.-colonel, 11th Scottish Commando* (London: G. Newnes, 1956)

Lambert, John and Ross, Al *Allied Coastal Forces of World War II: Fairmile Designs and US Submarine Chasers* vol. 1 (London: Conway, 1990)

Langley, James *Fight Another Day* (London: Collins, 1974)

Leasor, James *War at the Top* (London: Michael Joseph, 1959)

Lenart, Judith *Berlin to Bond and Beyond* (London: Athena Press, 2007)

Lepotier, Rear Admiral Adolphe Auguste *Raiders from the Sea* (London: William Kimber, 1954)

Lucas Phillips, C.E. *The Greatest Raid of All* (1958)

Mackay, Robert *Half the Battle: Civilian Morale in Britain During the Second World War* (Manchester: Manchester University Press, 2003)

Mason, David *Raid on St. Nazaire* (New York: Ballantines, 1970)

Messenger, Charles *The Commandos, 1940–1946* (London: William Kimber, 1985)

Michelli, Alison *Commando to Captain-Generall: The Life of Brigadier Peter Young* (Barnsley: Pen & Sword, 2007)

Mikes, H. George *The Epic of Lofoten* (London: Hutchinson, 1941)

Moran, Lord *Churchill: The Struggle for Survival 1940–65* (London: Constable, 1966)

Neave, Airey *They Have Their Exits* (London: Hodder & Stoughton, 1953)

—— *Little Cyclone* (London: Hodder & Stoughton, 1954)

—— *Saturday at MI9* (London: Hodder & Stoughton, 1969)

Neillands, Robin *The Raiders: The Army Commandos, 1940–45* (London: Weidenfeld & Nicholson, 1984)

Niven, David *The Moon's a Balloon* (London: Hamish Hamilton, 1971)

Noguères, Henri *Histoire de la Résistance en France* (5 vols, Paris, 1969–81)

Purdon, Corran *List The Bugle: Reminiscences of an Irish Soldier* (Antrim: Greystone Books, 1993)

Renault-Roulier, Gilbert *The Silent Company* (London: Arthur Barker Ltd, 1948)

Rhodes James, Robert (ed.) *Chips: The Diaries of Sir Henry Channon* (London: Weidenfeld & Nicolson, 1967)

Roskill, Stephen *War at Sea 1939–45*, vol. 2, *The Period of Balance* (Uckfield: Naval & Military Press Ltd, 2004)

Ross, Al *Anatomy of a Ship: The Destroyer Campbeltown* (London: Conway, 1990)

Rotenberg, Alexander *Emissaries* (Secaucus, New Jersey: Citadel Press, 1987)

Ryder, R.E.D. *The Attack on Saint-Nazaire* (London, John Murray, 1947)

Sebag-Montefiore, Hugh *Enigma: The Battle for the Code* (London: Weidenfeld & Nicholson, 2000)

Siccard, Daniel *St Nazaire 1939–45 La Guerre L'Occupation La Liberation* (1994)

St George Saunders, Hilary *Combined Operations: The Official Story of the Commandos* (New York: Macmillan, 1943)

—— *The Green Beret* (London: Michael Joseph, 1949)

Stanley, Peter *Commando to Colditz* (Millers Point, Australia: Pier 9, 2009)

Terraine, John *Business in Great Waters: The U-Boat Wars 1916–1945* (London: Leo Cooper, 1989)

Trevor Roper, H.R. (ed.) *Hitler's War Directives 1939–1945* (London: Sidgwick and Jackson, 1964)

Young, Peter *Storm from the Sea* (London: William Kimber, 1958)

Ziegler, Philip *Mountbatten* (London: Collins, 1985)

Articles

Ramsey, Winston 'The Attack on St Nazaire' (*After the Battle*, 59, 1988)

'I Was There! – We Went With the Raiders to St. Nazaire' (*The War Illustrated*, vol. 5, no. 127, pp. 669–71, May 1, 1942)

'St. Nazaire: Most Daring Raid Since Zeebrugge' (*The War Illustrated*, vol. 5, no. 126, p. 627, April 17, 1942)

Willans, T.W. 'Operation Chariot: The Raid on Saint-Nazaire' (*Purnell's History of the Second World War*, no. 31, 1968)

Acknowledgements

I wish to begin by acknowledging my debt to two previous historians of Operation *Chariot*. Cecil ('Peter') Lucas Phillips wrote the first account of the raid in 1958, and entitled it aptly *The Greatest Raid of All*. Whenever I thought that I had uncovered a new historical nugget under a particularly heavy rock I invariably discovered, when referring back to Lucas Phillips, that he had been there first. Lucas Phillips was an impressively enlightened historian for his day: his interviews with German and French participants make for a remarkably rounded account. Jim Dorrian's *Storming St. Nazaire* is a masterpiece of detailed, interview-based history. I have used his extensive and impressive research, now deposited in the Imperial War Museum, to great profit.

I am deeply grateful to a wide range of people who have enabled me to prepare this work, especially to the stalwart hearts of the Saint-Nazaire Society who keep the Charioteers' flame alive. I was dependent upon the time, patience and goodwill of many of its members, including Major General Corran Purdon CBE, MC, CPM, Lieutenant Colonel Bob Montgomery MC, Mrs Ann Mitchell MBE (daughter of the late Captain David Birney), Mr Nick Beattie (son of Captain 'Sam' Beattie VC RN) and the Reverend Lisle Ryder (son of Commander R.E.D. Ryder VC RN). I am also profoundly grateful for the keen eyes and red pen of Mr Peter Lush, a well-known expert on the battle who has travelled the windy streets of Saint-Nazaire in pursuit of his battlefield walks probably more than anyone else, and who saved me from many errors. Likewise Jeremy Clarkson's wonderfully evocative and well-told television account of the raid in 2007 is a model of its kind: passion for the drama of the human story and a determination to maintain historical and analytical balance being artfully combined. Despite my efforts it is possible that some errors have been overlooked. If this is the case I alone remain responsible. If they are brought to my attention I will endeavour to correct them in subsequent editions.

In addition to interviews with veterans I have relied very heavily on accounts of the raid that are held in various archives, both in the United Kingdom, Germany and France. I am especially grateful to the Imperial War Museum for permission to use some of the vast store of material in its care, and to the individual copyright holders who have kindly granted me permission to use their material in this account. I wish also to thank Peter Rogers of the Commando Veterans Association and Keith Janes of Conscript Heroes, together with the historians Charles Messenger, Matthew Cobb, Richard Hopton and Peter Stanley. I have received considerable assistance from the WW2 Experience Centre, Leeds; Martin Sugarman (Archivist, British Association of Jewish Ex-Servicemen and Women) and Kevin Ruane (grandson of 'Peter' Lucas Phillips). The French historians Luc Braeuer and Bernard Petitjean helpfully pointed me in the direction of the Bundesarchives, and the U-Boat Archives in Cuxhaven provided the reports by Herbert Sohler and Hermann Schlicht. In France the Charioteers' flame is kept burning brightly in Saint-Nazaire by *inter alia* M. Michel Euxebie and M. Charles Nicol. Finally, the support of my family, of my agent Charlie Viney, and of Richard Milner and his wonderful crew at Quercus, has made this endeavour, like the others before it, not just possible, but immensely pleasurable. Thank you all.

Index